D0035138

BOOK SALE
Solano College Library

Books by Peter Davison

POETRY

The Great Ledge   (1989)

Praying Wrong: New and Selected Poems, 1957–1984

(1984)

Barn Fever and Other Poems   (1981)

A Voice in the Mountain   (1977)

Walking the Boundaries   (1974)

Dark Houses   (1971)

Pretending to Be Asleep   (1970)

The City and the Island   (1966)

The Breaking of the Day and Other Poems   (1964)

PROSE

The Fading Smile: Poets in Boston, 1955–1960, from Robert
    Frost to Robert Lowell to Sylvia Plath   (1994)

One of the Dangerous Trades: Essays on the Work and
    Workings of Poetry   (1991)

Half Remembered: A Personal History   (1973)

(REVISED EDITION, 1991)

EDITOR OF

The World of Farley Mowat: A Selection from His Works

(1980)

Hello, Darkness: The Collected Poems of L. E. Sissman

(1978)

The Fading Smile

Peter Davison

Poets in Boston

New York • London

PS
255
.B6
D38
1994

The Fading Smile

from Robert Lowell to Sylvia Plath

W. W. Norton & Company

06-07-00

4 98

Iron Kettle

Copyright © 1994 by Peter Davison

First published as a Norton paperback 1996
by arrangement with Alfred A. Knopf, Inc.

All rights reserved.

Owing to limitations of space, acknowledgments for permission to reprint pre-
viously published and unpublished material may be found following the Index.

Chapter 11, "Out of Bounds: Robert Lowell, 1955–1960" appeared in slightly
different form in The Yale Review, volume 82, number 3, in July 1994.

Library of Congress Cataloging-in-Publication Data
Davison, Peter.
    The fading smile : poets in Boston, 1955–1960, from Robert Frost to
Robert Lowell to Sylvia Plath / by Peter Davison.
        p.   cm.
    Includes bibliographical references (p.) and index.
        1. American poetry—Massachusetts—Boston—History and criticism.
2. American poetry—20th century—History and criticism. 3. Poets,
American—Massachusetts—Boston—Biography. 4. Boston (Mass.)—
Intellectual life—20th century. 5. Davison, Peter—Friends and
associates. I. Title.
PS255.B6D38   1994   93-43945
811'.5409974461—DC20   CIP

ISBN 0-393-31358-1
W. W. Norton & Company, Inc.
500 Fifth Avenue, N.Y., N.Y. 10110
W. W. Norton & Company Ltd.
10 Coptic Street, London WC1A 1PU

Printed in the United States of America

1 2 3 4 5 6 7 8 9 0

To Harry Ford

WHOSE LOVE OF BOOKS AND LOYALTY TO AUTHORS
ARE SURPASSED BY NO ONE'S

Acknowledgments

This book took its beginnings in a lecture delivered to the Harvard Alumni College in June 1988, and an expanded version delivered to the Friends of the Smith College Library on March 30, 1990. Many people have contributed notes, anecdotes, and substantial information; but without the kind assistance of, and interviews with, the following poets and their friends, this book could not have been written: Daniel Aaron, William Alfred, Barbara K. S. Boger, Philip Booth, Edward J. Brunner, Albert C. Cook, Doris Holmes Eyges, Donald Hall, Elizabeth Hardwick, Anthony Hecht, Galway Kinnell, Maxine Kumin, Stanley Kunitz, Janet Malcolm, W. S. Merwin, Diane Middlebrook, Adrienne Rich, Stephen Sandy, Anne B. Sissman, Martin Slobodkin, Anne Stevenson, Saul Touster, and Richard Wilbur. I am grateful to the staffs of the Rare Book and Manuscript Room at the William Allan Neilson Library at Smith College, especially the late Ruth Mortimer, and, at Harvard University, to the Theatre Collection at the Nathan M. Pusey Library and to the Houghton Library and its helpful and severe guardians. Finally, and most warmly, I am grateful to Mary Nash for her biographical advice, and to Harry Ford for his long-standing support—emotional, intellectual, fiscal, and gastronomic—over twenty-eight years as my editor and publisher. The support, moral, emotional, and intellectual, of my wife, Joan E. Goody, should not and does not go without saying.

Contents

Illustrations

The Fading Smile

Poets of my generation and particularly younger ones have gotten terribly proficient at these forms. They write a very musical, difficult poem with tremendous skill. . . . It's become a craft, purely a craft, and there must be some breakthrough back into life. *Robert Lowell*, 1960

All the other arts, except music as composition, require some matter in order to fulfill themselves. The great thing about poetry is that your selfhood is simultaneously your instrument and your vessel. *Stanley Kunitz*, 1974

When Ted Hughes writes about the struggle of Plath's "true self" to emerge from her false one, he is surely writing about a historical as well as a personal crisis. The nineteenth century came to an end in America only in the nineteen-sixties. *Janet Malcolm*, 1993

No poem had ever said it to me quite so directly. At twenty-two it called me out of a kind of sleepwalking. I knew, even then, that for me poetry wasn't enough as something to be appreciated, finely fingered: it could be a fierce, destabilizing force, a wave pulling you further out than you thought you wanted to be. *You have to change your life.* *Adrienne Rich*, 1993

Prelude: The Vortex,
April 1959

To a Mad Friend

I may look fine at the moment, but like you
I have capered and somersaulted in the street,
While, hoisted upon my shoulders, someone's face
Smiled at my friends and answered the telephone;
Or hovered, like a fish with nose against
A rock, in elements I could not breathe.
You've seen us in every land you've travelled through:
Our ties were tied, our shoes were always shined,
But icy eyes and tightness around the smile
Are marks enough to know your brothers by.
Rest easier, friend: we've all walked through your dreams
And are no strangers to that company.

PETER DAVISON, 1959[1]

On May 11, 1959, Robert Lowell's *Life Studies*, the most influential book of American poetry for a generation, was to be published in New York. It had cost its author a harrowing struggle of over five years to renew not only the rhetoric of his poetry, but its very texture and substance. The book was, oddly, published first in England, early in

April, but the English edition did not include the thirty-six-page prose memoir "91 Revere Street," recounting Robert Lowell's childhood on Boston's Beacon Hill, the tormented decline of one of America's aristocratic literary families, and the fateful consequences for the author.

The American critics—those who could face the strange music of *Life Studies*—either recoiled, huzzahed, or reached for fresh labels for this jar of poisoned history. M. L. Rosenthal's September *Nation* review finally slapped a sticker—"confessional"—on the book, which has lasted longest and is, I fear, most misleading. Lowell's mentor, Allen Tate, had written him privately about the poems: "I do not think you ought to publish them. . . . They have no public or literary interest."[2] Elizabeth Bishop and Stanley Kunitz, by contrast, both encouraged him; Bishop, in fact, had helped instigate the book's very beginnings in 1957. Edmund Wilson declared: "Robert Lowell has done something very extraordinary; he has made poetry out of modern Boston."[3] John Thompson, Lowell's longtime friend, wrote with immediate discernment in *The Kenyon Review*:

In these poems there are depths of the self that in life are not ordinarily acknowledged and in literature are usually figured in disguise. Traditionally, between the persona of the creation and the person of the creator a certain distance exists. . . . Robert Lowell's new poems show that this distance between persona and poem is not, after all, important to art, but has been a reflection of the way our culture conceived character. This conception seems to be dwindling now to a mere propriety. And for these poems, the question of propriety no longer exists. They have made a conquest; what they have won is a major expansion of the territory of poetry.[4]

4

It would of course take some time for the air to clear after the explosion of such a book, and a great deal of misleading criticism has clouded the atmosphere in the years since 1959. Today I'd find myself supporting Mark Rudman when he asserts:

Life Studies is the first major book of poetry about the nuclear family. Previously this was the terrain of fiction and drama—of works like Faulkner's *Absalom, Absalom* or O'Neill's *Long Day's Journey into Night*. Lowell breaks new ground for poetry. . . . These poems were written during the Eisenhower era, the beginning of the Cold War, "the tranquillized Fifties," as Lowell dubbed them. . . . Lowell's project in *Life Studies* can be regarded as a corrective to conformity and the pernicious apathy he saw everywhere. . . .

Lowell has been dubbed a "confessional" poet, but his is not a poetry of confession, it's a poetry of revelation. What he manages to do in the poems is not to replicate people or places as they were, but to reveal them through his feelings about them. . . . Sometimes the borderline between self and other is blurred. The key line for our purposes is "I myself am hell. . . ." "I myself"—and it is precisely this insight that makes "Skunk Hour" a great poem, and *Life Studies* a great book rather than a collection of poems.[5]

The cost of such an achievement was extreme indeed. As Lowell said at the Boston Arts Festival in 1960, before reading "For the Union Dead," which the festival had commissioned, "When I finished *Life Studies*, I was left hanging on a question mark. I am still hanging there. I don't know whether it is a death-rope or a lifeline."[6]

In 1959 Robert Lowell taught his seminars at Boston University on Tuesdays from 2:00 to 4:00. It was either on

Tuesday April 21 or April 28 that his class (which included George Starbuck, playing hooky from his editorial work at Houghton Mifflin, and regulars like Anne Sexton, Sylvia Plath, Jean Valentine, Kathleen Spivack, Helen Chasin, Donald Junkins, Roger Rosenblatt, Richard Lourie, and others) became aware that Lowell was not himself when he arrived on the scene, a classroom that Anne Sexton described as "a dismal room the shape of a shoe box. It was a bleak spot, as if it had been forgotten for years. . . ."[7] Lowell himself called it "viewless unless one cared to look down on the city outskirts' defeated yellow brick and square concrete pillbox filling stations."[8] The teacher entered on that Tuesday and squeezed himself into a corner of the windowsill. "He seemed agitated," Kathleen Spivack wrote later. "We had the distinct fear that he was going to throw himself out of the window. The class sat completely hushed. Anne fixed me firmly with her green eyes, as if to communicate something. Lowell hospitalized himself directly after this class meeting."[9]

The word soon whisked around Boston, *Hieronymo's mad againe.* Whether the students in the class had as yet seen the entire text of *Life Studies* is doubtful, but they had certainly heard Lowell read a number of the poems from the book during the course of the year. Anne Sexton, who seldom overlooked an opportunity to immortalize the passing event, quickly wrote a poem of her own and sent it, on May 1, to Lowell's friend and former pupil W. D. Snodgrass with news of "Cal"'s latest breakdown:

> In the thin classroom, where your face
> was noble and your words were all things,
> I find this boily creature in your place;
>
> find you disarranged, squatting on the window sill,
> irrefutably placed up there,

6

like a hunk of some big frog
watching us through the V
of your woolen legs.

Even so, I must admire your skill.
You are so gracefully insane.
We fidget in our plain chairs
and pretend to catalogue
our facts for your burly sorcery

or ignore your fat blind eyes
or the prince you ate yesterday
who was wise, wise, wise.[10]

"I'm tired, everyone's tired of my turmoil," Lowell would write a year or two later; but in 1959 these repetitive melancholy breakdowns were still frightening enough to arouse immediate compassion. George Starbuck, at the end of the class, went off with Anne Sexton and Sylvia Plath to the bar of the Ritz-Carlton Hotel, where they had recently developed a post-class cocktail-klatsch. In later years the word has spread that they invariably discussed madness and suicide,[11] but I wonder whether this day may not have both triggered the subject and exhausted it. By May 3, with Lowell hospitalized and the class meetings cancelled, Sylvia Plath was noting in her journal, "Felt our triple-martini afternoons at the Ritz breaking up."[12]

Lowell would spend some six weeks in McLean Hospital, but "the news of his periodic breakdowns spread with amazing speed," Anthony Hecht has written, "penetrating without difficulty to even the most remote recesses of the world."[13] In Boston the word spread instantly; and friends of Lowell's like Philip Booth, Adrienne Rich, I. A. Richards, William Alfred, and John L. Sweeney would meet, doubly or severally, for lunch to commiserate and deplore. I had been travelling on publishing business for ten days or so, yet I recall, perhaps inaccurately, hearing about this illness from Roger Shattuck in Austin, Texas, on April 23. What's more, word of Lowell's latest crash was hissing around the poetry world just as *Life Studies* was being read and reviewed, and few books, partly as a consequence of this very coincidence, have undergone such ambivalent discussion. Those who knew Lowell felt a sinking feeling, commingled with trace elements of competition and relief, that it was not they who were ill. Most of us had suffered similar disabilities, though not perhaps of so keen an intensity, and certainly not so publicly visible.

It was not the first time, of course, that Lowell's friends had been summoned to his side, or that the long-suffering Elizabeth Hardwick, Lowell's wife, had had to undergo the pain and humiliation of her husband's hospitalization. The harrowing poem "Man and Wife," which appeared in *Partisan Review* in early 1958, had grievously dramatized the consequences of these breakdowns. Stanley Kunitz went to visit his friend at McLean, at Lowell's urging, to discuss a matter of the utmost importance.

He was in his bathrobe. He came out into the waiting room, and he had this proprietary air as though he owned the establishment, and treated me as though he were the host, and he talked a blue streak. He said, I have something very important, something I know you'll be interested in, and he said, This is an old poem, that really needs to be worked on, improved, and I'm having a difficult time with it, and I have to go over it with you. It turned out to be "Lycidas." He was reworking the whole poem. . . . He had half persuaded himself that this was his poem, and that he was correcting it. And I was in a dilemma because I couldn't tell whether he was actually claiming possession of the poem, and if I made this clear to him whether it could confuse him even more, so I simply went over it and made some corrections of my own, and we played out that game.[14]

Robert Lowell discourses with Jane Brooks; John Malcolm Brinnin
in background, February 15, 1959.

Robert Frost, 1958

John Holmes faces the TV camera, poems in hand, 1957.

The Holmes workshop: Anne Sexton on floor, George Starbuck on couch, Doris Holmes in armchair, 1958

Peter Davison
rehearses as
Alceste, October 1955.

Program cover

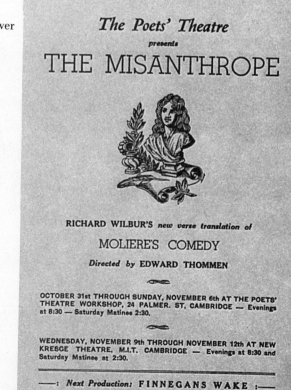

The Poets' Theatre

presents

THE MISANTHROPE

RICHARD WILBUR'S *new verse translation of*

MOLIERE'S COMEDY

Directed by EDWARD THOMMEN

OCTOBER 31st THROUGH SUNDAY, NOVEMBER 6th AT THE POETS'
THEATRE WORKSHOP, 24 PALMER. ST, CAMBRIDGE — Evenings
at 8:30 — Saturday Matinee 2:30.

WEDNESDAY, NOVEMBER 9th THROUGH NOVEMBER 12th AT NEW
KRESGE THEATRE, M.I.T. CAMBRIDGE — Evenings at 8:30 and
Saturday Matinee at 2:30.

——: *Next Production:* FINNEGANS WAKE :——

Richard Wilbur at Wellesley, 1957

I. A. Richards

W. S. Merwin, c. 1960, at Lacan de Loubressac

John L. Sweeney

Maxine Kumin, 1958

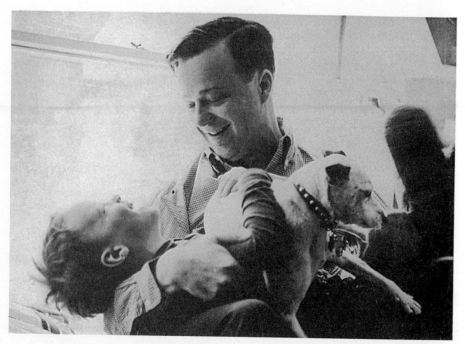

Donald Hall in Ann Arbor, 1958

Philip Booth at Wellesley, 1957

Sylvia Plath behind Ted Hughes,
Annisquam, Massachusetts, May 20, 1959

Adrienne Rich, Cambridge, 1960

L. E. Sissman reads the Boston *Sunday Globe*
for September 8, 1956.

Stanley Kunitz, May 12, 1959 (Ted Hughes at right)

1. The State of the Art in Boston, 1955

What brought the kindred spider to that height,
Then steered the white moth thither in the night?
What but design of darkness to appall?—
If design govern in a thing so small.

ROBERT FROST, FROM "DESIGN," 1922[1]

§ *Generations*

I chanced, in 1955, into one of the most vital milieux for poetry in the history of this country. Young poets in the mid-1950s, still overshadowed by the sequoias of Frost, Pound, Eliot, Stevens, Cummings, Marianne Moore, and William Carlos Williams, had taken refuge in a formal elegance that they were beginning to want to outgrow. The Beat Generation had urged stripping off those costumes altogether, but in Boston the transformation suggested a change of clothes rather than walking naked.

Poets born between the turn of the century and the end of the First World War—Theodore Roethke, Robert Penn Warren, Stanley Kunitz, Elizabeth Bishop, Randall Jarrell, Delmore Schwartz, John Berryman, and Robert Lowell— were as varied in temperament and as gifted in genius as the generation of elders who preceded them, but a disproportionate number of this second generation seemed to suffer under the curse of "despondency and madness," as

11

chronicled in Eileen Simpson's admirable memoir, *Poets in Their Youth.* The poets of this generation, more than others, suffered from difficulties with their fathers. John Berryman, Stanley Kunitz, Ernest Hemingway, Robert Fitzgerald, Elizabeth Bishop, all suffered the suicide or early death of their fathers; Robert Frost himself had to live with his father's early death, the madness of a sister, the suicide of a son, the early death of one daughter, the madness of another, and the death of two children in infancy. Other congeners like Hart Crane, John Berryman, Randall Jarrell, Delmore Schwartz, Dylan Thomas, and Theodore Roethke either committed suicide outright or acted sufficiently self-destructive to have an equivalent effect.

Moreover, this *entre-deux-guerres* generation of poets made up the first to volunteer wholesale for the classroom, to be given over to the material of literary scholarship and to respond almost maternally to the gaping bills of their students, many of whom would turn out to be the poets of my "postwar" generation. Jarrell's notable witticism, "The gods who had taken away the poet's audience had given him students,"[2] did not suggest that poets like him hated teaching, but—unlike many of his successors a generation later, who would regard the teaching of poetry largely as a way of making a career—Jarrell on the contrary declared, "If I were a rich man, I would pay money for the privilege of being able to teach."[3]

The cast of characters in my Boston story and of my own generation, the actors and actresses in the second poetic renaissance of New England's greatest and oldest brick city, were nearly all born in the 1920s. They aggregated swiftly and intimately in time and place, a dozen poets who settled in and around Boston for a few short years at the end of the 1950s, before John Kennedy's election as president. Is there some curious cause that made them come when they came, at a time crucial to American poetry, when its dominant figures, its language, its subject-matter, and its scenery, were about to change? And why did they leave, as so many of them did as soon as the new decade had struck? There may be some clues in the scene that took place in Robert Lowell's classroom on that April Tuesday of 1959.

This group portrait will for the most part limit itself to poets who, in the late 1950s, were just beginning their careers, or just attaining their full powers and reputations. The eldest, who visited Boston at the vortex, was Stanley Kunitz, born in 1905, who, despite being one of the masters, had received virtually no public recognition prior to 1958. He was awarded the Pulitzer Prize in poetry just two weeks after the episodes described at Boston University. Although the youngest, Sylvia Plath, was, except for Robert Lowell, the only one of these poets actually born in Boston, she had already cast her lot with Ted Hughes in England as early as 1956, and confirmed that decision in America in 1959, departing Boston forever before the end of the year.

In 1959 nearly every one of the poets of my chronicle, whatever his or her age, achieved some poetic breakthrough that marked a permanent change. And after 1960, as my generation of Boston poets began to leave the city behind altogether, the giants of the American forest came crashing down: E. E. Cummings, Robinson Jeffers, William Carlos Williams, Theodore Roethke, John Holmes, and the English Louis MacNeice all died in 1962 or 1963; the oldest and the youngest, Robert Frost and Sylvia Plath, died within two weeks of each other in 1963.

I believe there is one thing my generation seems to have had in common: nearly all of us had had in life to struggle with our fathers; and now our fathers-in-poetry were themselves dying. As Robert Lowell wrote in an essay on Stanley Kunitz' poem "Father and Son": "The poem is as much a struggle to recover childhood, or the prayer once held in childhood, as it is about the father."[4]

In the meantime, Boston was evolving from a charming but complacent city, angelic with clean laundry, where in

1956 Richard Wilbur's awakening soul could celebrate "clear dances done in the sight of heaven," into a transmogrified urban hell which the more saturnine Robert Lowell would excoriate, only four years later, with the phrase "a savage servility slides by on grease." Boston's common ground was levelled twice in the late 1950s: once literally, when the Boston Common itself was excavated to house an underground garage (which by 1992, after only thirty years, was already crumbling, condemned, and slated for a second excavation and reconstruction), and once figuratively, when "the shrill verve of [Elizabeth Hardwick's] invective," as a Robert Lowell poem described it, pinned Boston's "mysteriously enduring reputation" to the ground in 1959: "Boston—wrinkled, spindlylegged, depleted of nearly all her spiritual and cutaneous oils, provincial, self-esteeming—has gone on spending and spending her inflated bills of pure reputation, decade after decade."[5] Yet even as Hardwick was writing these words, Boston's reputation was crouching to spring again, from its oldest precincts, and even from her very household. 'Ware prophecy.

The dozen poets whose five-year histories I recount in this chronicle cannot be counted out of the history of American poetry, regardless of one's preferences of taste. I knew them all at the time, some better than others, and I have been reading their work, in some instances, since they began writing it. Some of them have been my teachers and masters, some have been friends and more than friends. But all of them, alive or dead, were my companions on a voyage, one of the most exciting poetic "surges," to use Philip Booth's word, ever to take place in America. David Kalstone wrote, much later, in a book exquisitely entitled *Becoming a Poet*, "They were sharpening and altering their notions of what it meant to tell the truth in verse."[6] So were we all. Now nearly all the others have abandoned the City upon a Hill, and only I am left alone to tell thee.

§ *Robert Frost*

Robert Frost, who turned eighty-five in 1959, remained still by far the most visible poet of the city and the region. He characteristically spent several months each year, spring and fall, at his good grey house at 35 Brewster Street in Cambridge, living alone. I was often a visitor to his living room and can even recollect the fragrance of it, a little like dusty patchouli. Frost's workroom, which I only once saw, was upstairs, with a Morris chair in it, a writing board across the arms, and a snowdrift of papers which, in the early afternoons, were shovelled and stacked by Kathleen Morrison, the devoted, astringent, and affectionate amanuensis who gave order and grace to his life in these years.

When Frost was in Cambridge—say, late March till June, and October till Christmas—he took his place at the center of Boston literary life, no matter who might be the gilded visitor of the current Harvard season. He had in the late 1940s resumed his relationship with Amherst College, where he would spend a week or two each spring and fall, living at the Lord Jeffrey Amherst Inn, consorting with his friends in Amherst and environs, like the eremitical bachelor poet Robert Francis, and doling out to a selected group of students the intoxicating flavors of his conversation. Every October he gave a poetry reading at Tufts University for his friend John Holmes; he usually gave a reading at Harvard or Boston University or Boston College as well as Tufts, in fact as many colleges as his stamina and their budgets would allow.

The public appearances of these years were uneven, and so were the private ones, but the old man, still working at his poems, always thinking aloud, welcomed company in Cambridge and held court for one or two or three friends, or sometimes even a whole class of schoolboys, in his parlor at Brewster Street. Sometimes there were evening parties or appearances here or there, or a small dinner at the houses of Archibald and Ada MacLeish or Howard Mumford and Bessie Jones. Kathleen Morrison had enlisted a troop of younger men, like Philip Booth and myself, whom she would entrust with the difficult task of Getting Frost Home Before Midnight—for he was a notorious night owl and, after a public appearance or an evening of conversation, loved walking home through the dark streets talking his way down from the preceding high, talking his way back to earth again. I seem to remember a dozen evenings, especially in the autumn, wading along sidewalks heaped with November leaves, walking him home from somewhere, and then Frost turning back at his door, wanting to walk me back home, halfway at any rate, and then my walking him in the other direction, until at last the lights were out in every house but his, and his conversation had begun to slow and fade out—it never actually concluded with a period—only to take up at the very same point at the next meeting, which might be months later.

We all cherished these evenings with him, especially the males: he was less open, perhaps, to the women poets. Adrienne Rich, who had studied under Theodore Morrison, and who was for some time his close neighbor on Brewster Street, had steeped herself in his poetry and imitated it in her own, but never became one of his intimates, as a dozen young male poets did—to say nothing of the older men like I. A. Richards and MacLeish and John Holmes, or the admired men of the middle generation like Lowell and Wilbur, who managed to visit him or entertain him with regularity over the years. He had his prejudices too: I once brought him a young, gifted, and charming black writer, who made him uneasy for the first hour, and another time I invited him to dinner with Charles Hopkinson, the portrait painter, Frost's equal in age but, in Frost's eyes, of a more established social station; and the evening was not a comfortable one: it might have been any two old geezers talking at cross-purposes. But he liked to meet young poets and literary people, loved showing off for them, and he was always delighted by my wife, Jane, on the evenings when he dined at our house. It is difficult to describe the comforting rhythms of his monologue, drawling on for hours at a time, with his open palm gesturing in the air like a conductor beating time to his own rhythm, his extraordinarily expressive face, seamed with the channels of age, glowing with the amusement his words gave him, and his mind flickering with extraordinary lightness from one topic to another, carried by the trade winds of metaphor, yet circling in such a way as to wrap up the collective subject-matter of the evening into an entity that resembled something very like a poem.

Very often he would in fact be trying out a poem, or lines in a poem, as part of the conversation, and few who knew him in the late 1950s would not have encountered, at some part of the evening's talk, a few minutes of experiment with a couplet which, Frost said, he had been asked by a Pakistani diplomat ("one of Ivor's boys," meaning a former student of I. A. Richards), an assistant secretary-general, to compose as the wisdom words for the new Meditation Room at the United Nations Building in New York, a poem to stand beside a forty-ton mass of Swedish iron ore, nearly pure metal. The talk would concern itself with unity and division, with the inability of humankind to settle arguments without arguing, to settle differences without strife, and one or another version of the famous couplet would emerge to be played with and juggled from hand to hand. Its final version, which finally came to print in 1959, was, to Frost's delight, refused by the United Nations, an organization which he happily suspected of baneful naiveté:

From Iron

TOOLS AND WEAPONS

TO AHMED S. BOKHARI

Nature within her inmost self divides
To trouble men with having to take sides.[7]

Tools and weapons were one of his favorite themes in these tense, Khrushchev-dominated years of the Eisenhower administration, the period between Suez and the Bay of Pigs. One of Frost's most dependable laugh-getters at readings was "The Objection to Being Stepped On," first printed in 1957, the poem which began, "At the end of the row/I stepped on the toe/Of an unemployed hoe./ It rose in offense/And struck me a blow/In the seat of my sense," and ended, "And what do we see?/The first tool I step on/Turned into a weapon."[8]

But despite all the clowning, and the thinking that disguised itself as clowning, the Frost we saw in his old age was also capable of writing one of the most bone-chilling lyrics of a generation:

The Draft Horse

With a lantern that wouldn't burn
In too frail a buggy we drove
Behind too heavy a horse
Through a pitch-dark limitless grove.

And a man came out of the trees
And took our horse by the head
And reaching back to his ribs
Deliberately stabbed him dead.

The ponderous beast went down
With a crack of a broken shaft.
And the night drew through the trees
In one long invidious draft.

18

The most unquestioning pair
That ever accepted fate
And the least disposed to ascribe
Any more than we had to to hate,

We assumed that the man himself
Or someone he had to obey
Wanted us to get down
And walk the rest of the way.[9]

Poems like these haunted the old man's imagination and memory, and carried a weight of mystery, irony, and terror that no other living poet could match: that was why in Boston in the 1950s Robert Frost was the living poet most looked up to by other poets, regardless of whether Archibald MacLeish's *J.B.* was packing them in on Broadway, or how intensely the academics might pore over the inner meanings of Stevens' *Opus Posthumous* (1957) or Eliot's *The Elder Statesman* (1958). The younger poets might not have a great deal to learn from Frost's poems themselves, though a great many of us began by aping him; but as an example of what it meant to be a poet, to live as a poet, to think as a poet, he had no rival. Moreover, it has become extremely difficult to remember him as he was, owing to the nature of Lawrance Thompson's posthumously published official biography, which Robert Lowell has rightly called "a work mediocre, poisonous, tone deaf, unable to animate a single character."[10]

§ *John Holmes*

If Robert Frost was the most notable poet of the period, the most assiduous and generous teacher of young poets in Boston was probably John Holmes, professor of English at Tufts University, and a friend and worshipper of Frost. He had, in fact, bought a vacation house in the remote village of Concord Corners, Vermont, next door to another house there that belonged to Frost, and which had been from time to time inhabited by Frost's daughter Irma Cone, who was troubled, like a disproportionate number of the Frost family, by mental illness. I first met John Holmes in 1948, when he was teaching as he often did at Chautauqua, New York, at the summer session in that beautiful place, and I was travelling with my parents and sister. Holmes and his new young wife, Doris, were cordial in the extreme, and we talked about the Concord Corners enclave and even, at John's suggestion, altered our itinerary to visit these houses on our way. My father was particularly interested in the detour, for in a letter Frost had written him at the height of their early friendship, on October 20, 1927, perhaps while my father was writing his poem "The Ninth Witch," Frost had announced his discovery of Concord Corners:

> I've just found the place for our ultimate school by a lake high in the mountains, a deserted village called Concord Corners that the railroad has undone by making passes back and forward below it two or three miles off in the valley. All that's left is a black church, a ruinous almshouse and half a dozen farm houses. Witches have debauched the church by sucking through it in the wind, in at one empty window socket and out at another. The church could be our lecture hall. We'd keep it black. We'd send you up to rope the bell in the steeple again so we could set it tolling to call fools into a ring. When poetry fails us that's where we'll go and what do. Is it a vote?
>
> But poetry mustn't fail us. I'll behave very badly if it does. Deny verities! Preach defeatism! Anger unvenerably![11]

Frost used also to brag that the first normal school in the United States had been founded in Concord Corners, and he intended to found the last. When we reached the village in 1948, with its tiny green and a darkling lake stretching away to the east of the crossroads, which was just about all there was left of the village by then, it became apparent— or would become apparent to me years later—that we were standing at the site of "Directive," Frost's most private, secretive, and mysterious poem, and one of his greatest. But the place was not merely a deserted village, it was positively sinister: something about it was not quite right; and I gradually learned that not only Irma Cone had lost her mental balance here, but John Holmes' first wife had done the same, and in fact committed suicide in a particularly horrible way, "slashing her wrists and bleeding to death over all his papers, which she assembled for that purpose on his desk."[12] We went through Frost's house, to which John Holmes had given us the key, admiring the twelve-inch panelling around the beautiful fireplace, and the lovely spaces of the rooms in the twin houses, now both empty. And then drove on. The darkness lay behind us.

In Boston in the 1950s, Holmes was arguably, along with his Tufts colleague John Ciardi, the most active of poets. Not only did he teach a full load of courses at Tufts, he also taught summer school at Chautauqua or elsewhere; he taught a night course for aspiring poets at the Boston Center for Adult Education, and he arranged poetry readings and interchanges between poets, and presided over the New England Poetry Club. For a short while he conducted a television program on WGBH-TV, assisted by Philip Booth and Donald Hall. "John had thought up the idea that [he] should do a little poetry workshop, with Donald Hall and myself," Booth remembers, "and the three of us would trade poems and talk about them on TV. In fact, we ran three dummy programs and they were a lot of fun, and then we did a fourth and we began getting fan mail from Winthrop and Hartford and everywhere else, and we were terrified. Television was so new, and we went off the air very soon."[13]

But John was the most open of teachers, encouraging his juniors, like Philip Booth, in a casual way. Doris Holmes Eyges says, "Sometimes John was criticized for being too generous, too open to students. Sometimes I think that was the problem in his first marriage. The house was always open to students, to poets. He liked the postman and the hardware store man as much as the president of the college."[14] An assiduous spreader of the word, he would call up someone like Booth when there was going to be a reading at Tufts. Booth remembers meeting Ted Hughes and Sylvia Plath at an evening at the Holmes house in Medford, and at other parties where he encountered poets like Stanley Kunitz for the first time. He also learned from talking with Holmes and by the casual exchange of poems a great deal about the writing of poetry; but, he says, "I learned more about the patterns of speech as such from Wilbur—reading him—I learned how much I wanted to write with the sense of pressure and release: 'He was a brown old man with a green thumb'—that is like somebody playing the high hat. I learned that early, and I still have a lot of Wilbur poems by heart."[15]

When George Starbuck, at twenty-six, first moved to Boston from Chicago in 1957, Doris Holmes Eyges recalls, "On his trip East he stopped in to see John, either through correspondence or some connection. I know they came to our house when they were in transit, really just arriving. He was married to his first wife, Jan. They had two children. He seemed very young. . . . John and Roethke taught together at Lafayette College, Easton, Pennsylvania, as beginning instructors, long long ago. John and Roethke were close from those days, and there was a real, real bond. When Roethke came to Boston unexpectedly, and had no accommodations, he asked to stay at our house. And months later he sent us a wonderful set of pilsener glasses. He was a great bear. He didn't kill me, or rape me, I should put it in the reverse order,"[16] Doris Holmes Eyges confided in me long afterward. On the heels of the earlier reading group with Richard Wilbur, John Ciardi, Richard Eberhart, and May Sarton, which had dissolved of its own acids, Holmes, in 1957, found in his adult education class two women of unusual promise: Maxine Kumin and Anne Sexton; and the next year he shifted them, together with George Starbuck and another poet named Sam Albert, to sessions that revolved among the houses of the participants, where the five poets brought their new poems for reading and analysis. He went on with his Boston class for years at the same time, sometimes asking Maxine Kumin or Philip Booth or Doris Holmes to pinch-hit for him in Boston. Holmes was the father figure of the group, but they were all vocal, perfectly willing to have at Holmes' poems, or at one another's. "George put up with a lot of chiding, I thought," says Doris Holmes Eyges. "They had to attack him on just being a technician. I think they truly respected each other as poets and friends, lovers, and whatnot. It was a strange group. . . . You'd have to see how much other interaction there was that was so overwhelming: the poetry, the passions, the private life, the mental breakdowns. . . ."[17] Intensity lay at the heart of their interaction, not all of it loving: Holmes, remembering his first wife's illness, could never quite tolerate Anne Sexton's willingness to pull back every curtain in her life: "He couldn't really blink away her talent—it was so evident—but he had as little to do with her as possible."[18]

The group went on for several years, until Starbuck left Boston in 1961 and Holmes began to suffer from the cancer that killed him in 1962. Maxine and Anne went on to other groupings, never abandoning their paired daily mutual criticism on the telephone, but in the meantime, with Holmes' affectionate encouragement, and the encouragement of the ever-generous May Sarton, Doris Holmes had begun to publish her own poems, and the seal of public approval was applied when she and John were invited to read their work together—at the Poets' Theatre, of course—in 1958.

§ How to Spell Theatre

Once he had been bitten by the New York theatre bug and written the plays collectively titled *The Old Glory*, Robert Lowell sketched a little unpublished essay called "Poets and the Theater." "For a hundred and fifty years," he wrote, "poets have looked on the theater with fascination and fury. . . . No two arts are more opposed than our poetry and our theater. . . . Professional prose playwrights have gone on writing delightful comedies and flawed tragedies. And poets have gone on filling the graveyard of letters with inflated verse plays, awkward to act and lethal to read."[19] Will all those flaming Broadway and Shaftesbury Avenue hits, written in verse after World War II, endure as literature? *The Lady's Not for Burning, The Cocktail Party, Under Milk Wood, The Rake's Progress, Candide, J.B.?* Certainly the young poets of Cambridge, Massachusetts, believed passionately in poetic theatre (as they spelled it) when in 1950 they—Donald Hall, Robert Bly, Frank O'Hara, Edward St. John Gorey, John Ashbery—began gathering in Richard Eberhart's parlor in Cambridge, or in church parish houses, and amused themselves by writing and performing plays that, at the outset, only poets could abide.

The founders of the Poets' Theatre of Cambridge had, for the most part, attended Harvard in its brilliant postwar era and been alerted to the theatrical tradition by the excellent Brattle Theatre Repertory productions of Shakespeare, Shaw, Anouilh, Wilde, and other Western greats at a ramshackle old theatre in Brattle Square in Cambridge. This company, professional actors, went the way that professionals tend to go: more professional, and from the provinces to Broadway. By the time the 1950s were growing old, the Brattle Theatre's revels all were ended and its theatrical space had been surrendered to films by Kurosawa, Truffaut, Orson Welles, and Ingmar Bergman. But the new Poets' Theatre, beginning in the year 1951, mounted theatrical productions, however exiguous, and in whatever hole or corner proved available, of plays written by John Ashbery (*Everyman* and *The Compromise*), Frank O'Hara (*Try! Try!*, the theatre's opening production, and *Change Your Bedding*), Richard Eberhart (*The Apparition*), Lyon Phelps (*Three Words in No Time* and *The Gospel Witch*), Donald Hall (*The Minstrel's Progress*), Paul Goodman, and Hugh Amory, whose *Orpheus* was only the first of three Orpheus plays the theatre would present in five years, one by V. R. Lang and one by Jean Cocteau.

The second season added such works as *The Teddy Bear, a horror play*, by Edward St. John Gorey, our glorious bump-in-the-night cartoonist who had been O'Hara's roommate during their undergraduate days at Harvard; *Smith, a Masque*, by Alison Lurie, the budding novelist and classic chronicler of the Poets' Theatre; and *A Change of Wife*, by Mary Manning Howe, playwright, director, novelist, close friend of Samuel Beckett, alumna of Dublin's Abbey Theatre, and the *madre buffa* of the Poets' Theatre group. As Donald Hall once said, "There was a lot of cheerful enthusiasm around the Poets' Theatre. Molly Howe was the most important figure, because she was dynamic and skeptical, enthusiastic and cynical at the same time, an absolutely invaluable combination."[20] Violet Lang, youngest of the many daughters of an organist at King's Chapel, once a Boston debutante, later a member of the Canadian Women's Army Corps, an editor of the *Chicago Review*, and a quondam showgirl at the Old Howard Burlesque House, was the theatre's Lady Gregory. Violet adopted the stage name V. R. Lang to keep her widowed father, under whose tyrannical roof she lived on Bay State Road, from discovering her theatrical associations. She wrote some of the most interesting if not accessible plays the theatre presented before her untimely death from Hodgkin's disease in 1956. The theatre's feverish, cliquish, erotic, and bohemian attractions, embodied to some extent by the Mae West of the troupe, voluptuous, husky-voiced, purple-eyed, seductive, languid Bunny Lang herself, enticed all sorts of talents to the theatre's threshold, to write plays or read them, act them or direct them—or even to smear the flats with paint, or to act as stage manager, as John Wieners, the sweetly demented poet, brought in by Frank O'Hara, did for a time.

From the beginning Bunny was involved in every Poets' Theatre show, as actress, director, writer, designer, and producer. She was not a good actress, though it was marvellous to watch her on the stage. She could save a bad play sometimes simply by walking out and smiling at the audience: the less the lines meant, the more she could put into them. . . . Among the original members as well as those that joined later no one was single-mindedly anxious to "revive poetic drama." Her motives were less worldly than most, for she did not principally hope to rise in society, to go on the professional stage, to get her poetry published, to become locally famous, or to meet possible lovers. Each of these ends was attained by some member of the theatre; all except the first were realized by Bunny. . . .[21]

I once read in a play with her, and when it was over she turned to me and, taking my hand and fixing me with her great purple eyes, whispered, fervently: "I love the way you read. You make everything sound so *true*." I succumbed to the feeling of helpless devotion shared by all the others on whom she turned the lamps of her attention.

No small theatre, utilizing poetical authors, plays in verse, borrowed stage space, costumes from grandmother's attic, and amateur actors, could expect to live a very long life without resorting to very special practices, and the Poets' Theatre, once it got a grip on itself, did not embrace poets for nothing. In May 1953 it presented, very profitably, at Harvard's Fogg Museum, two successive readings by Dylan Thomas, including the first public reading anywhere of *Under Milk Wood* by its author: "He was continually interrupted by extended bursts of laughter, and the play proceeded in an atmosphere of crackling excitement from its first solemn moments to its later passages of zany comedy and its final mellow embrace of a whole village of the living and the dead."[22] In 1955 the theatre brought Osbert and Edith Sitwell to read upon the stage of Sanders Theater, the beautiful if comfortless auditorium erected in memory of Harvard's Union dead after the Civil War, where they (the Sitwells as well as the Union dead) looked and sounded very much at home. It presented two separate plays by Archibald MacLeish, currently Boylston Professor of Oratory and Rhetoric at Harvard, viz., *This Music Crept by Me upon the Waters* and *The Trojan Horse*, and it presented William Alfred's first play, *Agamemnon*, and the first reading of his later, finer play, *Hogan's Goat*. Not all its energies were given to amateur theatricals.

In 1954 the theatre produced V. R. Lang's best work, *I Too Have Lived in Arcadia*, a romantic, vindictive, and highly contemporary but flawed pastoral play, and Denis Johnston's *The Dreaming Dust*, an evocation of the old age of Jonathan Swift. On November 24 it staged a joint reading of poems by Salem Slobodkin, a young Bennington graduate who wrote relentlessly obscure verse, and her friend and mentor William Alfred. Alfred read his dedicated lyrics with Irish charm and feeling, and Slobodkin followed, more than a little inscrutably, with her own, but when the reading ended, Bunny Lang came up to say, generously but who knows how candidly, "Those are very good poems." "Fuck you, you snake," was Salem's response.[23] Members of the Poets' Theatre liked to choose their admirers for themselves.

In 1955 the theatre hit its apogee with the two finest original productions it ever mounted—two productions which balanced perfectly on the edge between poetry and theatre. The first, which had its premiere in the spring of the year, was an adaptation by Mary Manning Howe of *Finnegans Wake*, which imported Tom Clancy (later famous as a member of the Clancy Brothers singing group) for the role of Shem the Penman and imported other Irish voices to give resonance to the sounds and dissonances of Joyce's text, to search out its dramatic surges and quiddities, and to leave spectators with the feeling that they had been living and breathing comfortably and even ecstatically beneath the waters of the Liffey for the space of two hours in the theatre. This production was one of the first to take place in the tiny bandbox playhouse that the theatre had found for itself at 24 Palmer Street, in an old painting loft in a back alley of Cambridge, and it was also one of the first to employ the talents of Edward Dodge Thommen, an experienced repertory director from Buffalo. *Finnegans Wake* had such a success that it would be revived again in the fall of the year and eventually published, along with plays by Lyon Phelps (*The Gospel Witch*) and Archibald MacLeish (*This Music Crept by Me upon the Waters*) in the special series that the Harvard University Press would devote to Poets' Theatre plays.

In the meantime, on October 31, 1955, the theatre presented *The Misanthrope* of Jean Baptiste Poquelin de Molière: "Comedy in Five Acts, 1666, Done into English Verse by Richard Wilbur," as the title page of the first limited edition put it. It was one of the great plays of the canon; the company was ripe to produce it, Thommen having at last trained a corps of actors to speak in verse and move in

time to its action; and, most important, it was the first of
Richard Wilbur's many dramatic verse translations, setting
a new standard for accuracy and excellence in actable En-
glish translations of the French classics. After the season
in which Joyce and Molière, Howe and Wilbur, brought
serious literature into the tiny forty-nine-seat theatre on
Palmer Street, the Poets' Theatre had become, in its special
way, famous.

Whether fame was good for it was another matter. The
Rockefeller Foundation, excited by the possibility of ful-
filling some dream of verse theatre, gave the theatre control
over a fellowship for young playwrights, the funds from
which the theatre's members promptly donated to two of
its earliest and dearest cronies: V. R. Lang, who went on a
honeymoon for the autumn, and Frank O'Hara, who sat
around Harvard Square saloons from January to June chat-
ting emphatically about movies: "His conversation was self-
propelling and one idea, or anecdote, or *bon mot* was fuel
to his own fire, inspiring him verbally to blaze ahead, that
curious voice rising and falling, full of invisible italics, the
strong pianist's hands gesturing with the invariable ciga-
rette."[24] But, truth to tell, he was not enjoying himself very
much. Cambridge had palled: "It's not hot enough, it's not
crowded enough, there's not enough asphalt, and you can
see over buildings too easily."[25] April of 1956 brought forth
a work by John Ashbery (who was living in Paris) entitled
The Compromise; or, The Queen of Cariboo which spoofed
a number of stock figures from Nelson Eddy films, all of
whom were justifiably devoured at the final curtain by a
gigantic thunderbird. In this production I played the part
of a Mountie; Bunny Lang, of a music-hall singer; Robert
J. Lurtsema, of a sinister Indian brave; and Frank O'Hara
delivered a desultory epilogue in the role of "the author
of the play." *The Compromise* comprised all the campy
characteristics of the New York poets who were Bunny's

best friends. But the play had hardly closed when Bunny finally succumbed, after three years of illness, to Hodgkin's disease.

Whatever high qualities of theatre the tatterdemalion earlier years had elicited, the road from this point forward was strewn with broken glass, quarrels between poets and actors, cross-purposes, acrimony, and pandemonium. Leadership, though desperately sought, could not be found after the departure of the coolly competent Roger Shattuck for a Texas professorship. For a short time in 1957 even I served as chairman of the theatre. Managers resigned. Directors resigned. Playwrights protested the quality of their productions. Rockefeller Fellows, after elbowing one another for their places, saw no reason why they should give their plays exclusively to the theatre despite having accepted its stipends. Although the theatre kept on producing good plays to the end—plays by James Merrill, W. S. Merwin, and Robert Penn Warren, Jean Cocteau, and Eugène Ionesco, William Butler Yeats, Samuel Beckett, and (again) Denis Johnston—it also sponsored poetry readings which, though ignored by the actors and directors, may have produced more important historical consequences than many plays the theatre mounted.

On December 4, 1958, the manager's newsletter lamented, "It's cold, cold, cold in the theatre. We're running out of money." By April 29, 1959, the theatre had achieved a deficit, the fire department was complaining, not without reason, of innumerable violations, there were no new plays to be found, and the executive committee voted to dissolve the corporation. Shortly thereafter, the Poets' Theatre building on Palmer Street not unexpectedly went up in flames, hopelessly gutting the little theatre which had staunchly kept open since 1954.

Although clones of the Poets' Theatre have repeatedly attempted to revive it over the last three decades, the original vision of a theatre governed by poets and operating for poetry was realized only for a fleeting while in the middle 1950s; and, whatever the theatre managed to achieve by way of encouraging the dramatic arts, its central accomplishment lay in bringing drama into the art of poetry. Of course John and Doris Holmes read there together in 1958. Where else would they go for an Opening Night? But there were other poets who took the Poets Theatre seriously as a theatrical enterprise as well as a rostrum for the declamation of lyric poetry. It is impossible to write the history of Boston's poetry in this period without including the Poets' Theatre.

2. The Narrator, 1955–1993

FROM *Not Forgotten*

IN MEMORY OF N.W.D.

1 *Watching Her Go*

Drawn by her mumbled entreaties,
We gathered wordlessly around her bed.
She lolled there, shrunken, grizzled,
Garlanded with feeding-tubes, damp with sweat,
Plucking, when she remembered,
At the dressings from the last operation.
Look! Could she have stirred at the touch
Of my hand? Or was it another wave breaking?
The eyes opened. Pain burst at me
As from a cannon's muzzle.
They closed. Flaccid, fumbling
At the unravelled edge of herself,
She died like an otter sliding into a pond.

2 *Dream*

I stood alone at a funeral. It was up to me
To pronounce the oration. My tongue was knotted fast,
And every mourner rolled his maggot eyes.
The reek of greenhouse flowers pressed on ears
Still filled with Handel's "Largo," while the bright box
Gleamed like a conference table, proof against speeches.
Toward the rear of the chapel, twisting Kleenex,
Sat ranks of visitors, urged to stop in on their way
To another appointment by friends who had assured them

This would not take long. It was taking longer and longer.
Who was dead? It was up to me to remember.

I had ransacked my pockets twice—no memoranda—
And my Oxford Book of Consolations had vanished.
The penguin crowd creaked folding chairs impatiently,
So with nothing at all to say, I did what I did:
Danced a very respectful dance on the coffin.
The guest of honor drummed her cold toes
On the underside of the lid . . .

5 *Aftermath*

The world now has
A gray look to it.
There is much less strangeness
Left in strangers.
Mountains have shrunk.
Trees loom with less shadow.
Even the flavor of fear
Tastes as diluted.
Yet the bloom of your presence
Is absurd as unicorns
Or buttercups at Christmas.
Just as your girlishness
Glanced out daily
From within thickened
Middle-aged flesh,
So does memory
Find you hovering
In a hundred places
Or standing
At the center of the music.

I pray you, do not stray
Farther from us.

WRITTEN *1959;* Hudson Review, *1961*

On June 27, 1955, I turned twenty-seven, and as I did so I was literally in full flight from New York, very conscious of making a transformation in my life. I had, five years earlier, leaped without advance thought into book publishing, snatching at the offer of a junior editorship at Harcourt, Brace. I had worked hard, spent some time in the Army, returned to New York, and worked even harder at learning publishing and chasing girls; but of all the poets examined in this book, I alone remained unmarried at the age of twenty-three—unmarried, in fact, at thirty.

I had long known that I loathed New York, that I must for the sake of sanity put the city behind me. I had been lucky enough to land a job in Cambridge as assistant to Thomas J. Wilson, the tall, courtly, loyalty-inspiring director of Harvard University Press. My hope was that, while continuing to learn the publishing trade, I could do what English publishers so often succeeded in: writing at the same time. Perhaps even dare to write poetry.

I drove all night and arrived in Cambridge, my twenty-eighth year rolling up, as it were, on the speedometer. I was resolved to commit myself at last to the writing that all aspects of my previous years in New York—my exhausting job, my equally exhausting love affairs, my intense family ties, my hatred of the city—had prevented me from carrying out. To live solitary in my little three-room duplex (bedroom and bathroom upstairs, sitting room and kitchen downstairs)—or not quite solitary, for I hastened to purchase a double bed Just In Case—seemed an idyllic prospect.

Now I was settled into Boston for sure: dazed after the first round, I realized I had brought more with me to Boston than books and furniture. I had inherited—that is the only word—a passion for poetry, and an awe of its power so overmastering that I was paralyzed by a resistance to becoming a maker of poems. My mother Natalie Weiner's principal interests, growing up in New York in an affluent Jewish family, were political and musical; while my father, poor, illegitimate, and ambitious, aspired to music and poetry. Edward Davison, tall, English, with curly hair which I inherited, vivid, externally self-confident, internally self-pitying, and gifted with a magnificent vocal instrument, also possessed an astounding memory for poetry and song, and, in his relationship with my mother, lavished her with both.

I. A. Richards, who had been one of my teachers at Harvard, had known my father early and wrote me, after his death,

> Going back—beyond fully trust-worthy memory—to his undergraduate days, I first recall his first appearance as *the* likliest contender for the more or less unfilled role of *the* Cambridge Poet. He was being printed, in *The London Mercury* with wide and sensible acclaim. That was how, I think, I met him: forthright, eager, communicative, expansive and sincere with an amazing, free-flowing memory for poetry. He could talk for a whole evening in the phrases of the poems he had been reading.[1]

I had grown up, from seven to seventeen, in Boulder, Colorado, where my father was professor of English at the university. My exposure to poetry at home was total. My father's voice, ringing with lines from Milton or Shelley or Blake or, most often, Shakespeare or Dickens, was as much part of my surround as Boulder's birdsong. President George Norlin, impressed by the young Englishman, put him in charge of the principal oasis at the University of Colorado, the annual three-week summer writers' conference in the Rocky Mountains—then one of only two writers' conferences in America, second only to Bread Loaf, and less regional, perhaps, in its scope. The upshot was constant visits from writers and poets, old friends and new. My parents extended hospitality not only to Frost but to Sandburg, to John Crowe Ransom, Ralph Hodgson, Robert Penn Warren, Ford Madox Ford, John Peale Bishop, Paul Engle, Witter Bynner, Thomas Hornsby Ferril, to say nothing of prose writers and editors ranging from Katherine Anne Porter, Paul Horgan, and Thomas Wolfe, to Wallace Stegner, Frances Lindley, and Howard Mumford Jones.

In the early 1940s my father included my young sister and me in an annual broadcast for National Poetry Week, on Denver's KOA radio station. We would memorize verses of his selection to recite, alternating with him: Wordsworth, ballads, songs from Shakespeare, Thomas Nashe, occasionally one of my father's own poems, and lots of William Blake, including, even, once, a father-son duet, "The Land of Dreams," my father's resonant tenor voice alternating with my own piping soprano:

> Awake awake my little Boy
> Thou wast thy Mothers only joy
> Why dost thou weep in thy gentle sleep
> Awake thy Father does thee keep
>
> O what Land is the Land of Dreams
> What are its Mountains & what are its Streams
> O Father I saw my Mother there
> Among the Lillies by waters fair
>
> Among the Lambs clothed in white
> She walkd with her Thomas in sweet delight
> I wept for joy like a dove I mourn
> O when shall I again return
>
> Dear Child I also by pleasant Streams
> Have wanderd all Night in the Land of Dreams
> But tho calm & warm the waters wide
> I could not get to the other side

Father O Father what do we here
In this Land of unbelief & fear
The Land of Dreams is better far
Above the light of the Morning Star

The mid-1950s were the heyday of J. D. Salinger's pre-
cocious Glass family. Charles Van Doren, another preco-
cious son of a poet, wrote a novel about an existentialist
son who plotted to kill his father; I read the manuscript for
the Atlantic Monthly Press in 1956 and encouraged Charles
to rewrite and publish it, but he opted instead to compete
with his father, Mark, by winning a fortune on national
quiz shows, and he became rich, if infamous. Allen Gins-
berg and his father, Louis, both wrote poetry, and with
mutual affection, despite the clear superiority of the son's
achievement. As for me and my sister, the performing seals,
we had to cope with the presence of my father, who during
our childhood and youth was a recognized literary figure
and public performer; by 1955 he was actually president of
the Poetry Society of America, although by then, alas, he
had not written a new poem for fifteen years.

We two Davison children could hardly help, eventually,
giving ourselves to verse: my sister began writing lyrics
and satirical songs in the 1950s and has by now written
hundreds of songs, mostly for performance in revue and
industrial shows from coast to coast: for her it came as
spontaneously as breathing. How could I imagine that my
voice as a poet could outsing my father's? It took me years
even to start trying.[2] Instead, I gave myself, during school,
college, and after, to singing, both choral and solo, throwing
myself into the words of *Lieder* and Elizabethan songs, and
into the texts of the great choral works which the Harvard
Glee Club, in whose tenor section I sang, was included,
either a capella or with the Boston Symphony Orchestra
under the direction of Koussevitzky, Bruno Walter, Bern-
stein, and Stravinsky. And I was given to theatricals, both

37

spoken and sung. Whether in New York or on military service during the Korean War, I was always able to find a place in a chorus or a choir. Although at Harvard and Cambridge I was exposed to poetry through teachers as eloquent as I. A. Richards, W. J. Bate, F. O. Matthiessen, Howard Mumford Jones, F. R. Leavis, Noel Annan, and others, that was mere literary study: I learned poetry, as poetry, outside the classroom—on the stage, directed by Mary Manning Howe in America and by Peter Wood in England; and in the sweet singing of the choir.

The first thing I did, once I had arranged my furniture and gone to work at Harvard on July 15, was to telephone Sylvia Plath, the most literary young woman in my address book, whom I had got to know while she was still at Smith. Within a week she came to dinner, and during the following month we saw each other ten times, in what one biographer has described as "a summer affair." It came on very fast and terminated as quickly, but it penetrated my consciousness far deeper than I knew. There was something typical of the moment in our heedless, faintly demented relationship, something typical of the late 1950s. Our erotic grapplings were supercharged by the intensity with which Sylvia quizzed me about the poets and poetry I knew, and bubbled over to me about contemporary American poetry—of which at this time I knew very little. Of an evening we would lie on the floor listening with rapture to the recorded voice of Dylan Thomas reciting "In the White Giant's Thigh" or "Fern Hill."

The poems Sylvia had written and showed me that summer were exercises of the performing self. She had a vast collection of manuscripts already, and she told me of her methods of sending them out to magazines, systematic as a Fuller brush salesman. She also spoke of her mentors— Auden, who had taught at Smith during one of her years there but who did not admire her work; Dylan Thomas,

Elizabeth Bishop, Isabella Gardner, Marianne Moore. At this stage of her career, after the 1953 lacuna of her first suicide attempt and its Pyrrhic treatment by electroshock, she was writing stories, poetry, anything she could set her hand to.

Sylvia's passion for writing poems, her satchels full of typescripts, was something new to me. As a Harvard undergraduate I had known poets—John Ashbery, Kenneth Koch, Donald Hall, Robert Bly—but not in such a way as to share their work. At Cambridge University I had veered toward the theatre as an actor and had frustratingly attempted prose fiction. The writing of poetry, I seemed to imagine, belonged to the older, my father's, generation; its study, to the classroom. Now I was lying in the arms of a girl sedulously and passionately dedicated to the practice of the art and to the study of its practitioners, a girl four years younger than I but a decade ahead of me in poetic accomplishment.

To have known the young Sylvia Plath, with all her manic-depressive energy, her enthusiasm, her determination, her duplicity, her intensity, and especially her ambition, may not have been comfortable, but it was certainly exciting. I found her bewildering, enthusiastic, ambitious, a trifle exploitative. Though I was the older partner, it was I who found the affair unmanageable. At first the relationship rested on poetry, literature, publishing, the names of poets, the traffic between my literary information and her own. Then, one night, in a strange mood (this was August 19, 1955, five days before the second anniversary of her 1953 suicide attempt), she told me in pathetic detail the story of that notorious event and its aftermath. Her narrative was as different in tone[3] from *The Bell Jar*—though the details were roughly the same—as though the tale were being told by Esther Summerson and not Esther Greenwood—and I was quite overwhelmed, to the degree that I took to my bed for two days with the disturbance of a non-

39

specific illness. I loved her for the dangers she had passed, and she loved me (I thought) that I did pity them. Before this our relationship had not deepened beyond passion and curiosity.

On August 23 I went to Wellesley to meet Sylvia's mother for the first time, and, after a genteel suppertime, was taken for a walk and, in the fading light, with the air of an executioner, Sylvia told me that she did not want to see me again. In her journals for the following February, in the depth of depression just before her first encounter with Ted Hughes, she remembered me, not unfairly, thus: "Probably it was because I was too intense with one boy after another. . . . Either they were all or nothing. . . . They were also very conspicuously not Richard [Sassoon]. . . . I was too serious for Peter, but that was mainly because he did not participate in the seriousness deeply enough to find out the gaiety beyond."[4] At the time she dismissed me I was shocked and hurt; but, despite the disappointing bruise to my self-esteem, once I had recovered I realized she had left me with a stirring of hope for myself as a poet, perhaps the "seriousness" she demanded, and I would never lose it, even though it remained buried for a while.

Early that fall, after Sylvia had left for Cambridge, I learned that the Poets' Theatre, on whose board Wilbur served, was soon to present the premiere production of *The Misanthrope*, and I tried out for a part. The Poets' Theatre at 24 Palmer Street, which I had never visited before that evening, September 8, 1955, lay at the top of a steep flight of stairs. The theatre was a high, dark space, ridiculously small even with the curtain raised, holding seven rows of six, and one row of five, folding chairs on the same level as the stage area, with two more chairs, on sellout nights, held in reserve to balance on planks atop the sink at the rear, where the set designers washed their paintbrushes. It was already hard to exaggerate the importance of Wilbur's presence in Boston poetry circles, and I felt a little thrill when I saw him, as the tryouts commenced, tall, handsome, courtly, warm, wonderfully ingratiating and easy in his manners, sitting toward the back of the theatre with Mary Manning Howe, adaptor of *Finnegans Wake.*

The theatre space was scattered with chairs. It carried a distant aroma of paint and dust, loomed over by the last production's scenery, hanging limply from the flies, vaguely suggesting the Liffey River at night. The theatre, with its bare working lights, seemed irrefutably dark, and a number of men and women—aspirants for roles in the play—were waiting to be heard. A short, highly animated individual with a tweed cap and a long scarf was hurrying from group to group, chattering in a voice decidedly stagey. This remarkable creature, the director, Edward Thommen, managed to fill a remarkable amount of space, both with sound and with motion, generated evidently not only for the actors' benefit, but for the playwright's. When we were finally called to order, Thommen brandished a few pages of Harcourt, Brace folded and gathered printed sheets, six sets of which had been provided by the publisher, and from which the theatre would shortly prepare its acting sides. When my turn came I was handed the part of Philinte and, reading with a tall, handsome French instructor at Harvard, started off with these lines:

PHILINTE
Why, what have I done, Alceste? Is this quite just?

ALCESTE
My God, you ought to die of self-disgust.
I call your conduct inexcusable, Sir,
And every man of honor will concur.
I see you almost hug a man to death,
Exclaim for joy until you're out of breath,
And supplement these loving demonstrations

41

With endless offers, vows, and protestations;
Then when I ask you "Who was that?" I find
That you can barely bring his name to mind!
Once the man's back is turned, you cease to love him,
And speak with absolute indifference of him!
By God, I say it's base and scandalous
To falsify the heart's affections thus;
If I caught myself behaving in such a way,
I'd hang myself for shame, without delay.

PHILINTE
It hardly seems a hanging matter to me;
I hope that you will take it graciously
If I extend myself a slight reprieve,
And live a little longer, by your leave.[5]

At a second audition, with the poet still a shadowy presence in the back row, we were asked to reverse the roles. At the end of this one I was awarded the part of Alceste, no doubt because I seemed more appropriately cast in a mode unreasonably indignant than pliantly reasonable. I scurried home to start memorizing the lines, which was only the beginning of the pleasure the weeks with this play would give me. Not only did the memorization, and my testing of ways to read the lines, enable me to learn how extraordinary were the inclinations and nuances of Wilbur's verse, but I found, when I compared his translation with the French text, that he had translated line for line, condensing Molière's six-foot alexandrines into five-foot rhymed couplets without losing either meaning or intonation.

I began, moreover, to penetrate the strange, quixotic, self-defeating character of Alceste, not, I began to fear, too unlike my own at the time—a character, as Wilbur wrote in his introduction, who "must play-act continually in order to believe in his own existence, and he welcomes the fact or show of injustice as a dramatic cue." When we began rehearsals, I came to understand how every scene of the play casts a different light, a different shadow, on Alceste, as Célimène and Oronte, Philinte, Acaste, and Arsinoe all test Alceste's virtue in a dangerous effort to be his friend. In judging them all too harshly, he ends by judging himself more harshly still. The play is one of the great dramatic tautologies, evenhanded, elegant, passionate, poised, and in a sense without outcome. Alceste and Philinte assume positions in the closing lines of the play nearly identical to those they occupy at the beginning. But the effect of the play on me, its principal actor, was as tautological as the structure of the play itself. Though I learned tremendously from the text, from Thommen's directing, and from the other actors, particularly Eustacia Grandin as Célimène, I also found myself in the weeks of fathoming the part of Alceste searching more deeply into myself. Wilbur's Alceste changed my life, and it helped me realize myself, at last, as a poet. When the play was over I began to miss Alceste; I felt empty and selfless, lacking in vocal capacity.

The weeks of acting his lines also taught me much about Richard Wilbur, lessons I would not fully understand for years, as his later poetry circled with level, coherent grace through its consistent attitude toward itself, its lucid observation of the natural world, its theistic capacity to "speak of the world's own change,"[6] a frequently repeated theme in his poetry, as in "Love Calls Us to the Things of This World"—a poem he had no doubt recently written or was in fact writing at the very time of *The Misanthrope*'s run.

This theatre was my first true classroom for the learning of what it felt like to write poetry—unless Robert Frost's company was a classroom. Like most of the poets of my age in Boston, I was drawn to Frost and was luckier than many in my access to him because of my parents' long

43

friendship. In 1956–57 I spent some time with Edwin Muir, visiting Harvard, and became enthralled by the inner world of his poetry, with the echoing inner paradoxes of his dream-poems, like "The Combat": "The killing beast that cannot kill/Swells and swells in his fury till/You'd almost think it was despair,"[7] or "The Horses," which T. S. Eliot would call "that great, that terrifying poem of the 'atomic age.' "[8] I also became more deeply involved with the work of my contemporaries through seeing their work put on at the Poets' Theatre, or by personal acquaintance with such as Frank O'Hara, Bunny Lang, whose work I learned from though without admiring it overmuch, and with older poets whom, with my childhood training, I found it easier to talk to: the gay and passionate May Sarton, the grave and considerate John Malcolm Brinnin, the discerning and heterodox Roger Shattuck. Moreover, I was now, in my new work at the Atlantic Monthly Press, reading many manuscripts of contemporary poets and beginning to hear for myself the nuances in the voices of my generation, reviewing the work of Merwin, Hughes, Swenson, and others, in cumulative understanding.

Most important, it took several years of the assistance of a Cambridge psychoanalyst to free me. I was deeply troubled by my father, aroused and uplifted by his poetic voice; disappointed at his betrayal of his own true poetic gift; and angered by his shame, which expressed itself in alcoholism. I had not been able to read or write my way out of that dilemma, nor out of my correlative overdependence on intimacies with women—or, more precisely, relationships with women which failed to be intimate. Finally one great love affair melted and lacerated me for two years and, in the end, made me unhappy enough to give utterance to loss, grief, jealousy, and distress, emotions that I had previously managed somehow to forbid myself. Beyond that, I had to discover the precipitating and unwelcome knowledge that it was not only difficult to write poetry: it could be positively painful. I owe this rudimentary discovery to a publishing assignment. In 1956 I had left Harvard University Press, after repeated solicitation, to join the editorial staff of the Atlantic Monthly Press, then the book publishing arm of *The Atlantic Monthly*, and Seymour Lawrence, then its director, asked me to read the typescript of the selected poems of Stanley Kunitz.

It was a July weekend in 1957, and I was sitting reading Kunitz' typescript on a screened-in porch above the treetops at my apartment at 76 Buckingham Street, Cambridge, where I had moved earlier that year. I had never heard of Stanley Kunitz, whose book had been recommended to the Press by Richard Wilbur. The powerful metaphysical structures of Kunitz' early work, the knotty movement, the intense seriousness, the bodily involvement, disturbed me so deeply that I reacted angrily to the poems, not realizing that it was my emotions, not Kunitz' inadequacy, that were making me shudder, as in one poem prophetically entitled "Open the Gates":

> Within the city of the burning cloud,
> Dragging my life behind me in a sack,
> Naked I prowl, scourged by the black
> Temptation of the blood grown proud.
>
> Here at the monumental door,
> Carved with the curious legend of my youth,
> I brandish the great bone of my death,
> Beat once therewith and beat no more.
>
> The hinges groan: a rush of forms
> Shivers my name, wrenched out of me.
> I stand on the terrible threshold, and I see
> The end and the beginning in each other's arms.[9]

These rock-solid lines at first reading seemed to me windy and pretentious, yet I could not ignore them: the poem would not loose its grip on me. And I found myself even

more deeply disturbed by some of the emotions raised by
"Father and Son," with its concluding lines: "Among the
turtles and the lilies he turned to me/The white ignorant
hollow of his face."[10]

These lines were too much for me to bear, and I could
read no more. I left Kunitz' manuscript on the table next
to my reading chair and walked to my desk, feeling a sense
of turmoil that was wrenching something out of me. I
thought of a friend who, like Kunitz, had known little or
nothing of his father, and whose defenses prevented him
from expressing emotion. Thinking I was writing about my
friend, I wrote the following lines, which would turn out to
be my first published poem:

The Winner

I hear a child inside
Crying to be let out.

"No," shouts the swaggering Self,
"Mind shall destroy all doubt.
Out with all doubt, I say!
Stifle that treacherous word!
I have high deeds to do
Twirling my deathly sword."

Mind's on his mettle now,
deft at his surgical art,
Stunning my pain with pain
Drowning the infant heart.[11]

I could turn back to Kunitz' poems with a cleared head and
a new sense of empowerment: yes, it was possible after all
to penetrate the dark. I could understand—or nearly
understand—that poetry was not intended merely for the
melodies of song, but to open the gates of history, to temper
the metal of truth. The uncompromising power of Stanley's
poetry had broken the ice of my self-suppression.

But it could hardly deprive me of my heredity. After years of listening to my father's voice, is it surprising that, when I came to write poetry, it would show genetic traces of my father's?

The Secret

Other poor fools in mirrors staring
Have tried to see behind the eyes
That watched them baffled and despairing.

One there was who, beyond all error,
found what he looked for and grew wise—
Sufficient wise to smash his mirror;

And ever after walked avoiding
Windows and waterpools wherein
His secret might have leapt from hiding.

And I, ignorant still, and cheated,
Gaze on my glassed and cryptic twin,
And he looks back at me defeated.

EDWARD DAVISON, *1930*

Sacrificial Mask

Mirror, Mirror on the wall,
Who is falsest of us all?

Only silence. Does this mask
Hear no questions mirrors ask?

I have modelled every crease
To ensure the people's peace

Who go easy when they see
Kindly love encasing me.

Now the eyes behind the face
Blink their horror and disgrace.

47

They know well what price was paid
For the features I have made.

PETER DAVISON, *1959*

Part of my difficulty was professional: many of my contemporaries had already involved themselves in academic life: only Merwin and L. E. Sissman had come to the point of rejecting it once and for all, though Plath soon would. I had rejected academic attachments by leaving Harvard University Press after a year and moving to the Atlantic Monthly Press. Instead, I had taken on a lifelong burden of editorial work, editing books of all sorts, and involving myself with the techniques of publishing administration, finance, promotion, and sales.

I entered poetry, like other poets, for reasons other than collegial or competitive ones. I needed poetry to identify my undiscovered self. As Robert Penn Warren would write in *Democracy and Poetry* (1975): "Poetry even, in the same act and the same moment, helps one to grasp reality and to grasp one's own life. Not that it will give definitions and certainties. But it can help us ponder on what Saint Augustine meant when he said that he was a question to himself."[12] I doubt whether in this respect I differed from the other poets of my time: my presence in this book, far from representing an attempt to rank myself with my betters, constitutes a reality check, an autobiographical testament to the nature of the era. Warren himself quoted an essay by C. G. Jung—an essay which I first read in the summer of 1957, which first saw print in *The Atlantic Monthly* of November 1957, and which I caused to be published as a short book, under the title *The Undiscovered Self*, by the Atlantic Monthly Press—and then Warren wrote:

"Resistance to the organized mass [Jung's italics] *can be effective only by the man who is as well organized in*

48

his individuality as the mass itself." . . . And we may argue that the "made thing,"—the poem, the work of art—stands as a "model" of the organized self. . . . That mark of struggle, the human signature, is what gives the aesthetic organization its numinousness. It is what makes us feel that the "made thing" nods mysteriously at us, at the deepest personal inward self. . . . The posited self of a lyric may be taken as purely fictional or as a shadowy persona of a literal self, the author. And this fact leads to the most subtle, complex, and profound relationship in literature.[13]

The fact that my earliest poetry, and that of some of my contemporaries, took the poet into highly personal and intimate material in his or her quest for "aesthetic organization" reveals, I think, more of the nature of the era than it does a deliberate aesthetic move toward "confession" among poets.

My own motives, as I see them from this perspective, seemed to me a question of saving myself from drowning. The poems I was writing from 1957 through 1959 were not, in the contemporary sense, particularly "confessional," though their private sources were as intimate as possible, the self regarding the self in its various disguises and exposing it. Poems I wrote during this time took on a series of semi-demented personae—"chilling salacities," as Dudley Fitts would later call them,[14] e.g., "The Peeper" and "Summer School," both contemporary in their obsession with psychic extremity, and "Artemis," a stylized but impassioned lyric written in 1959, whose interaction of style and theme finally persuaded me that I had begun to learn my craft as a poet:

> See how this girl, trim,
> Fragile as porcelain,
> Poises within herself,
> Standing apart with hounds.

Chaste in her garments, loins
Crisp as a boy's, her knees
Rigid as spear-shafts,
She stares down a victim,

Lowers her eyelids,
Lets the white linen fall,
Stretches, as unaware
Of the blood rising,

Curls like a kitten,
Unclenches her fingers,
While her demented eyes
Flutter in hiding.

Now, when the hunt is closed
Hard on the quarry,
Savage in chase at last,
"Die," she screams, riding.[15]

The events in my life during these two years could be, and have been in my autobiographical writings,[16] detailed and anatomized. The termination of the love affair which governed me in 1956–1957 plunged me, in January 1958, into nine months of erratic, even occasionally dangerous behavior, but nonetheless I managed to keep doing my editorial work at the Atlantic Monthly Press, writing my poems and music reviews, and—a fact which in the intervening decades I have tended to forget—meeting at monthly intervals with a group of writers, mostly young, mostly fiction writers, and usually at my own home. It was in fact a workshop, of the sort that I have subsequently, rather priggishly, found myself disapproving of, yet at this time of self-discovery it gave me a sort of stability in thinking of myself as a writer. In the summer of 1958, by way no doubt of staging a routine protest against my psychotherapist's plan for a leisurely summer vacation, I took a rather adventurous excursion through the Caribbean by trading schooner, only to return from San Juan to New York to find that my mother was in the hospital with a cancer which would prove, within a year, fatal.

A week after returning from her bedside in New York to Boston I found an invitation to come to tea with Sylvia Plath and Ted Hughes, who had just taken up residence in a crow's-nest two-room apartment in Willow Street on Beacon Hill, looking toward the Charles River and Louisburg Square. Sylvia had baked a walnut cake, and both poets had many questions about publishing. It was, I thought, a cheerful occasion in spite of my rashness in showing my hosts some of the poems I had been writing, although it now seems clear to me that Sylvia's principal interest in inviting me may have been intended to lubricate her working relationship with *The Atlantic Monthly*. Their reception of my poems was polite, which at this stage was all the poems could deserve. Ted generously pointed to some promising lines here and there, and recommended that I train my ear by memorizing poems by other poets which I especially admired—excellent advice indeed.

Sylvia was herself apparently pointing toward another depression: on September 14 she had written in her journal, "I must be happy first in my own work and struggle to that end, so my life does not hang on Ted's," followed, on the fifteenth, by "A panic absolute and obliterating . . ." After my visit on the sixteenth, the journal for the eighteenth contains the entry, "Much happier today . . . I got right to work after coffee and wrote 5 pages analyzing P.D. [Peter Davison—this work has disappeared]—one or two well-turned sentences."[17] During that fall and winter I saw Ted and Sylvia with some frequency, since one of her closest friends was my next-door neighbor. In November I invited Sylvia Plath and Ted Hughes to my apartment to meet Robert Frost, an evening at which Frost characteristically did all the talking, though Ted Hughes chimed in often enough. A photograph of the event (taken by *Life* photographer Grey Villett, who was shooting a story about my life as a young bachelor, never published) shows nothing of Sylvia but her left hand, clenched tightly around a glass, and the dark mass of the back of her husband's head. The visit is not mentioned in her journal, though it was the first time Ted, at least, had laid eyes on Frost.

I also, that very week, first spent an evening in New York with the woman with whom I would fall promptly, deliciously, and wholly in love. Jane Truslow was a petite, bewitching, and witty woman, with dark hair and cornflower-blue eyes, working for a New York literary agent. She had—another of these coincidences!—shared a dormitory at Smith College with Sylvia Plath and, like Sylvia, had lost her father early, like Sylvia had been a *Mademoiselle* guest editor, like Sylvia had been a student of Alfred Kazin, like her had aspirations to be a writer, and she also had suffered from self-destructive psychic breakdowns—although, unlike Sylvia, she would never do so again. The two women maintained a wary friendship and correspondence after our marriage on March 7, 1959.

One of the first consequences of marriage was the transformation of my little household at 76 Buckingham Street, which Jane, painting and sewing and carpentering, altered into a place very different from its bachelor decor. She was, as she would later describe herself in a book, "the last of the red-hot housewives,"[18] and the nesting impulse was powerful in her. Ted and Sylvia were, when all was prepared, invited to dinner at 76 Buckingham Street, with a copy of the June *Atlantic Monthly* (containing poems by Adrienne Rich and myself) on the table, on May 31, 1959, and the evening, I thought in my innocence, was cheery, full of laughter and Ted's good humor. But Sylvia's unpublished journal had other observations to make, based on other feelings. There is something wrong here, she felt, all of Jane's painting and redecorating (just the sort of home-furbishing she would bring to her own cottage in

North Tawton in a year or two[19]) and purchasing of Lawrence Sisson's watercolor (a wedding present). Does Jane know, Sylvia wondered melodramatically, that she is redecorating the place where Peter "kept his mistress" for two years? And, her unpublished journal goes on inevitably to inquire, does Jane know about *me*? Of course she did, and only Sylvia would not instantly have known as much in the first exchange of glances. A few days later Ted and Sylvia left Boston, and we would see them together only once more, in London a year afterward.

Robert Lowell had been living at 239 Marlborough Street in Boston since 1955 and teaching at Boston University. I knew him, had known him a little ever since my Boulder childhood, had known more than one woman who had been his wife or lover—the brilliant Jean Stafford, my father's Colorado student; the engaging Gertrude Buckman, the former wife of Delmore Schwartz, who was now my publishing colleague at Little, Brown; and another much younger woman who, a fellow mental patient at the McLean Hospital during Lowell's breakdowns in the spring of 1958, was one of those for whom Lowell, in the throes of mania, had demanded from his long-suffering wife a new start, a new woman, a new life. This girl, whom I took to dinner and movies and kept friendly company with, was still in the fall of 1958 recovering from the experience of the previous winter and told me much—more than I wanted to know—about Lowell's demented phases, not that the common gossip of the literary community was likely to have spared him.

I wrote a poem which began, in draft: "There's been some talk about you, but it's died/Away of late, since you came home again . . ." but I dropped those lines in the final version of "To a Mad Friend" before it was published in *Harper's*.[20] Later, in a postcard not unlike those he sent to other poets, Lowell spoke kindly of my poems published in an anthology, and suggested that "we struggle with some of the same themes and material. I still find it a miracle if anything of mine comes off, though each new start is full of hope."[21] Well, some of the same forces were driving us all. He did indeed tower over the rest of us like Antony, thanks to his intensity, his achievement, his intelligence, and, yes, even his madness: in his livery walked crowns and crownets. But I was slow and clumsy in absorbing Lowell's new mode of poetry: when I reviewed *Life Studies* in *The Atlantic Monthly* for July 1959, I would conclude helplessly by saying, "The reader remains more fascinated by Lowell's life than by his poems."

At the end of 1958, however, I had written to myself, "My poems are free at last," and it was true that they drew encouragement from other poets and readers. May Sarton was particularly generous with her praise; I. A. Richards wrote me warmly in response to some of my poems, notably "Not Forgotten," and Robert Frost, on our evenings together, usually asked to see copies of what I had been writing—copies that he read in private, and only once commented on to me. I have been told by scholars that he wrote a good deal about them, but I have never dared look up his remarks in the Frost archives. "Not too much of the sadness," was all he ever said to me, "not so much of the sadness."

Over this landscape, enriched by love and by the arrival of poems in my life, hung the dreadful gloom of mortality, and the inexorable approach of my mother's death, which arrived the day after her sixtieth birthday, on September 24, 1959. My mother, in constant pain, lost even the power of speech as metastasizing cancer damaged her brain. As the end approached, and after it had passed, I wrote a group of poems, "Not Forgotten," to deal—in terms of the self—with the crushing and paradoxical emotions that so archetypal a loss produced. This was as close to "confession" as my poems were to come—until the next death! Nonetheless,

54

"Not Forgotten" shoehorned me into a number of anthologies that followed that fashion in the 1960s. Yet I had been as true to "that mark of struggle, the human signature," as I knew how. And this poem, when it appeared in *The Hudson Review* in 1961, brought me an instant response from the benevolent John L. Sweeney, leading to recordings, readings, and eventually I suppose, if I am to judge from Dudley Fitts' introduction to *The Breaking of the Day*, the Yale Series of Younger Poets award in 1963. More important in the long run, this suite of poems gave evidence that I was no longer timorous about bringing poetry into a truthful embrace with the most powerful emotions I could feel.

As my work began to appear in magazines, I got acquainted, not only through my attendance at poetry readings at the Poets' Theatre and elsewhere, but through the normal circulation of like-minded professionals of my own age, as well as through the poets who published or aspired to publish in *The Atlantic Monthly*, those other poets who lived nearby, and learned to speak to them about those things that our work had in common—those things, at least, that it was possible to speak about. When he was not ill, Robert Lowell was to be seen often in public, often at his own readings—I first heard him read the early poems from *Life Studies* in 1956. I got to know May Sarton, a noted Cambridge figure, and through John Malcolm Brinnin, a hospitable Atlantic Monthly Press author, I met Howard Moss and Philip Booth; through *The Atlantic Monthly* I often saw Alastair Reid, whom I had met years earlier and who, nearly alone among these poets, gladly read my beginning poems and gave me welcome advice; through membership in a literary softball game I met George Starbuck and Arthur Freeman; through Arthur Freeman I met Maxine Kumin and Anne Sexton, who were easy to recognize since they attended, like two dark beautiful caryatids, all poetry readings together. (As Maxine Kumin told me later, Anne used to say, "They couldn't tell the kook from the Jew."[22]) Through sheer admiration I called up Adrienne Rich and invited her to lunch, hoping that the author of *The Diamond Cutters* might want to become an Atlantic Monthly Press author in the future. On visits to Middletown I would encounter Dick Wilbur, and on visits to New York, Bill Merwin, who, beginning in 1962, spent his American visits mostly in New York, where he edited the poetry for *The Nation* for several years.

So many coincidences pepper this poetic era. In the summer of 1957, when I put down Stanley Kunitz' manuscript to write my first poem, it was virtually the very day when Robert Lowell, entrapped in family entanglements after the deaths of both parents, at last became free to write "Skunk Hour" and begin writing the other poems in *Life Studies* that revealed the actualities of his family life. ("Lowell always spoke of August and September of 1957 as a turning point in the writing of *Life Studies*."[23]) Sylvia Plath, in a black depression on Cape Cod after the rejection of a poetry collection by the Yale Series of Younger Poets, and fearing lest she might be pregnant ("I have never in my life, except that deadly summer of 1953, & fall, gone through such a black lethal two weeks") was writing a "long lumbering dialogue verse poem about two people arguing over a Ouija board."[24] Anne Sexton, at some time before September 29, 1957, had written "Music Swims Back to Me," one of her first truly fine poems, and showed it to Maxine Kumin, which opened their long friendship. Merwin, in Castine, had just gone through the powerful experience of a storm-tossed voyage with George Kirstein and resumed the work of reconciling himself with America that would bring him to the conclusion of *The Drunk in the Furnace*. L. E. Sissman was on the verge of divorcing his first wife, Barbara Klauer. Both Adrienne Rich and Elizabeth Hardwick had new babies, born early in 1957, which could well explain why Rich seems to have written almost nothing during that year, not turning to new—and very different—work until 1958. Donald Hall was just leaving Boston, permanently, for Ann Arbor; Richard Wilbur, for Wesleyan. Stanley Kunitz, with his *Selected Poems, 1928–1958* accepted for 1958 publication by the Atlantic Monthly Press, was ready for a change of life, and he would marry his third wife, Elise Asher, on the summer solstice in 1958, come to Boston in the fall, and turn to a new kind of poetry. Philip Booth was encountering, in 1958, a psychic impasse, having come up against the irrefragable refusal to mourn the death of his mother four years earlier. And I too, in the spring of 1958, went through as bad a psychic period as I have ever known.

In short, while 1957 seems to have been, for many of the Boston poets, a time of clarification, it was followed, in 1958, by a very stormy aftermath, and then, in 1959, by climactic changes in the lives and work of nearly all the poets this book takes up. It may not be too much to claim that the year 1959 was the turning point, the pivot on which the poetry of the 1950s turned into that of the 1960s.

Most of what I myself wrote was veracious enough, but in what sense was it truthful to my spirit as opposed to my diction? That was the challenge that the poets of 1959 faced. What sound should they adopt for their veracities? We shall see how often they succeeded in finding the true voice. It would take me into my forties, another decade, more or less, to speak completely. I would not be one of our explorers: that would be left up to Lowell, Merwin, Kunitz, and the women, those Bacchae of our generation, Plath, Rich, and Sexton.

3. Speak of the World's Own Change: Richard Wilbur, 1955–1957

Love Calls Us to the Things of This World

The eyes open to a cry of pulleys,
And spirited from sleep, the astounded soul
Hangs for a moment bodiless and simple
As false dawn.
                        Outside the open window
The morning air is all awash with angels.

Some are in bed-sheets, some are in blouses,
Some are in smocks: but truly there they are.
Now they are rising together in calm swells
Of halcyon feeling, filling whatever they wear
With the deep joy of their impersonal breathing;

Now they are flying in place, conveying
The terrible speed of their omnipresence, moving
And staying like white water; and now of a sudden
They swoon down into so rapt a quiet
That nobody seems to be there.
                        The soul shrinks

From all that it is about to remember,
From the punctual rape of every blessèd day,
And cries,

"Oh, let there be nothing on earth but laundry,
Nothing but rosy hands in the rising steam
And clear dances done in the sight of heaven."

Yet, as the sun acknowledges
With a warm look the world's hunks and colors,
The soul descends once more in bitter love
To accept the waking body, saying now
In a changed voice as the man yawns and rises,

"Bring them down from their ruddy gallows;
Let there be clean linen for the backs of thieves;
Let lovers go fresh and sweet to be undone,
And the heaviest nuns walk in a pure floating
Of dark habits,
        keeping their difficult balance."

PUBLISHED *1956*[1]

It would have been nearly impossible for an eastern undergraduate of literary inclinations to have got through college in the late 1940s or early 1950s without becoming aware of the poetry of Richard Wilbur, even if the reader, as I did, swallowed sideways. As a student at Harvard between 1945 and 1949, I knew Wilbur a little, as a cool, handsome, invariably courteous presence, but he never taught me. I read his poems as they appeared in local magazines; but I was still a clumsy consumer of contemporary poetry. At first I missed connections, in my ignorance, with all those qualities in Wilbur's work that I now cherish, suffering as I did from a form of poetry-reading disability, or, perhaps, undereducation. I was devoted to Frost, puzzled by Marianne Moore, fascinated by Cummings, dubious about Sandburg, as yet entirely unacquainted with Stevens or Williams or even Robert Graves. My college studies took me from Shakespeare through Hardy, and I argued, in an

59

essay written in my senior year, that Hardy was a grander and greater poet than Yeats—not a popular stance then or now, but I am not certain I have ever wanted to change it.

I began to read Wilbur with more insight after a graduate year of reading modern poetry in England, when, in 1950, I joined the editorial staff of Harcourt, Brace and Company just at the time Wilbur's second volume, *Ceremony and Other Poems*, appeared, and I found myself reading both *Ceremony* and its 1947 predecessor, *The Beautiful Changes*, with pleasure; for Wilbur seemed like the natural heir, with his seventeenth-century graces and metaphysical moves, to the major tradition in poetry as we viewed it. But even so, I can still see why his poems had not immediately attracted me as a student: they stood at a distance from the self. Something was being withheld.

Wilbur more than other poets of his generation was able to find, in the world as it was, drama, conflict, irony, and beauty, and he has continued to give himself over to that form of utterance for a lifetime. Unlike most of the work of his contemporaries, his is a poetry seldom given to the first person, to the revelation of interior states, to psychic or emotional agitation. Donald Hall has dubbed it "invulnerable."[2] Wilbur shunned the high-profile self-expression of Jarrell, Berryman, Roethke, Lowell, and others by retaining—with whatever inner difficulty—his balance, his equability, his willingness to convey, like his father the portrait painter, the inner states of other persons, other actors, and to avoid both the private and the aesthetic dangers of self-revelation. Seldom has a poet been less "confessional." When he speaks of his father in his poetry—only once, if I'm not mistaken, in an early poem called "My Father Paints the Summer," it is his father's art he admires, an art performed at studio distance from its subject:

> But up in his room by artificial light
> My father paints the summer, and his brush

Tricks into sight
The prosperous sleep, the girdling stir and clear steep hush
Of a summer never seen,
A granted green.[3]

Richard Wilbur's father, Lawrence Lazear Wilbur, was indeed a portrait painter, creator of calm landscapes as well as serene visions of those who sat for him. Their family lived, after young Richard's birth in New York in 1921, on farmland in New Jersey, where the young man was reared, in fact, closer to the natural world than most other poets of his Boston generation. He hitchhiked and hopped freights across the country and got involved with the left-wing politics of the time. He attended Amherst College at a time when its famous expository writing program was beginning to form itself.

One of his reasons for choosing Amherst was the presence there of Robert Frost, but before young Wilbur entered, Frost quarrelled with Amherst's President King and took himself off to Dartmouth College instead—where he would have an important effect on the life and work of, among others, Philip Booth, whose father was a member of the Dartmouth faculty. For Wilbur, Amherst provided a rich education, but not much in the way of poetry-writing. "If you profited from the nurture of your teachers you were probably going to emerge as a poet/critic. There was a very encouraging atmosphere, but there was only one course in creative writing. I never took it, and I never thought I was missing anything."[4] Nonetheless, Wilbur married (in 1942 after his Amherst graduation) Charlotte Ward, the daughter of a writer who had for a while edited the *Boston Post*. She and her family had spent much of her childhood in Italy.[5]

Not long after the Wilburs' marriage in 1942 Richard had been called to the war, where, despite some official suspicion of his leftish politics, he eventually ended up in

Italy, involved in Army Signal Corps cryptographic work during the invasion of the Italian peninsula, close to the horrible bloodletting at Anzio and the campaign in southern France, to start him writing poems, love poems to his wife at home, poems about the war. As one of his discerning critics writes, "Wilbur started writing poetry in combat; he became a poet in truth, when after the smoke had cleared and the grief given way to some species of calm, civilization began to rebuild itself."[6] When the war was over he had already formed, under the advice of his Amherst teachers, the ambition to undertake graduate study at Harvard and become a teacher of seventeenth-century literature: "the whole blooming seventeenth century, the European seventeenth century."[7] At Harvard, assisted by the G.I. Bill of Rights, he had, within a year after his entrance in early 1946, achieved nearly everything except the dissertation for the doctorate, and learned all those languages.

Then I had the great luck to be taken in the Society of Fellows, and was in that from 1947 until 1950. Almost at once when I got to Harvard I found myself being "discovered" as a poet. Charlee let the secret out to our friend André du Bouchet. Some of them were sent down to Reynal and Hitchcock, and they simply accepted the manuscript. . . . They wanted me to write a few good poems to add to what they had, but they right away made a rash commitment to doing a book, and that right away changed my sense of commitment to what I was doing at Harvard. . . . Some of my first poems were in the *Advocate* [the Harvard undergraduate literary magazine]. The encouragers of poetry on the Harvard faculty were people like Ted Spencer, who saw one of those *Advocate* poems and said, "Are all your poems like this?" and F. O. Matthiessen, who in his insanely busy life read the whole manuscript of my first book. And I. A. Richards, Ted Morrison, Douglas

Bush. I never gave a poetry reading at Harvard, no matter how small a room, that wasn't attended by Douglas Bush. And of course there was Harry Levin, who, though he blushes about it now, published some quite decent poems a long time ago in the *Sewanee Review*, and of course Jack Sweeney. There was all that encouragement there, all that responsiveness to one's being a poet. And in the Society of Fellows you could find yourself at Monday evening dinners sitting next to Alfred North Whitehead. It made me feel I had committed myself for three years to being a scholar and if possible even a thinker, and it rather overturned me in a nice way when Crane Brinton, who was the chief of the Senior Fellows at that time, said to me, "Look, you're probably worrying about whether to be a scholar or a poet. I just want to tell you that it's all right for you to be a poet." So I found myself as I left those three wonderful years in the Society [i.e., in 1950] wanting to go on into teaching. I already had a couple of children and really needed the dough. They were kind enough to put me in right away as a Briggs-Copeland Assistant Professor; therefore I was there for five years but not presumably on the promotional ladder. In the four years I taught at Harvard I taught in Jack Sweeney's marvelous freshman humanities program, where I read all the great books I'd never read and had to become articulate about them. I do think that for me as a poet that was invaluable. . . . I did a course in modern poetry that had an appallingly big enrollment, and so I had to be something of a lecturer. Well, that was all very pleasant and hard-trying and would I suppose have wiped me out as a poet had it not been for a Guggenheim in 1952 and a Prix de Rome absence in 1954–55. Those fellowships really did save me, I think, from being deflected back into full-time teaching and scholarship. And then, in 1955, I went out to Wellesley, and stayed there for a couple of years, but that too was sort of disrupted and punctuated because of the *Candide* thing I got into in 1956. I had to take a leave of absence in order to finish up writing the show, which opened at the very end of 1956.[8]

The poets with whom Wilbur mingled during his years at Harvard and Wellesley, 1946–1957, were a different group from those who would dominate Boston at the end of the decade, pushing off, as it were, from the poetic boundary he had set for them. A lifelong friendship grew up between Robert Frost and the Wilburs, fanned by the warmth of Frost's grateful memories of Charlotte Ward Wilbur's great-aunt Susan Hayes Ward (the first editor to accept Frost's poems for publication, in *The Independent* in 1894 and after), and a relation between the work of the two poets made itself manifest from the outset. (In this respect Wilbur does not differ from other poets of the time, but his later poem "Seed Leaves" is the most brilliant imitation of Frost ever written by any other poet.) In Wilbur's years in Cambridge and Wellesley (1946–1957) he especially saw a lot of Frost, not only around Boston but at the summer writers' conferences at Bread Loaf, in Vermont.

John Ciardi, May Sarton, Richard Eberhart, John Holmes, occasionally Edwin Honig or Archibald MacLeish, would come together of an evening at one person's house, often John Holmes' house in Medford, and share their poems. There was real criticism, no mere puffery. Each poet brought a poem and read it aloud; they worked on it, and then drinks would be served, and the evening would relax. Wilbur recalls:

Wonderful Dick Eberhart was incapable of self-criticism and incapable of profiting by anyone else's criticism. He was always just plain out to show us new poems and hope to be appreciated. John Holmes, on the other hand, produced poetry promiscuously, some

64

of it very fine, some of it mere typewriting, and he was always ready to throw away a poem if it didn't click with people. John Ciardi took detailed criticism, largely without bellicosity, and sometimes he made a change or two. I forget what my attitude was, except that I was anxious to please, anxious to be praised. I forget whether I ever doctored a poem in the light of criticism. May was a very warm, encouraging person when she would like a piece. She was generous. She wanted to like things. John Ciardi was often rather harsh with her in critical sessions. She felt that he was cruel. There was a strange strand in John's otherwise admirable nature. He was never very kindly toward women writers or women artists with a few exceptions.[9]

Richard Eberhart's big birthday parties, in Cambridge at his mother's house, brought out an additional array of poets—Robert Lowell, Elizabeth Bishop, Dylan Thomas, Dudley Fitts, Merrill Moore, Peter Viereck, Conrad Aiken, Ruth Hershberger, John Malcolm Brinnin, Howard Moss, J. V. Cunningham—but many of these people were from out of town and few of them remained in Boston and environs after 1956. By that time Wilbur himself was about to depart, and a new group of poets, most of them born in the 1920s, were to grow up and move into the pueblo, furnished with a postwar education rather than the classical prewar education shared by Wilbur, Lowell, Berryman, and Jarrell, and nurturing different expectations from the art of poetry and from their colleagues alike.

When Wilbur was going through his formative years, the world of poetry was very different from what it would become a very few years later: the shift between the sociology of poetry in the early 1950s and the late 1950s was profound. Wilbur remembers fewer poetry readings, and fewer poetry workshops, than his younger friends recall during the very same years, but he surmises that the fresh excitement about poetry of his postgraduate years got organized through the world of Harvard-sponsored symposia:

There were endless panel discussions of poetry, the way it was written and the way it ought to be written, and it seems to me that between 1946 and 1953 I must have done twenty of those things with various casts of characters in the Boston area, not just at Harvard, often at this or that church. But these gatherings of five people, twenty people, were just part of that excitement, encouraging I think to writers, giving them the feeling that they were being what they ought to be, doing what they ought to do, not determining at all. Jack Sweeney—the man who ran the Widener Library Poetry Room, later the Lamont Poetry Room— did wonderful acts of sponsorship, all that encouragement there, all that responsiveness to one's being a poet—I guess they were monthly gatherings in the Poetry Room at Widener, at which on each occasion someone would read, and one of his poems would be printed up and handed around. I remember Delmore Schwartz reading, and Ruth Stone, and I remember I read with trepidation a lot of my poems; it was probably the first time I ever read to any group. And then we'd have a few drinks, and then it would be over for that month. But in some way it was a little affirmation of the importance of what we were doing. It didn't turn into the workshop kind of thing.[10]

Richard and Charlee Wilbur were the sort of young people who were taken up by the senior members of the faculty, Archibald and Ada MacLeish, Kenneth and Eleanor Murdock, Harry and Elena Levin: "We were forever seeing the MacLeishes, and other members of the senior faculty there,"[11] even after they left Harvard for Wellesley. This was the era of the urban academic dinner party, a formidable and deeply entrenched institution of the 1950s and

1960s, and the Wilburs were one of the most desirable younger couples available for these ceremonies. There was a special personal interaction between the MacLeishes and the Wilburs, a social poise they had in common, two handsome poets and two charming women, who, though they saw many things differently, enjoyed the worldliness and the bonhomie of each other's company. Though they stood a generation apart, the two poets could imagine exchanging places in society, and the two men shared qualities of outward amiability and inner secretiveness.

But Wilbur, though he was flattered by MacLeish's favor, by no means felt altogether at home with his poetry. MacLeish, he remembers, after he arrived at Harvard in 1949, took a generous interest in a lot of the young poets who were then undergraduates, even though many of them felt that his standards for poetry were different from those they had or aspired to.

Young students like John Ashbery, Robert Bly, Donald Hall, and Kenneth Koch were both greatly benefited by Archie's presence and by what he added to the excitement about poetry at Harvard, by his goodness in reading manuscripts, and by his encouragement; and at the same time were—on one ground or another— somewhat resistant to his example and his teachings. There are a few of his poems that I cherish. But as an example he matters to me, not in the whole range of his work but just in those particular wonderful poems. He was one of the few people who when I showed him a poem gave me really useful criticism. He could put his finger right on the defect. But I think Archie's general position seemed square even to people of my age. After I went to Wesleyan, and Archie retired in 1962, he wanted me to succeed him, but Charlee and I felt that somehow if we went back to Harvard we would be happily devoured by it, that we would be expected to perform all the functions which the MacLeishes had performed.[12]

This phase of Wilbur's life, during which the family was growing to encompass four children and the poet had both to support this family and to sustain his work, would seem to have involved him in an ambivalent relationship with Harvard, a relationship that carried over into his subsequent academic relationships. Wilbur's instincts led him to protect his poetry, to keep his poetic life and his academic life separate; and they even set a geographical distance between one and the other. The Wilburs' four children had to be educated, and the Cambridge public schools were notoriously undesirable in those years. During a good portion of his time on the Harvard faculty, after 1950, the Wilburs resided in Lincoln, some ten miles from Cambridge. "We decided we wanted to go out and live in the country; we were both country folks."[13] Moreover, Wilbur was extremely fortunate with fellowships: after his junior fellowship at Harvard, 1947–1950, he joined the Harvard faculty; then in 1952–1953 a Guggenheim Fellowship took the family to New Mexico; in 1954–1955 a Prix de Rome took the family to Italy; and in 1956–1957 he took a leave of absence from Wellesley to work with Lillian Hellman and Leonard Bernstein on *Candide*. In short, he spent more than half of his time *not* teaching, between 1947 and 1957. This was lucky for his poetry, for as a teacher he was especially assiduous in preparation, giving about eight hours in study for each hour in the classroom.[14] When he was teaching, he lived at a sanitary distance from his work; and later, when he moved to Wesleyan University, he resided in Portland, a few miles from the campus, across the Connecticut River. In the summers he repaired to Cummington, Massachusetts, to a lovely house located on an old farmstead not far from Archibald MacLeish's place of retirement in Conway. There was an outbuilding which he converted into a poet's tower, and later a tennis court and a swimming pool. Unlike many of his contemporaries, in fact, he endeavored to insulate himself from the poetry world, an insulation which sometimes reflects itself in his poetry.

At first it may have seemed tempting to think that he could write for the stage, and in 1952, in New Mexico, Wilbur's intention was to write an original verse play, "which I never managed to do. That led happily to *The Misanthrope* and to your Alceste."[15] He had found the Poets' Theatre amusing but not engrossing. He seemed to enjoy Wellesley; but his time at Harvard had been both nourishing and overwhelming, and it seemed to him essential as a poet to keep a safe distance between himself and Cambridge, although he would always retain friendships there, and some of his children would take up residence there in later years.

During his Cambridge and Wellesley years he kept at arm's length from the younger poets, though those who ventured to approach him were never received with anything but kindness. Donald Hall, for example, never felt any resistance to his dropping by with a few poems, and Wilbur always welcomed him. He was admired, his company was a delight. Poet after poet thought of him, at least during these years, and some till this day, as the most accomplished poet in America. The year 1956 seems to have been the crux of the poetic career of Richard Wilbur. In that year he published his most acclaimed book of verse, *Things of This World*; he absented himself from Wellesley College to collaborate with Leonard Bernstein and Lillian Hellman on the musical version of *Candide*, and his first major verse translation, Molière's *The Misanthrope*, after its 1955 publication by Harcourt, Brace and its simultaneous production by the Poets' Theatre, went into its first New York production. *Candide* did not, however, achieve the smash Broadway success that was expected of it, though it made an indelible mark on the musical theatre and has been revived in New York as recently as 1991. Wilbur's *The Misanthrope* remains the standard translation till this day.

Thus Wilbur had, at thirty-five, already managed every accomplishment that a young American poet can aspire to, and, for *Things of This World*, he now, in 1957, topped it all off with the Pulitzer Prize in poetry and the National Book Award. He had also begun to be rewarded with the sort of niggling reserved for those who succeed. Though critics like Donald Hall wrote, "Wilbur has been a particularly accomplished poet of delight. . . . No one since Herrick has written more exactly. . . . *The Misanthrope* is Wilbur's *chef d'oeuvre* as a translator; it contains passages which do not curl up and die at the mention of Dryden,"[16] others seemed to make terrific efforts to find a fly in the ointment: "It is astonishing how rarely Wilbur writes in the bleak, bitter, or inconsolable mood. . . . He walks among the devils that his fellow poets keep pointing out to him, but he doesn't see them. Instead, he persists in seeing angels. . . . How can he be so damnably good-natured in an abominable world?"[17] Randall Jarrell, pungent as always, wrote: "Mr. Wilbur never goes too far, but he never goes far enough. In the most serious sense of the word he is not a very satisfactory poet. And yet he seems the best of the quite young poets writing in this country, poets considerably younger than Lowell and Bishop and Shapiro and Roethke and Schwartz. . . . His impersonal, exactly accomplished, faintly sententious skill produces poems that, ordinarily, compose themselves into a little too regular a beauty. . . . Wilbur's lyric calling-to-life of the things of this world—the things, rather than the processes or the people—specializes in both true and false happy endings, not by choice but by necessity. . . ."[18] And, it is true, the very angels in "Love Calls Us to the Things of This World" are, in fact, *things*, clothes, laundry.

Thus, lines were already being drawn between those who

relished the equability, the polished monumentality, the material and spiritual balance of Richard Wilbur, and those who somehow could not forgive him for the smile on his face. Wilbur himself describes his coming up against one new wave in 1956:

> When I left the *Candide* operation and my per diems were exhausted, and not much money was coming in, I went to the West Coast to try to raise some. Allen Ginsberg had just read "Howl" for the first time as I arrived in San Francisco, and already things were jelling: there was a sudden choosing up of sides, or choosing of stances or postures. All sorts of people had decided to be Beats within a few days and were wearing the uniform. I found myself running into a curious stereotyping of myself. I remember being introduced by Robert Duncan at San Francisco State just after *Things of This World* was published, and he really said to the audience, "He's not my kind of poet at all." He didn't say, Here's this gray-flannel-establishment-easterner-Anglophile, and all the things that he'd have said later. He said, nevertheless, "For what he is, Wilbur has certain good qualities. Do listen to him." It wasn't a churlish introduction; it was one of those unhappily honest performances that people sometimes give.[19]

Nonetheless Wilbur was perfectly aware that other poets whose temperaments were less sanguine than his own—Roethke, Lowell, Jarrell, Berryman—were suffering in ways that, whether or not Wilbur shared them, he was unwilling to reveal. "It certainly is true that a lot of people were falling apart and preparing to die, and I wonder to what extent that is really unrelated to choice of literary style or unrelated to literary currents one might distinguish."[20] But Wilbur did not at this stage know much about the other poets who had recently arrived in Boston, was only slightly acquainted with Adrienne Rich, Sylvia Plath, Anne Sexton,

Maxine Kumin, W. S. Merwin, not at all with L. E. Sissman, and his acquaintance with Robert Lowell was, as with some of Lowell's other friends, a trifle wary. At Wellesley, on the other hand, he fell in with a different group of poets, younger men like David Ferry and Philip Booth, who were also on the faculty, and older poets like the great Jorge Guillén, one of the famous generation of Spanish poets from the Civil War, who took up a visiting professorship at Wellesley during these years, and two of whose poems Wilbur translated very beautifully: "The Horses," and "Death, from a Distance." In addition to such translations he reached back to Anglo-Saxon models ("Junk") to the fourth century ("Eight Riddles from Symphosius"), and, most touchingly of all, to fifteenth-century France, where Wilbur uncharacteristically uses the first person, but characteristically puts it in the mouth of a character other than himself. He has spoken of this poem as representing the frustrations of academic life, where so much is offered to the thirsty learner, and there is so little time to drink or swallow:

Ballade for the Duke of Orléans

> who offered a prize at Blois, circa 1457, for
> the best ballade employing the line "Je
> meurs de soif auprès de la fontaine."

Flailed from the heart of water in a bow,
He took the falling fly; my line went taut;
Foam was in uproar where he drove below;
In spangling air I fought him and was fought.
Then, wearied to the shallows, he was caught,
Gasped in the net, lay still and stony-eyed.
It was no fading iris I had sought.
I die of thirst, here at the fountain-side.

Down in the harbor's flow and counter-flow
I left my ships with hopes and heroes fraught.
Ten times more golden than the sun could show,

Calypso gave the darkness I besought.
Oh, but her fleecy touch was dearly bought:
All spent, I wakened by my only bride,
Beside whom every vision is but nought,
And die of thirst, here at the fountain-side.

Where does that Plenty dwell, I'd like to know,
Which fathered poor Desire, as Plato taught?
Out on the real and endless waters go
Conquistador and stubborn Argonaut.
Where Buddha bathed, the golden bowl he brought
Gilded the stream, but stalled its living tide.
The sunlight withers as the verse is wrought.
I die of thirst, here at the fountain-side.

ENVOI

Duke, keep your coin. All men are born distraught,
And will not for the world be satisfied.
Whether we live in fact, or but in thought,
We die of thirst, here at the fountain-side.[21]

In 1957 he was invited to teach at Wesleyan University, where he would spend the next twenty years, after 1962, on an enviable teaching schedule. He turned soon after translating *The Misanthrope* to translating *Tartuffe*; his next volume of poems, *Advice to a Prophet* (1961), was rich with translations (eight of the thirty-one poems in its pages derive from languages other than English), and the lyrics evinced a growing tendency toward the religious themes that would continue to serve as ribs and backbone in Wilbur's later work.

As in his earlier poems, Wilbur intermingled action and objects by substituting nouns for verbs, verbs for nouns (a fire-truck speeding through the streets is described as "blurring to sheer verb"[22]), as though the distinction between motion and stasis were too difficult to determine:

Ask us, prophet, how we shall call
Our natures forth when that live tongue is all
Dispelled, that glass obscured or broken

In which we have said the rose of our love and the clean
Horse of our courage, in which beheld
The singing locust of the soul unshelled,
And all we mean or wish to mean.[23]

As Anthony Hecht has written, "his is the most kinetic poetry I know: verbs are among his decisively important tools, and his poetry is everywhere a vision of *action*, of motion and performance."[24]

Wilbur's work did not take a sharp turn, as Lowell's and other poets' did: he continued steadily along the path that had been laid out since his early work and, unlike most of the other Boston poets, did not enter on a "new period." "Who knows what leads people to have new periods?" he once said. "It's not necessarily being led. When people decide it's time to try a new sensibility, a new technique, a new way of being ambitious, it can I suppose mean nothing more than what Yeats was saying in that song from a play, 'The painter's brush consumes his dreams'—in which he's essentially saying the cycles turn, things come and go, people wear one thing out and they have to try another."[25] Moreover, Wilbur, unlike those poets who immersed themselves in the acidic turmoil of literary life like Robert Lowell and John Berryman, distracted himself with other things: he played tennis, he gardened assiduously at his Cummington farm, he protected himself from what Stanley Kunitz in later years would call "the poetry prison." My own meetings with him in the years after our brief Poets' Theatre association have normally taken place in some non-poetic locus: a summer place on Martha's Vineyard in 1956, a theatre, parties at Yale or Wesleyan in the early 1960s, a large reception in New York in the 1970s, a luncheon party in Cambridge in the 1980s, a literary celebration or two, and a private interview at his farm in Cummington in the 1990s—always amiable, always happy, always cordial. Somehow this poet, with all the stress that poetry enforces on the personality, had managed to protect himself from the extra strains that poets have a way of imposing on themselves. It is a tribute to his marriage, now fifty years in duration, that his even keel was maintained.

In 1957 Wilbur ran into Stanley Kunitz at a party in New York. He had read Kunitz' work at the recommendation of Theodore Roethke and John Ciardi and had developed the highest respect for it. When Kunitz told him that, after thirty years of continuous artistry, he was without a publisher, Wilbur asked to read the new poems and then sent a postcard, which I have seen, to his old friend Emily Morison Beck, at the Atlantic Monthly Press in Boston, recommending that she publish a *Selected Poems*. It would be, he wrote, "one of the best poetry manuscripts of the century. No exaggeration. Kunitz has every technical virtue. What's more he can put his perfected and rather lapidary style at the service of the most fundamental themes and passions."

In February, 1959, Wilbur appeared at Harvard to read his new work, and a considerable crowd gathered. I was there, and, though delighted by the poems I knew, was disappointed by the woodenness of the delivery. (Apparently in those days Wilbur used to suffer allergies of the throat before giving a reading.) Also present was Sylvia Plath, who wrote in her journal, "Oddly, I was bored to death. I enjoy his poems more when I read them myself. . . . Kunitz, in his best three or four poems much much finer."[26] Plath had been reading Wilbur herself only three weeks earlier with greater relish: "A bland turning of pleasaunces [sic], a fresh speaking and picturing with incalculable grace and all sweet, pure, fabulous, the maestro with the imperceptible marcel. Robert Lowell after this is like good strong shocking brandy after a too lucidly sweet dinner wine, dessert wine."[27] In later years, when she wrote her best work, she would openly praise Lowell's influence on her, but not Wilbur's.

In 1962 Robert Lowell and Richard Wilbur celebrated their joint birthday, March 1, at Wilbur's house in Portland, Connecticut. The two poets—regarded by some, including Robert Frost, as the leading lights of their generation—were, not surprisingly, never especially close, but they admired and liked one another. By that birthday, Lowell's forty-fifth and Wilbur's forty-first, Lowell's work had taken a sharp turn indeed from where it had stood in 1956, Wilbur's *annus mirabilis*, a year in which Lowell was not writing poetry at all, certainly not yet the poems of *Life Studies*. During the interval Wilbur had moved along to *Advice to a Prophet*, and Lowell, with *Life Studies* and *Imitations* behind him, had begun the poems, most notably the title poem, of *For the Union Dead* and was, despite demur, involved in theatrical productions in New York. The courses of the two poets had decidedly diverged, Wilbur retaining his dedication to beauty, Lowell increasingly mining the personal mode he would persist in for the rest of his life. Wilbur's attitude toward Lowell was both abashed and faintly disapproving. "I enjoyed Cal a lot in other ways, but we didn't spend an enormous time showing each other work during long afternoons." This birthday was apparently an exception. Lowell showed Wilbur his poem "The Drinker,"[28]

which ends with that nice image of the forsythia-colored mackintoshes of the police. He was a good honest direct non-malicious critic. I remember showing him a poem of mine called "Leaving," about a garden party, and he said, "Aw come on now, that 'gaze-enameled cheek' in there is the only interesting thing in this poem. You should try to write about something besides garden parties." I took his aversion to that poem seriously, and it took me a long time to come around to liking it again, so I set it aside, and didn't print it until the new poems section of my [1988] *New and Collected*.[29]

I can also remember on that mutual birthday Cal saying to me, "My father died at sixty. That gives me fifteen years." [Lowell in fact, died at sixty, and his mother did as well, all three deaths the result of heart attacks.] I think that Cal always had a John Keats feeling, that he had to unpack his brain, that he had to get himself written, that he didn't have much time. What I don't like in the prosaic, hammered-out poems of the latter career, can be accounted for to a great extent in those terms.[30]

The two poets celebrating at Wilbur's house in Portland, Connecticut, on that raw March day stood at the opposite poles of the poetry of their time: the first would keep himself erect, withheld, relaxed, and alert, dedicating himself to lyric purity, revealing little of himself in the polished stones of his poems, but much in the totality of his poetry. His poetry has continued till this day to carry a faint happiness (a favorite word) on its face, like the impenetrable smile of the sixth-century Greek *kouroi*. Lowell, as we shall see, could not keep the smile from fading: in fact, his powerful mind and his competitive ambition would relentlessly hunt the smile down until it became a rictus of agony. Wilbur's agonies, whatever they were, remained concealed, while Lowell's found their way to the page, nearly as swiftly as they occurred. At that 1962 birthday party, both men stood at the height of their powers. Wilbur would never descend from his height, but neither would he rise any higher. In essence he would never change. On the other hand, Lowell would never again attain, I think, despite a fury of work and personal agony, the heights he had already reached.

Wilbur, languid prince of poets, even when through a magic spell he managed to turn himself into a toad, could simply not withstand turning back into a prince again, betaking himself to "Amphibia's emperies":

A toad the power mower caught,
Chewed and clipped of a leg, with a hobbling hop has got
   To the garden verge, and sanctuaried him
   Under the cineraria leaves, in the shade
      Of the ashen heartshaped leaves, in a dim,
         Low, and a final glade.

The rare original heartsblood goes,
Spends on the earthen hide, in the folds and wizenings,
      flows
   In the gutters of the banked and staring eyes. He lies
   As still as if he would return to stone,
      And soundlessly attending, dies
         Toward some deep monotone,

   Toward misted and ebullient seas
And cooling shores, toward lost Amphibia's emperies.
   Day dwindles, drowning, and at length is gone
   In the wide and antique eyes, which still appear
      To watch, across the castrate lawn,
         The haggard daylight steer.[31]

The beauty of this poem, and of Wilbur's poetry in general, almost always consists in the beauty of ennoblement, despite his lovely modesty:

      Forbid my vision
      To take itself for a curious angel.
      Remind me that I am here in body,
      A passenger, and rumpled.[32]

Yet, rumpled or drying, the passenger's vision is awash with angels; the world is pure; Roland is poised tall and heroic

78

at Roncesvalles, winding his horn and standing fast against the barbaric hordes.

However, as Cavafy had suggested in "Waiting for the Barbarians" decades before, "Those people were a kind of solution." And the civilized poet must protect himself, mustn't he? I heard Wilbur speak eloquently at the Amherst memorial service for Robert Frost on March 24, 1963, and have wondered ever since how much he was speaking for Frost, how much for himself:

> The world invites poets to do all sorts of things *instead* of writing poetry; the invitations read "in addition to" but "instead of" is the upshot. Insofar as he could, and for many years at the cost of hardship, and never with any complaints of the world, he refused, so as to give his best to the best thing he had to give. Much seeming selflessness is self-betrayal: to lick envelopes for worthy causes is admirable, no doubt, but one should ask what talent one may be neglecting while performing the office of a cat. . . . He never for a moment held himself cheap, and that is why he has enriched us so.

Stirring words, indeed, about Frost, who kept himself secret but warned the world to check up on him, who said, "I want people to understand me; I want them to understand me wrong." But do Wilbur's words sound quite so passionate in the mouth of a younger poet, a poet who had so scrupulously protected himself?

4. In Search of Ararat: W. S. Merwin, 1956–1959

The Native

FOR AGATHA AND STEPHEN FASSETT

He and his, unwashed all winter,
In that abandoned land in the punished
North, in a gnashing house sunk as a cheek,
Nest together, a bunting bundle crumpled
Like a handkerchief on the croaking
Back-broken bed jacked up in the kitchen; the clock
Soon stops, they just keep the cooker going; all
Kin to begin with when they crawl in under,
  Who covers who they don't care.

He and his, in the settled cozy,
Steam like a kettle, rock-a-bye, the best
Went west long ago, got out from under,
Waved bye-bye to the steep scratched fields and scabby
Pastures: their chapped plaster of newspapers
Still chafes from the walls, and snags of string tattling
Of their rugs trail yet from stair-nails. The rest,
Never the loftiest, left to themselves,
  Descended, descended.

Most that's his, at the best of times,
Looks about to fall: the propped porch lurches
Through a herd of licked machines crutched in their last
Seizures, each as ominously leaning

As the framed ancestors, trapped in their collars,
Beetling out of oval clouds from the black
Tops of the rooms, their unappeasable jowls
By nothing but frayed, faded cords leashed
  To the leaking walls.

  But they no more crash
Onto him and his than the cobwebs, or
The gritting rafters, though on the summer-people's
Solid houses the new-nailed shingles open
All over like doors, flap, decamp, the locked
Shutters peel wide to wag like clappers
At the clattering windows, and the cold chimneys
Scatter bricks downwind, like the smoking heads
  Of dandelions.

  In his threadbare barn, through
The roof like a snag-toothed graveyard the snow
Cradles and dives onto the pitched backs
Of his cow and plowhorse each thin as hanging
Laundry, and it drifts deep on their spines
So that one beast or other, almost every winter
Lets its knees stiffly down and freezes hard
To the barn floor; but his summer employers
  Always buy him others.

  For there is no one else
Handy in summer, there in winter,
And he and his can dream at pleasure,
It is said, of houses burning, and do so
All through the cold, till the spooled snakes sleeping
  under
The stone dairy-floor stir with the turned year,
Waken, and sliding loose in their winter skins
Like air rising through thin ice, feed themselves forth
  To inherit the earth.

      WRITTEN *1959*; FROM *The Drunk in the Furnace, 1960*[1]

In August 1956 W. S. Merwin flew westward across the Atlantic after seven uninterrupted years in Europe, writing in his journal an hour-by-hour description of this flight, which suggested the alterations of feeling, the yearning "to renew contact with something." The essay, published in *The Paris Review*,[2] expressed, not explicitly, a breathless excitement in journeying toward his sources, but also a sense that Merwin had come to a crossroads in his life. Within hours after arriving in Boston, he found a place to live—at 76 West Cedar Street, on Beacon Hill, at a wary distance from Cambridge and the classrooms of Harvard. He later described its rental in careful detail:

> This building was a yellow brick job dating from well into the present century. . . . At the time I thought it was just fine. Five relatively large rooms on the top floor, and from each of them a view of the Charles River, or the roofscapes of Beacon Hill. . . . Even through the dirty panes the light from the river filled the empty rooms, and . . . I agreed to pay seventy-five dollars a month. Though I had never lived in Boston, the move there had represented to me a kind of home-coming. Seven years I had lived in Europe, with feelings about the States changing and revolving. The urge to get back to the States was generated in part—and more than I was then ready to admit—by the deepening frustrations and claustrophobia of an unfortunate marriage in England. But besides that I felt a need to renew contact with something—I was not sure what it was, but I thought of it as being my own. Yet I did not want to go back to the States to take up an academic career, as so many of my friends had done.
>
> Finally, in 1956, I was offered a grant of three thousand dollars to spend a year in association with The

Poets' Theater [*sic*] in Cambridge, and try to write a play. It was just what I wanted, and the five empty rooms and their echoes seemed like the beginning of everything.[3]

The Poets' Theatre's invitation, scouted by Donald Hall, had been tendered by board members Mary Manning Howe and Roger Shattuck.[4] It offered a playwright a year's leisure to write a play and work toward its performance by a small theatrical company founded to encourage, commission, revise, and perform verse plays. Merwin was the third playwright, the first from outside the inner circle, to receive its Rockefeller grant money. He had been writing plays for several years. However, living principally in London, broadcasting translations on the BBC, and somewhat uneasy under his English wife's theatrical and powerfully cosmopolitan influence, he had felt his intentions as a dramatist compromised by the British verse theatre, dominated as it was by the plays of T. S. Eliot, Christopher Fry, the high rhetorical style of George Barker, W. R. Rodgers, and Dylan Thomas.[5] For an American poet, London in 1956 hardly provided the perfect theatrical moment. Merwin freely acknowledged that English actors spoke verse far better than Americans, but he did not hear his language their way nor they his, and he had been tempted to give up verse plays altogether for want of a theatre to show them in. Poetry for him was altogether separate from playwriting. Merwin says he once expressed his discouragement to T. S. Eliot, who was of course at the height of his dramaturgical reputation in the 1950s, which had seen *The Cocktail Party* and *The Confidential Clerk* command large audiences in the West End and on Broadway. Eliot, he says, was supportive. "I've felt the same way," he said. "I've thought about abandoning verse plays. If I did, there are so many other people who could do it much better."[6] As William Alfred said of Eliot, "Mr. Eliot was a very humble man about an art that he didn't know, and Binkie Beaumont, the London theatrical agent, said that the only way you can get a play that's going to work in front of a large audience is to get a drawing-room drama, either a tragedy or a comedy."[7] Whatever Merwin had in mind, it was not drawing-room drama.

I first met Merwin in Boston, on October 3, 1956, in my welcoming role as a recently elected member of the Poets' Theatre's corporation. He looked like a faun, smooth-skinned, simply and shaggily attired, with flashing grey eyes and curly locks, moving quickly without restlessness, carrying a magnetic presence, manifestly a temptation to women of all ages. Though I was aware of his poetic reputation, I was then relatively ignorant of his poetry, two collections of which (*A Mask for Janus* and *The Dancing Bears*) had been published, the first as W. H. Auden's 1952 choice for the Yale Series of Younger Poets. (A third volume, *Green with Beasts*, was published the year of Merwin's appointment to the theatre.) At our few meetings he spoke precisely but with confidence on a variety of subjects, and when he listened he did so with unusually alert attention —neither with the rapt concentration of the freshman acolyte nor the blasé skepticism cultivated by nearly all senior Harvard people. Since he had already encountered plenty of the latter, he seemed at first a bit wary of me, since at the time I was representing not only the Poets' Theatre but had relations with Harvard University Press, which published the outstanding plays produced by the theatre. So far the press had committed itself to publish one play by Archibald MacLeish, one by the poet Lyon Phelps, and the dramatic adaptation by Mary Manning Howe of *Finnegans Wake*. My attitude toward new plays was far from blasé, and I hoped to persuade the syndics of Harvard University Press to publish Merwin's play if it succeeded when produced. Merwin and I spoke more and more freely. I did not realize it at first, but I had met a man with a preternatural memory—one of the most useful attributes of a writer.

The city of Boston, rather than Cambridge the college town (as it then was), became Merwin's chosen turf, and he soon acclimatized himself to the city with the ease of a much-travelled urbanite, walking the streets for hours and days at a time, soaking up Boston's attributes with passionate attention. He was sought out by those who were aware of his growing importance in current poetry: John L. Sweeney was among the first. Sweeney was white-haired, in his fifties, mischievously grave, attired as solemnly as a deacon. A poet himself, and a former poetry editor of *The New Republic*, he lived at 51 Beacon Street, halfway up Beacon Hill and overlooking the Boston Common, with his blond, devout, fey, sweet-natured Irish wife, Maíre, a scholar of Celtic literature. Sweeney took the part of a patron, in the best sense, in promoting the fortunes of poets in Boston for many years. Where money was needed, he could find money; where introductions were needed, he obliged; and he taught courses in poetry at Harvard with clerical discipline and clerical kindness. His generosity toward talent was a benefaction to a generation of poets and was quite uncharacteristic of Harvard, where he held his sinecure at the Poetry Room, while teaching the humanities course which Richard Wilbur had so relished.

Merwin became especially devoted to Sweeney:

He was a man of such kindness and such intelligence. It was his role in life to be at the center of talents, bringing them together. I met such strange people as Bronowski at his house. Everybody who was in any way connected with the arts. Jack certainly never collected anybody. He was not even subjectively a name-dropper. He really wanted to make a foyer for people to come and meet each other. I can remember with great fondness, walking along Charles Street and feeling very strongly that distaste for the literary track. I told Jack I wanted to get a job of some sort or do something where I would not see people all the time who were literary people. "It's interesting that you say that," said Jack, "because Sylvia has just been telling me the same thing." (Of course, neither Sylvia nor I did anything about it.) But Jack told me, between one end of Charles Street and the other, "There's this place down near Worcester where they are moving a cemetery, and they pay you good money for helping exhume the bodies and moving them somewhere else. It might be a very interesting job for a writer." He was the most avuncular kind of figure, everybody's beloved uncle.[8]

Also part of Merwin's welcoming committee were Stephen and Agatha Fassett, of 24 Chestnut Street, Beacon Hill, who lived in a Federal house, with oriental rugs, a grand parlor, and a generous collection of cats, a few doors down the hill from Robert Lowell's birthplace, up the hill from the former home of Francis Parkman, and across the street from the childhood residence of James Russell Lowell. Fassett, tiny, cheerful despite physical weakness, crinkly-eyed, a man of remarkable sweetness, was, like Sweeney, affluent and a little frail, as though he had suffered from tuberculosis in his youth. He had dedicated himself to engineering the recording of poetry in a studio in his home, and during Sweeney's tenure at the library he recorded the work of many of the poets—soon to include Merwin—who resided at or visited Harvard, laying down a rich and remarkable poetry archive during this period. His Hungarian wife, Agatha, had been a close friend of Béla Bartók and wrote a touching book portraying Bartók's last years in America. She, too, swiftly took to the Merwins, visitors on the exotic foreign ground of Boston. Merwin was additionally welcomed to Boston by Robert Lowell and Elizabeth Hardwick, who took a particular liking to Dido Merwin when, after a month or two, she joined her husband in Boston and helped him finish furnishing their West Cedar Street apartment with ingenuity in throwaway, bargain-basement, or charity furniture.

I never met Merwin in such grand company as the Lowells, and in fact I do not remember meeting his wife at all, except once on the street, though I would have more than enough to do with her in later years. Merwin seemed to have a lot going on in his mind, much welling up within him. At our encounters for a drink after a rehearsal, or over coffee or lunch, I asked him about Robert Graves, of whose poetry I was becoming a devotee. He described his former employer with respect but a little inhibition. Word later reached me that their parting had not been entirely amicable. He brightened, I thought, when talking about American topics, about writing plays on American themes for American actors, and he described *Favor Island*, the play he was writing for the Poets' Theatre, about a crew of shipwrecked nineteenth-century sailors clinging to an island off Portsmouth, New Hampshire, who, unrescued in a foul winter, turned to cannibalism. I especially recall that his conversation concentrated intensely on his American roots, as he spoke of poems he was writing about his family and ancestors from the Alleghenies, his father the minister, his grandparents and their sources, the sound of American speech, the feeling of the American ground, a fathoming of the American mystery.

American poetry in the mid-1950s had taken a sharp turn toward the European and was due for a correction. *A Mask for Janus*, dedicated to Dorothy, Merwin's first wife, had been scrupulously decorous, Gravesian, lyrical, elevated, hieratic, almost medieval, and decidedly literary. One felt the presence of Dante, of medieval ballads, of the troubadors, though not necessarily Pound's troubadors. One of

87

the few poems to adopt an American theme, a sestina entitled "Variation on a Line by Emerson," ended with a haughty transatlantic chill, as from All Saints' Day:

> Tell me who keeps infrangible solitudes
> But the evening's dead on whose decided face
> Morning repeats the malice and the light.[9]

A lyric entitled "Song" flew as artificially as an imaginary bird in a medieval bestiary:

> Mirrors we lay wherein desire
> Traded, by dark, conceits of fire;
> As gardened minds with delicacy
> Could neither close with flesh nor flee. . . .[10]

These embroidered early works of Merwin's carried out the lessons of the postwar generation of poetry, sedulously following the tutelage of John Peale Bishop or John Crowe Ransom, but also of Merwin's *modus vivendi*. For years, while growing as a poet, Merwin was able to support himself in Europe and England by translating classics for broadcast: *The Poem of the Cid*, *Lazarillo de Tormes*, plays by Lope de Vega, *The Satires of Persius*, *The Song of Roland*. His tastes as well as this bull market in translations kept him attuned to the medieval tradition in European culture, the unitary Catholic attitudes of Spain, Portugal, Catalonia, and the Holy Roman Empire, in stark contrast to his inborn and directly experienced Pennsylvania Presbyterianism.

Because of their European influences, these early poems bear a superficial resemblance to those of Richard Wilbur in their metrical brilliance, in their cultural balance, in their emotional remoteness, in their European orientation; but at heart they differ by a long way: Wilbur had set out to be "a seventeenth-century man," while Merwin was drenched in medieval ballads, in alchemy and unicorns, absorbed in courtly myths and enthralled by chalices curiously wrought of chrysoprase and chalcedony. If Wilbur's favorite character proved to be Alceste, Merwin's was as likely to be a personality both more self-conscious and less self-confident, even though skilled indeed in prosody:

What shall I say,
How chiseled the tongue soever, and how schooled
In sharp diphthongs and suasive rhetorics,
To the echoless air of this sufficiency?
Where should I find the sovereign aspirate
To rouse in this world a tinkle of syllables,
Or what shall I sing to crystal ears, and where
All songs drop in the air like stones; oh what
Shall I do while the white tongued flowers shout
Impossible silence on the impossible air
But wander with my hands over my ears?
And what am I if the story be not real?

FROM "East of the Sun and West of the Moon";
FROM *The Dancing Bears*, PUBLISHED 1954[11]

The artificial, though exquisite, diction and the remote correctness of these early poems could not have expressed anything more strongly than the distance between their author and his nativity. The author of those lines had been reared, the son of a Presbyterian minister, in Union City, New Jersey, "on the Palisades above Hoboken."[12] He was born in 1927, the first of two children, to a family with deep roots in the Allegheny country of western Pennsylvania and eastern Ohio. In Union City, with his father's church looming across the street from their house, the child could, on special occasions only, accompany the preacher to his pastoral study in the top of the house and look out eastward over the Hudson River.

I could watch the boats coming and going and not say anything. . . . They plied upstream, downstream, in a silence I could watch, through the clear afternoon light of autumn, just as it is: the river blue and gray, the

black hulls, orange hulls, gray hulls, the bow waves
and the wakes. There were more of them then, as I
remember. Liners, tugs, barges freighted with whole
railroad trains. And ferries, yawning and turning to and
from the dark arches in the green arcades of ferry barns
on the far side. Smoke rose, utterly out of reach, un-
aware of being watched. White steam leaped from
hooters, and long afterwards the sound arrived. And
behind me the typewriter clattered and thumped, and
my father muttered to himself.[13]

Across the street from the house in Union City stood "a
church with a yellow brick spire/on a cliff above a river/with
New York on the other shore,"[14] a church perhaps the same
hue as Merwin's chosen home in Boston, the church where
the remote, forbidding father preached every Sunday, and
the young boy and his sister sat drawing pictures throughout
the sermon with crayons and paper provided by their
mother, a diversion for the children that no one dared dis-
cuss with the minister despite its inordinate good sense.
Still, the melodies of prayer, Scripture, and sermonizing
were not without their effect:

> During prayers I did not dare to raise my head and
> look at him for long, but through other parts of the
> service if I fixed my eyes on him I found that an aura
> of light came and went around him. It was a trick of
> the eyes, and I knew it, and knew that it would not be
> encouraged if I spoke of it, so I never mentioned it, but
> I learned to make that luminous phantom grow larger,
> more intense, spread out like rays in water, while my
> father's voice rose and fell, coming through it from
> somewhere else. The name for that part of the church
> was the sanctuary. It was holy, and forbidden to every-
> one but those taking part in a service. . . . I was told
> that there was something up there in that place, which
> nobody could see, and that it was always there. It was

in the pulpit, and near the communion table and my
father's chair. It was not an "it." When the place was
empty I would turn my eyes suddenly to look, though
I knew I would not surprise what was there.[15]

This experience of the Word, described many years later,
could well have been gnawing at the mind of the young
poet who, in Europe, had adopted Robert Graves as a father
figure, and who, back in America, would write poems to
revive Union City and its inhabitants in poetry that spoke
in American tones. "I started writing hymns for my father
almost as soon as I could write at all, illustrating them,"
Merwin would assert.[16] But in the intervening years, his
tongue had savored vowels and his ear had heard tunes that
were distant indeed, tunes that emerged from the great
West European traditions of poetry. One of the finest pieces
in his third book, *Green with Beasts*, published just before
Merwin came to Boston, tackles that very dedication.
"Learning a Dead Language" begins:

There is nothing for you to say. You must
Learn first to listen. Because it is dead
It will not come to you of itself, nor would you
Of yourself master it. You must therefore
Learn to be still when it is imparted,
And, though you may not yet understand, to remember.[17]

Not until Merwin came back to Boston did he begin,
freighted with a rich store of recent memory, to choose
learning to be still, to start searching out the antediluvian
concerns of his own life. The minister's family had moved,
when William was nine, from Union City to Scranton,
Pennsylvania, where his education came under the influ-
ence of a maiden cousin, Margie, who lived in the house
with the family for a year or two.

She supervised our homework. She could tell imme-
diately whether we knew our lessons or not. . . . For

me she added arithmetic exercises of her own. . . . I had more confidence in her than in any of the teachers at school. . . . Her attention was unwavering and apparently tireless. She never supplied an answer nor part of one. She was relentless and uncompromising but completely patient: she would stay with whatever it was until it was learned. . . . She did not approve of many of my father's arbitrary and special restrictions, nor of his moody punishments of me in particular.[18]

Later, Billy Merwin attended Princeton, where he studied under R. P. Blackmur and John Berryman, concentrating on Romance languages. William Arrowsmith and Galway Kinnell, whose later careers, like Merwin's, were given to wandering, were fellow students. After taking a bachelor's degree in 1948, Merwin, with Blackmur's encouragement, stayed on another year as a graduate student in Romance languages, married Dorothy Jeanne Ferry, the secretary to Princeton nuclear physicist Henry Smyth, he who wrote, shortly after the war, the first authoritative report on the making of the atom bomb. In 1949 the Merwins joined the hordes of postwar American travellers, landing in Italy and tutoring children there and in Portugal for $40 a month. They made their way in 1950 to Majorca, where Merwin became tutor to Robert Graves' son William and helped with *The White Goddess* while completing his first book, *A Mask for Janus*. After his employment with the Graves family ended, he remained on Majorca, then an inexpensive place to live, hoping to scratch out a living as a free-lance translator while writing *The Dancing Bears*. He was also translating *The Poem of the Cid* for the BBC.[19] *The Dancing Bears* was dedicated to Dido Milroy, whom Merwin had met in London, and with whom he had been corresponding. He and Dido were collaborating, at her suggestion, on the authorship of a play entitled *The Darkling Child*. Neither Merwin's marriage nor Milroy's was entirely secure, and the collaboration turned into a closer relationship, first on a journey they took together to the Canary Islands and later, when Merwin went to London in 1951 to finish the play at Milroy's house in St. George's Terrace, overlooking Primrose Hill. By 1954 Dido (whose maiden name was Diana Whalley) would become Merwin's second wife. She was some years older and more experienced than he, a relative of the poet Lascelles Abercrombie and widely acquainted among the poetic community, which derived much of its support from the BBC in London, and she had strong ideas about the course of her handsomely gifted young husband's career.[20]

Merwin's Pennsylvania past had empowered an extraordinary gesture. Years before, in 1946, while Merwin was still at Princeton, his tutelary cousin Margie had died, leaving, to everyone's surprise, "all of my worldly effects . . . unto my cousin Billy S. Merwin." This entire estate (which came to $1,225.65)[21] had been set aside for years to await a moment worthy of it. In July 1954, as Bill and Dido explored the Quercy, in south-central France, they discovered at Lacan de Loubressac, near Bretenoux, a half-abandoned house, overlooking the valley of the Dordogne, that he knew he had to possess. With Cousin Margie's inheritance, Merwin bought it for himself as a counterpoise to London. The next year he began restoring it, and, once he returned from America, this house and its surroundings would take their place as the scenery for decades of Merwin's poetry and prose.[22] He made it his home for many years, and it remains in his possession today. It became, as he has said, his "dream country":

Somewhere else than these bare uplands dig wells,
Expect flowers, listen to sheep bells,
Wind; no welcome; and nowhere else
Pillows like these stones for dreaming of angels.[23]

But even before that dream could form, he would have to rediscover America.

The world of Europe, the world of England, in which Dido was so certain, was leading me to examine what my relation with my background was, but to re-examine it from a distance with no money and no means of getting back. And this led to a great deal of reading of American history and so on, and it was from there that the poems about my grandparents were beginning, by the summer of 1955. . . . Robert Graves had said that you had to find your own poetry, but you had to go somewhere completely different before you did it; and he thought that Americans went back to America, but that the time they were out of America was very important, before they got to see it.[24]

Thus Merwin's flight from Europe had taken on artistic meaning, and his work that first year in Boston showed more evidence of change. He began to spend more time with Robert Lowell and Elizabeth Hardwick, attending their parties and meeting their friends, e.g., Allen Tate, who spent part of the summer of 1956 in Cambridge, and other poets who passed through the Sweeneys' and the Lowells' portals.

Cal was interested in my family poems and wanted me to read them and would come around to the apartment and ask me, Would you read that poem over again, could I have copies. Cal wasn't writing [poems] at that time and had not been writing for a number of years. Of course Cal had written about family in "Quaker Graveyard" and other poems, but he wanted to write about it in a different way. And obviously, this had something to do with his thinking about the way he might write about it. Did he show me any? No. Once he started writing them he didn't show them to me,

except, later on, one of the poems about the marital
quarrels with Elizabeth. . . .[25]

Another early acquaintance was Donald Hall, poetry ed-
itor of *The Paris Review*, who had been corresponding with
Merwin before he left London, and whom he first met on
September 18, 1956.[26] Hall, Robert Pack, and Louis Simp-
son were to include seven of Merwin's poems in their fa-
mous anthology, *New Poets of England and America* (1957)
with an introduction by Robert Frost. ("Young poetry is the
breath of parted lips. For the spirit to survive, the mouth
must find how to firm and not harden."[27]) The editors in-
cluded work mostly from *Green with Beasts*, and notably
included "The Master," which could easily be construed as
a portrait of Robert Graves. Hall soon invited Merwin to
his house in Lexington, where Merwin met Adrienne Rich,
her husband, Alfred Conrad, and Philip and Margaret
Booth. It seems to have been an unsteady evening, because
Merwin, fresh from Europe, had understood the 8:00 in-
vitation to include dinner and found himself drinking on
an empty stomach. (Once the misunderstanding was re-
vealed, the Halls promptly fed him.)

Merwin was soon offered the chance to read his poetry,
by Philip Booth, on behalf of Wellesley College, a reading
attended by Adrienne Rich, John Holmes, and his wife,
Doris, among others. Merwin became quite close with Adri-
enne Rich and her husband, exchanging dinners and meet-
ing in coffee shops. Anne Sexton and Maxine Kumin came
to Merwin's reading, which was held at the DeCordova
Museum, in Lincoln, but friendships did not result.

Though the Poets' Theatre was conducting a busy season,
Merwin did not find the theatre on Palmer Street a partic-
ularly congenial hangout, though he did attend rehearsals
of *Favor Island* during its preparation by William Driver,
a veteran of British theatre, and by Edward Dodge Thom-
men. I recall the production of the play, when I saw it that

95

following spring of 1957, as a rather dark experience, low lights and low voices, the doomed sailors calling through an unlit universe to one another, their doomed companions. Merwin commented unhappily to Donald Hall on the theatre's dramatic pace: "There's no business like slow business."[28]

I have not read *Favor Island* for many years, and, although the syndics of Harvard University Press declined to include it in the Poets' Theatre Series, I was able to help get part of it published the following autumn in *New World Writing*, the New York semiannual literary paperback. Merwin's most careful critic, Edward J. Brunner, calls it "a secularized mystery play" and suggests, incorrectly, that it was written before Merwin came to Boston.[29] Brunner also suggests that in Boston Merwin was writing two additional plays, *The Gilded West*, about Buffalo Bill, which was later produced in Coventry, and *The Peacock at the Door*, a play which has never been produced, and which deals with the last public execution performed in Pennsylvania. I believe that after this Merwin gave up playwriting as such.

But he never paused in his work on poems. He found that the flavor of England, which he associated with his wife's interest in the theatre, was receding. He had, in England as early as the summer of 1955 (e.g., "Grandfather in the Old Men's Home"),[30] begun writing poems about his grandparents and other Pennsylvania relatives. It was these poems that Lowell expressed interest in. And Merwin, despite the Poets' Theatre and the fact of Lowell's having taken an interest in his plays, gradually ceased to write plays, partly because of Dido's involvement. "She always wanted to be a kind of Egerea. Later on she really saw herself as Nadezhda Mandelstam. I was younger, and she was very forceful, she knew an immense amount. She certainly wanted to affect the playwriting, and that in some ways is why I gradually ceased. I found I couldn't write them with her and I couldn't write them without her, so I

finally dropped it. She had nothing to do with the poetry. . . .
There was no sense of her influencing the poetry."[31]

In the meantime, Merwin had been publishing some of
his new poems in *The Nation*, which had brought about a
correspondence with George Kirstein, *The Nation*'s pub-
lisher. Merwin's new poems had revived the poet's child-
hood riverside longing for boats and the sea, combining it
with some experience of sailing with Dido's brother in the
North Sea. Kirstein, a devoted yachtsman, took a special
interest in these marine poems. Merwin describes the day
in June 1957 when Kirstein, in Boston for a Harvard re-
union, puffed up the five flights of stairs to the Merwins'
apartment, where he invited Merwin to sail with him from
his home in Mamaroneck up the New England coast. This
was more ambitious sailing than anything Merwin had at-
tempted before, but Kirstein allayed any anxiety by declar-
ing, "It is almost impossible to miss the coast of Maine."[32]

And so, several weeks later, off they set, in *Skylark*, Kir-
stein's thirty-eight-foot yawl, on a howling voyage that
would make *Favor Island* seem almost tame, for the pair
of them managed to reach out of Long Island Sound and
toward Monhegan Island along the rim of an unpredicted
hurricane that had been expected to bend out to sea, but it
hugged the shore with *Skylark* in its arms for three days
and nights before the yawl made her way unharmed to
Tenants Harbor and Camden, where the Merwins and Kir-
stein wearily parted, having laid the foundations of a life-
long friendship between George and William.

Dido and William made their way overland to Castine,
where Robert Lowell and Elizabeth Hardwick, with baby
Harriet, were spending their summer, and where Philip
Booth, a native of Castine, offered to find a shack for Dido
and William to stay. Booth was increasingly an admirer of
Robert Lowell's. His first book of poems, *Letter from a
Distant Land*, had won the Lamont Poetry Selection award

97

in 1956. He was a sailor, a boatman and former naval person, a wood-carver, a dedicated and craftsmanlike poet, and a devotee of the landscape and townscape of rural Maine. He was just what Robert Lowell needed in Castine, a person to provide and steer boats, and an acolyte.

This was the Lowells' first of many summers in Castine, thanks to the presence there of Robert Lowell's beloved elderly cousin Harriet Winslow. The village would become even more intellectually crowded in future summers, but this year F. W. Dupee, Allen Tate, William Alfred, Elizabeth Bishop, her companion Lota de Macedo Soares, Rollie McKenna, Richard Eberhart, and others visited the Lowells. Lowell had, early on, urged Merwin to join them. "He said," Merwin reports, "that you're going to love Castine. There are these promontories with pine trees going down into the sea. It's just like Japan." "Just like *Japan*!" Merwin snorted. "Cal had no powers of observation."[33] But the Merwins loved the non-Japanese beauty of the Maine seacoast. Though they spent time with the Lowells, with Philip and Margaret Booth, with Frederick Dupee and his wife, with Elizabeth Bishop and Lota de Macedo Soares during their visits, they also kept to themselves.

For the Lowells, however, it was a very social summer, and after a while Merwin began to feel claustrophobic about the social milieu, "in which literature was referred to literature which referred again to literature. . . . A little air ought to get in. . . . This was something you couldn't talk to them about. None of them by definition could have understood it, and if they had they wouldn't have been able to be sympathetic. Philip Booth was another matter. He was very interested in a life outside literature, in a very literary way, a way in which literature was always there in the wings."[34] Merwin, in his house up the peninsula, gave himself over to writing and to sailing, when he could crew on someone else's boat, with relatively infrequent involvement with the shenanigans of the summer people with their tennis and their cocktail parties. He was aware that Lowell's work had taken a turn, and that he was now writing poems again, the *Life Studies* poems; but Merwin was bent on his own direction, writing the poems that would be published in *The Drunk in the Furnace*, poems which would at last discard the elaborate European accoutrements of his earlier poetry and approach the directness of American speech, with seascapes and cityscapes, portraits of blind and drunken people, and Hopperesque scenes like the masterly "Pool Room in the Lions' Club," ending for all the world like a description of a literary circle:

> They must think
> The whole world is nothing more
> Than their gainless harmless pastime
> Of utter patience protectively
> Absorbed around one smooth table
> Safe in its ring of dusty light
> Where the real dark can never come.[35]

But Merwin was still moving toward another goal in the distance: the Word, as embodied in the moral concern that his Presbyterian family had laid out for him.

With the end of summer, the Merwins returned to West Cedar Street, and Merwin soon wrote a review, published in *The New York Times Book Review* of October 6, 1957, of a new book of poems, *The Hawk in the Rain*, by a young Englishman named Ted Hughes, a volume which had won a competition judged by W. H. Auden, Marianne Moore, and Stephen Spender: "An exciting new writer . . . They are unmistakably a young man's poems, which accounts for some of their strength and brilliance. And Mr. Hughes has the kind of talent that makes you wonder more than commonly where he will go from here, not because you can't guess but because you venture to hope."[36] Since Auden had also chosen Merwin for the Yale Series, this additional endorsement helped bind an alliance. Though

Merwin and Hughes had never met, it was not long before the ever-alert Jack Sweeney, discovering that Ted Hughes and Sylvia Plath had located themselves in Northampton, where Sylvia was teaching at Smith College, invited them to dine at his house with the Merwins the next time they visited Boston. Hughes had a broken foot[37] and, after the first dinner at the Sweeneys', where Sylvia did most of the talking, another visit was arranged at the Merwins' apartment, Hughes struggling to the fifth floor on his crutches, and then engaging Merwin and Dido in intense conversation about London and the possible places for a poet to live and work.[38] Over the next six months, the Merwins and the Hugheses met whenever the Hugheses came to town.

Neither of the men at bottom wanted to live in London but preferred the country; neither of the men wanted to teach. Dido had her roots in London, and Sylvia dreamed of leading a salon; and the struggle between Merwin and Dido revolved about the place where they might live: in the event it turned out to be a ten-year tug-of-war, with Merwin spending as much time as possible in France and Dido as much time as possible in London. The Hugheses were on the point of deciding to give up academic life and live in London, but that decision cost dearly. As Dido records it (and Merwin pays tribute to the accuracy if not to the animus of her memory):

> There was talk about lots of things, but the all-absorbing topic was the sixty-four-thousand-dollar question of how to survive without having to teach. Bill had proved it was possible. He was just then, to all intents and purposes, the only One That Got Away, and, as such, an authentic and experienced refusenik—not only on account of what he had managed to avoid so far (including the plummy position of Poetry Consultant to the Library of Congress) but also because he had actually done what Sylvia claimed they wanted to do: travelled,

light and footloose with a ruthless disregard for in-
essentials, picking up whatever was to be had by way
of a living, in no less than three European countries
(France, Portugal, and Spain) besides England, over a
period of several years. . . . Our meeting with Ted and
Sylvia in Boston generated a solidarity and determi-
nation to do everything we could for them, and we
picked up exactly where we had left off when they
turned up in London two years later.[39]

The rest of the Merwins' time in Boston, about six months
after this meeting, was given over to his work on the un-
published plays, and to *The Drunk in the Furnace*. The
quality of the work in this book was climbing higher and
higher, more and more intense, more and more elaborate,
with an entangling of metrical intricacy that no other poet
of his time could rival, and these new poems were sub-
stantial indeed, not to say elemental. It should not be sur-
prising that a man who was writing a play about a shipwreck
should also be writing poems about disasters at sea, and
about homecomings, nor that these poems should be full
of the music of the sea-road, as in "Bell Buoy," which hisses
and slides with the sound of waves:

> So we set signs over the world to say
> To ourselves, returning, that we know the place,
> Marking the sea too with shaped tokens
> Of our usage, which even while they serve us
> Make one with the unmeasured mist, sea-slap,
> Green rock awash with the gray heave
> Just out of sight, wet air saturated with sounds
> But no breath. . . .[40]

The poems that Merwin was writing at the end of his
Boston sojourn were as different from the first poems as
one dialect from another. One of the last, "The Native,"
which I have printed at the beginning of this chapter, was

suggested to him by Agatha Fassett,[41] possibly describing a family on Cape Cod near the Fassetts' summer house in West Falmouth, though the first draft of the manuscript refers to a place that could either be Riverton, Virginia, or Rimerton, Pennsylvania, and it takes rural ruin, a classic Robert Frost theme, to its ultimate desolation: the deserted village, the collapsed farmhouse, the sort of rural proletariat that even in the 1950s the Merwins could see proliferating in Maine. But the bravura of this poem could not quite take Merwin over the crest of the mountains to view the other side. "The Native" is one of the most extraordinary poems of the 1950s, and he would never write another one like it.

The fact is that Merwin's twenty-one months in Boston made him see that it was not a place where the literary life could be pressed to its edge. There was a drunk inside the old furnace, as the title poem's metaphor has it, banging and clattering, like a pied piper:

> all afternoon
> Their witless offspring flock like piped rats to its siren
> Crescendo, and agape on the crumbling ridge
> Stand in a row and learn[42]

and Merwin had moral questions to ask, questions of man's inhumanity to man and brutality toward the environment that would not fit into the metrical brilliances even of "The Native." From this time forward he would push beyond the structures of traditional prosody in order to grapple with his demons and the demons of the universe. By 1959 the poems in *The Drunk in the Furnace* were written and ready for publication, and Merwin abandoned forever the intricacies of metrical virtuosity that he had displayed in that book.

I had virtually stopped writing poetry at the end of the 50s, because I felt that I had come to the end of something and that if I wrote again I'd want to do it quite differently. James Wright went through very much the same process. . . . Why are you writing poetry that includes things you really don't need there? This process of trying to see what was unnecessary, of strengthening by compressing and intensifying, of getting down to what was really essential, led me to write poetry that was farther and farther away from conventional stanzaic and metrical structure. . . . I saw that if I could use the movement of the verse itself and the movement of the line—the actual weight of the language as it moved —to do the punctuation, I would both strengthen the texture of the experience of the poem and also make clear its distinction from other kinds of writing. . . . Punctuation as I looked at it after that seemed to staple the poem to the page. But if I took those staples out, the poem lifted itself right up off the page. A poem then had a sense of integrity and liberation that it did not have before. . . . I haven't really changed enough to want to give that up.[43]

The Drunk in the Furnace was published in 1960, but by that year Merwin had removed himself to France, had given himself over to the country life, and he had advanced to a further stage. *The Moving Target*, published in 1963, would take a completely different approach to the techniques of poetry, for by this time Merwin had realized that, in order to penetrate the realities of his imagination, he would have to risk even apparent obscurity if he wished to grapple with the moral complexities that increasingly tempted him, and to deal truthfully with the movements of his own mind. *The Moving Target* from its first poem shifted into free verse, and before its conclusion abandoned punctuation as well. As he wrote in "Lemuel's Blessing," the first major annunciatory poem of the new mode,

let me leave my cry stretched out behind me like a road
On which I have followed you.

And sustain me for my time in the desert
On what is essential to me.[44]

Before the book was done and Merwin had entered into
the mode of his next phase, *The Lice*, he was writing entirely
in the manner that would govern his extraordinary poetic
explorations of the next thirty years:

Tell me what you see vanishing and I
Will tell you who you are[45]

Boston had served its purposes: the poet had rediscovered
his native land and had enabled himself to understand that
his work henceforward would take place not in any place,
past or present, but in a timeless, undiscovered country.

In March 1958 William and Dido left for London, and
early that summer Merwin took up residence in France to
finish the renovation of the farmhouse at Lacan, where
Dido would join him later in the season. In 1960 Merwin
spent the winter in New York; in 1962 he worked there as
poetry editor for *The Nation*. This pattern continued, Lon-
don or New York in the winter and Lacan in the warmer
months, until 1968. At that time William and Dido sepa-
rated, and she took over his house. Although he sometimes
came to Lacan in the summer, they would occupy separate
houses there. After 1977, when he ceased to visit Lacan,
she lived there till her death in 1990, while he migrated
between New York and France, Mexico, Hawaii. And, as
Merwin's concerns shifted toward a dedication to the op-
pressed peoples of the earth, and to the wounded environ-
ment, his life took him farther and farther around the world,
with diminishing frequency to New York, where he kept a
pied-à-terre across the river from Union City—but never
back to Boston, not even for a visit, for twenty-five years.

The Merwins kept close to Ted Hughes and Sylvia Plath
when they came to London at the end of 1959, and the

friendship even survived an unfortunate visit by Hughes and Plath to Lacan in 1961.[46] Merwin and Hughes have remained on good terms since Plath's death in 1963. Merwin also kept close to Adrienne Rich through the turbulence of the intervening years of her life, and remained friends, while they lived, with the Sweeneys and the Fassetts.

But, with these exceptions, looking back at Boston, he would soon see most of his friends there gone and the rest disappointing. Boston had given him a landfall, a chance to set foot on American soil again and to re-enter the vital movements of the American language. His future would seesaw between France, England, New York, Mexico, and Hawaii; and it would be decades before Merwin spent any more time in Boston or New England. His poetry likewise took a completely different direction from those of his Boston coevals: Merwin moved westward as Lowell moved eastward. By the time of Lowell's return from England to New York at the end of his life in 1977, Merwin had torn himself away from Europe altogether, to Hawaii.

5. Country Matters: Maxine Kumin, Donald Hall, Philip Booth, 1955–1960

Though Maxine Kumin, Donald Hall, and Philip Booth, all born in the 1920s, were vividly present among the Boston poets of the 1950s, not one of them seemed, for some reason, to act as a centripetal force for other Boston poets; and each of them eventually yielded to a larger and distinctly geographical concept: that of New England. At the heart of their work lay the New England surround, whether the mountains of New Hampshire or the seacoast of Maine. They steered away from the city, they did not often tangle with the large political, social, or environmental issues of their time; and, most of all, although each of their lives during this period and afterward contained its share of distress, they eschewed the "confessional" mode.

Did this make them uncharacteristic of their era? Some critics have an interest in making the late 1950s the age of confessionalism. These three poets at various times sought, apparently with success, the consolations of psychoanalysis, but never felt the need to prop poetry upon their bleeding flesh, never seemed to insist upon their personal, beleaguered, despairing centrality. For Maxine Kumin, as for Donald Hall, the refuge was Up Country (a title Anne Sexton had suggested to her)[1]; for Philip Booth it would be Down East. But the seeds of all this work had been planted in Boston.

1. Maxine Kumin

Halfway

As true as I was born into
my mother's bed in Germantown,
the gambrel house in which I grew
stood halfway up a hill, or down,
between a convent and a madhouse.

The nunnery was white and brown.
In summertime they said the mass
on a side porch, from rocking chairs.
The priest came early on the grass,
black in black rubbers up the stairs
or have I got it wrong? The mass
was from the madhouse and the priest
came with a black bag to his class
and ministered who loved him least.
They shrieked because his needles stung.
They sang for Christ upon His cross.
The plain song and the bedlam hung
on the air and blew across
into the garden where I played.

I saw the sisters' linens flap
on the clothesline while they prayed,
and heard them tell their beads and slap
their injuries. But I have got
the gardens mixed. It must have been
the mad ones who cried out to blot
the frightened sinner from his sin.
The nuns were kind. They gave me cake
And told me lives of saints who died

aflame and silent at the stake
and when I saw their Christ, I cried

where I was born, where I outgrew
my mother's bed in Germantown.
All the iron truths I knew
stood halfway up a hill, or down.

WRITTEN *1959;* FROM *Halfway, 1961*[2]

Among those attending the reading given by John and
Doris Holmes at the Poets' Theatre in January 1958 were
poet John Malcolm Brinnin and his friend Bill Read, col-
laborator with Brinnin in editing their McGraw-Hill an-
thology *The Modern Poets*[3]; Firman Houghton and Ruth
Whitman, co-editors of the Cambridge literary magazine
Audience; and John Holmes' inner circle from the monthly
reading group; George Starbuck, Anne Sexton, and Maxine
Kumin, Anne's fellow suburban housewife, also from New-
ton, who by 1958 was teaching English composition at
Tufts. But, as Kumin recounts her poetic development, it
had taken a while for her to make good her escape into
serious poetry:

> Housebound, dutiful, and diligent, I was baking cook-
> ies or making salt dough for small hands to pummel.
> Reading aloud, pacifying, and feeding three young-
> sters born within a five-year span seemed to usurp
> almost all my energy. . . . I had an unused master's
> degree in comparative literature. Nights and week-
> ends I ghosted articles destined for various medical
> journals. . . . It is hard for me to particularize what
> I was feeling then. Whatever it was—depression, an-
> omie, an inwardly raging discontent, was heavily en-
> crusted with guilt. Why wasn't I happy? We had come
> through World War II unscathed. We had married

young, after a passionate courtship; we had bought a house in a Boston suburb noted for its good public schools, and we were raising a family. I was fulfilling all the expectations of my generation, but it left me emotionally drained, flattened, even despairing. . . . From the dawning of literacy in my early childhood, I had written. . . . At Radcliffe I got my comeuppance . . . [and], having been warned away from the serious practice of poetry, I sought another outlet. In March 1953, the *Christian Science Monitor* bought the following quatrain:

Factually Speaking

There never blows so red the rose,
So sound the round tomato
As March's catalogues disclose
And yearly I fall prey to.

I sold similar verses to *The Saturday Evening Post, Good Housekeeping,* the *New York Herald Tribune,* the *Wall Street Journal,* and several other periodicals and journals. By the time my last child was born on June 13, 1953, I had established a thriving cottage industry. It seemed essential to carry on this business without in any way neglecting housewifery and motherhood. . . . It never occurred to me then that I was the willing victim of sexism. . . . The pressures to conform came from *me*. The stricture to write only humorous verses also came from within. For hadn't I been admonished not to get serious about deeply held feelings?[4]

This last admonition weighed especially hard upon women, but I for one can testify that men too were afflicted with such admonitions in the late 1940s. In writing about her writing, Kumin even today speaks of it as a "business," as though that categorization made it more serious; and the pattern of her early work as a versifier would not wholly alter in future years, when she wrote a score of children's books and a half-dozen novels, as well as the serious poetry which would bring her a Pulitzer Prize.

Early in the winter of 1957 I made my way, rather shyly, into [John Holmes'] poetry workshop at the Boston Center for Adult Education. . . . Anne Sexton and I met in that group; we discovered, that first evening, that we had each driven into Boston alone from suburban Newton. Further, we confessed to husbands and small children. Thus began our intense personal and professional friendship. It was to endure until her suicide in October of 1974. . . . I wish I had kept some kind of journal during the years of serious, warring, loving, almost violently productive workshops with Holmes and George Starbuck and Sexton and Sam Albert. For by now we were meeting in one another's houses and continued to do so until [George Starbuck's departure for Rome in 1961 and] John Holmes' death in 1962. We struck sparks off one another, spoke harshly, repented by way of letters mailed the morning after; encroached shamelessly on one another's apportioned time—here, Sexton was the prime offender; meddled and interfered, rewrote whole lines of one another's poems—here, Starbuck was clearly the frontrunner; stayed on much too late out of pure sociability—this was Sam Albert's métier; took forever, striking matches and puffing on an overstuffed pipe as a considered dodge between statements—this was John Holmes.[5]

Maxine Kumin, born in 1925, in Philadelphia, had grown up in an old Victorian house next door to the convent of the Sisters of St. Joseph.

I went to the convent school during that critical period that Jesuits refer to. Although I'm grateful for some wonderful relationships with the nuns, they instilled in me tremendous anxiety about my immortal soul. I went to high school in Philadelphia and then I came away to Radcliffe. . . . In addition to the Catholic influence, which was very unsettling since I was growing up in a Jewish family, there was a German woman who lived with us. We called her Fräulein. She was like a mother to me until I was about seven or eight when she left to get married. My father was one of the biggest pawnbrokers in the city of Philadelphia. . . . It is also true that I was invited to join Billy Rose's Aquacade as a summer job in my eighteenth year at the fantastic rate of pay of $125 a week. Although it was very well chaperoned, my father wouldn't let me go. . . . So I really flunked out as a swimmer and that's how I became a poet. My father lived long enough to see some of my work in print and was terribly proud of me.[6]

This paragraph, from a 1975 interview with *Crazy Horse*, collects in one bouquet nearly every one of the themes dealt with in Kumin's first collection, *Halfway*, the poems which she was writing and rewriting between 1957 and 1960 under the influence of John Holmes' writing workshop and in daily consultation with Anne Sexton. Her work, especially in the early years, gave off a discernible flavor of W. H. Auden, as did that of Hall, Booth, Rich, Starbuck, and numerous other poets of this generation; for in the late 1950s, he was still a powerfully influential figure: the young poets would not turn against Auden until much later, in order to justify their own development. Louis Simpson would declare, "Something was missing in Auden's concept of poetry. . . . A poem by Auden was an exercise in reason; listening to a poem by [Dylan] Thomas was an experience,"[7] and Adrienne Rich would reveal many years later, when she was no longer young, that she had long "cherished a secret grudge against Auden, not because he didn't proclaim me a genius, but because he proclaimed so diminished a scope for poetry, including mine. . . . Yet he was one of the masters."[8]

Maxine Kumin's poetry of the 1950s, though before long it would march with Sexton's work and Rich's into the new field of feminism, would never fully abandon Auden's example: she sustained her music, her gaiety, she retained her prosody, she kept her own witty, instructive voice, and she worked assiduously throughout a long lifetime of poetic production.

> I still was very much of a formalist, but the subject-matter changed, and I began to dare to write about more womanly considerations. Up till that time I had been writing orderly, mannerly verse, many of the poems that you see in that first book, *Halfway*. That does represent a shift. That book itself . . . the title poem was the most daring thing in the world for me to write because it was so personal. It was my life history. Clearly Anne's influence on me was enormous. In retrospect I see this much more clearly. I think that I was able to grow much more personal in my poetry because of her shining example. The problem was talking about family, parents, personal considerations. That seemed very dangerous and very fraught with feeling, so that seemed very daring.[9]

Later on Kumin's style and subject-matter shifted gradually from her early water poems, the gift of the swimmer, to her later poems about country life and farming, the gift of the equestrian. As long as Anne Sexton lived, the two women retained their intimacy, and their professional interdependence, and they collaborated on children's books, working out the texts by the side of Anne Sexton's swimming pool. Yet in carriage, style, and religion, they were alien, and their poetry has little in common. (George Starbuck once said, "I think Maxine felt at times she was some

kind of ethnic village or historic exhibit for Anne, the re-
ligion student wanting to know 'What's this Jewishness all
about? Who's this Yahweh?' "[10]) Yet their intimacy never
faded. They were able to appreciate, support, and criticize
each other's work in daily telephonic marathons for eigh-
teen years, even though toward the end Kumin became
angry with Sexton's self-destruction; yet, even so, Sexton
saw to it that Kumin was the last person she waved farewell
to as she went to her suicide in 1974. Sexton had been on
the Pulitzer jury that gave Kumin her prize in 1973 for *Up
Country: Poems of New England,* and soon after Sexton's
death Kumin moved permanently with her husband, Victor,
to devote herself to her horses on a New Hampshire farm.
Her later work—like mine and Donald Hall's, beginning
at about the same time, the mid-1970s—would be given
over to the New England countryside and its resonances.

The entrance to Kumin's work in the late 1950s had been
pressed by the need to take her feelings seriously; the later
work, scrupulous in its observation, slightly sententious, less
self-conscious, would take the land, her horses, the rural
surround, as the focus for those feelings, and, especially
after Anne Sexton's death, absorb the odors, vistas, and
temperatures of the country as her own inner climate.

2. Donald Hall

Digging

One midnight, after a day when lilies
lift themselves out of the ground while you watch them,
and you come into the house at dark
your fingers grubby with digging, your eyes
vague with the pleasure of digging,

let a wind raised from the South
climb through your bedroom window, lift you in its arms
—you have become as small as a seed—
and carry you out of the house, over the black garden,
spinning and fluttering,

and drop you in cracked ground.
The dirt will be cool, rough to your clasped skin
like a man you have never known.
You will die into the ground
in a dead sleep, surrendered to water.

You will wake suffering
a widening pain in your side, a breach
gapped in your tight ribs
where a green shoot struggles to lift itself upwards
through the tomb of your dead flesh

to the sun, to the air of your garden
where you will blossom
in the shape of your own self, thoughtless
with flowers, speaking
to bees, in the language of green and yellow, white and red.

BEGUN *1959*; FROM *A Roof of Tiger Lilies, 1964*[11]

Donald Hall was born in 1928 in New Haven, where his father was in a family milk business, the Brock-Hall Dairies. His mother came from a many-generational New Hampshire farming family named, prophetically, Wells, from whose waters Hall would draw much of his poetry. A great proportion of his writing, and the conduct of his life, recapitulates the struggle between business and the farm. After an extremely precocious beginning in poetry he attended Phillips Exeter Academy, the Bread Loaf Writers' Conference, and only then Harvard College as an undergraduate, between 1947 and 1951. There he devoted himself to "conversation and competition, for nothing in schoolwork was so exciting as the other students, who included Robert Bly, Adrienne Rich, John Ashbery, Frank O'Hara, Peter Davison, L. E. Sissman, Harold Brodkey, and Kenneth Koch. . . . My first English teacher was John Ciardi and the class included Frank O'Hara and his roommate Edward St. John Gorey. Archibald MacLeish arrived as Boylston Professor in my junior year."[12]

I used to see Hall in 1948 and 1949 at the Signet Society, a literary club to which he often lent his cheerful, bluff, energetic presence, as did Robert Bly, who sat, stern and frowning, in a corner armchair, was given to blue serge suits and white shirts with celluloid collars, and gathered around his shoulders an invisible grumpiness which he did not surrender in later years even after his severe costume changed to serapes or embroidered waistcoats. Kenneth Koch, who as an undergraduate seemed to me as remote, caustic, urbane, and forbidding as he now seems charming and agreeable, was also to be seen at the Signet, as was John Ashbery, shy, aesthetic, apparently timid, fascinated by music and art, and vaguely friendly. These male poets gathered under the shelter of the newly revived postwar *Harvard Advocate*, which did not welcome women.

Richard Wilbur was also part of Hall's undergraduate life. "Generous of him, sitting over there in Adams House and getting away from the children, and he would show me what he was working on, and I would show him what I was working on. That was a nice thing for him to do, and it was helpful to me in growing up."[13] They also spent a day at Suffolk Downs, betting on the horses. There may be something remotely significant in the fact that Wilbur chose to bet on horses because they were beautiful, Hall because they showed up well in *The Racing Form.* "We came out forty cents apart."[14]

Hall and Bly, who have remained close friends for forty years, enrolled in the first year of Archibald MacLeish's English S, a writing class famous for the fiction that came out of it, but not quite so effective when it came to poets. "[MacLeish] had the long bony face of an aristocrat, the good looks of a rich man, and the smile of an administrator," Hall recalled, "so of course we distrusted him immediately. [Hall, Bly, and company] waited for him, that first day, like lions for a Christian.' "[15]

Hall spent much of his year with MacLeish writing a play entitled *The Minstrel's Progress* that was eventually presented by the Poets' Theatre. "MacLeish was helpful, and continually kind. Then why did I withhold devotion or even gratitude? I was intolerant of him—impatient, quick to find fault—and I was not alone. Other students and colleagues mocked him. . . . Annoyance with this agreeable fellow turns up everywhere."[16] When Hall was studying with MacLeish, the older poet accused him of laziness. Laziness! An unforgivable insult to a hardworking student who had not yet learned that laziness of the spirit can be concealed by busyness—yet MacLeish was right, and Hall soon began to suspect it.[17]

Hall met Adrienne Rich on a double date in 1950 with Robert Bly and Joan Toland (now Joan Bok, chair of the New England Electrical System), when the four undergraduates sat in Jim Cronin's saloon and the three poets recited their poems to one another. In 1953, however, he met Adrienne again, after he had married Kirby Thompson, won a Henry Fellowship to Oxford, and taken up residence outside Oxford for his second year. At Oxford he threw himself into literary societies, managed to book Dylan Thomas to come and read, wrote as hard as he could, succeeding in garnering the Newdigate Poetry Prize at Oxford, as he had won the Garrison Poetry Medal at Harvard, for all I know the only person ever to win both. Oxford suited him, though Robert Bly once wrote me that he thought Hall's two years in England were the worst thing that ever happened to him. On the other hand, those years brought Hall into contact with the British poets of his generation, whom he, as the editor responsible for the British choices, would soon anthologize.

During Donald Hall's year with Yvor Winters at Stanford, 1953–1954, he was made poetry editor of *The Paris Review* by George Plimpton, who had been a fellow member of MacLeish's writing class at Harvard, and Hall's consequent correspondence with poets brought him into early and close contact with everyone from Dylan Thomas and T. S. Eliot to W. S. Merwin, James Wright, and Louis Simpson. When he became a Junior Fellow at Harvard in 1954, he not only continued his editorship of *The Paris Review* and continued his association with the Poets' Theatre, arranging most of the public readings, but, together with Robert Pack and Louis Simpson, he compiled an anthology for paperback publication entitled *New Poets of England and America*, for which, in 1956, he persuaded Robert Frost to write an introduction. The anthology, published in 1957, became the flagship anthology for the metrical poets of the 1950s, especially for the metrical poets of the Eastern territory. And by this time Hall had published his first book, *Exiles and Marriages*, which had won the Lamont Poetry Selection award for 1955 and had been recommended for a Pulitzer

Prize in *Time*, though it received dubious reviews from such as Stanley Kunitz and William Arrowsmith, who wrote in *The Hudson Review*: "My over-all impression of Mr. Donald Hall's *Exiles and Marriages* is one of a general level of competence so high that it almost obscures the fact that this volume contains an alarmingly high percentage of poetic odd-jobs and merely fashionable exercises. . . . Mr. Hall nowhere experiments or takes risks with his form. . . . The result is a compact tidiness of feeling . . . and there is a calmness and smoothness coming close to blandness in both form and statement."[18]

Hall spent his last months as a Harvard Junior Fellow living in Lexington with his wife and growing family, and he developed an uneasy friendship with Philip Booth, who lived not far off, in Lincoln. Hall remembers:

> I saw quite a bit of Phil, especially when I was living out in Lexington. He used to drive over frequently, and we used to sit there in the cellar and talk, and show one another our work. You realize we were in competition, and Phil chose to avoid being competitive. I never wanted to avoid it. I've always enjoyed it in, I hope, a sort of cheerful spirit. But one editor at Viking wrote Phil in 1955, saying "I'd like a copy of your book, thinking of submitting it to the Lamont competition." And another editor from Viking wrote me, and—my letter came first by a couple of days—he would not submit his. I begged him to submit, but he wouldn't. He sent his the next year, and the next year *he* won. But I was never wholly comfortable with him, I never felt relaxed camaraderie. It may have been rivalry or whatever.[19]

Booth's view complements Hall's: "We had young children together, we had picnics together. There were certainly Harvard people at the Halls' New Year's Eve party, and

Margaret said, much to my pleasure, at 12:01 a.m., 'Isn't anybody going to kiss anybody?' And Don was an education too. He took me to the Society luncheons several times, where there were Dan Ellsberg and John Hollander."[20] Even before that, Hall arranged for Booth and Rich to read together at one of the Poets' Theatre's summer events; but there was a certain coolness between the two men. Hall gave us all the impression of being intent on making a career in poetry. He and Hollander, simultaneously Junior Fellows, circled warily around one another. Hollander was not writing much poetry at that time, devoting his powerful intellectual curiosity to other matters, though he had written poems as an undergraduate at Columbia and would soon write poems again. Twice during his junior fellowship Hall participated in a workshop with John Holmes, Booth, and Robert Lowell. "We only met twice. Cal was kind of grumpy and wasn't writing. I brought in stuff, and I think Phil did and John did. It was exciting in potentia, but it didn't jell."[21] And other poets felt Hall's competitive drive as well: Hall tells how, years afterward, Galway Kinnell told him, at a party in New York, "in his slow way—he was slower then than he is now—'God, I used to hate you.' That was for *Exiles and Marriages*, the Lamont prize, *Time* magazine, nomination for the National Book Award, all those things, and, you know, for not a very good book. Sometimes a book is singled out for no particular reason, and it isn't a very good book. I'm not being modest."[22]

It was true that, despite Hall's visibility as a rising young poet, his work would not reach its heights for some years to come. In 1957 Hall had become concerned lest his connection with Harvard might stifle him, and he accepted an assistant professorship at the University of Michigan, leaving with Viking Press his second book of poems, *The Dark Houses*, published in 1958, a book which is mainly distinguished ("Hang it all, Ezra Pound, there is only the one sestina . . ."[23]) by its literary artificiality and its earnest, non-lazy attempt to be different from his first.

"I left Boston just when things were beginning to heat up. In the undergraduate years things were pretty hot, but that was over in about 1951, when Adrienne and I graduated, because we were the last of that bunch. When I left it was building up. Merwin arrived, and Plath and Hughes. Lowell was there at the end. I wonder what my life would have been like if I had stayed, as I might have done. I would have had an affair with Anne Sexton like everyone else."[24] But as it happened, he never met Sexton or Plath at all, coming no closer to Sexton than a flirtatious correspondence, nor to Plath than to be praised as an anthologist in the last review she ever wrote, in 1963. He became closer, with the passage of time, as they visited Ann Arbor on road trips, to older poets like Frost and Lowell, who saw in this Michigan satrap of the literary system a friendly face in an alien town, but his work during these years was not taken very seriously because, somehow, despite its author's evident ambition, it did not *au fond* take itself seriously.

Yet, he had been writing for years, and the poems that he wrote in Cambridge did not much improve, despite devoted labor, during his Michigan period. I used to see him at intervals, and correspond at others, during these years, and he struck me as a driven, externally cheerful, internally cross-grained man, undeniably busy, dedicated to the literary marketplace. W. D. Snodgrass has written that during these years "he was, steadily, becoming a skillful businessman, an adept literary and academic politician."[25] When, after twenty years of teaching and the publication of six volumes of verse, his first marriage dissolved, he took a courageous course and left academic life in 1975, to move to his ancestral family farm in New Hampshire and support himself as a free-lance. His work changed abruptly for the better. "It was apparent that the poet had been victimized by his own versatility. This is a trap from which most poets never emerge," wrote Robert McDowell. "For Hall nothing less than a profound change of life would provoke the much needed change in his poetry. In late middle-age Hall made the transition from running with the pack of popular academic plodders to a solitary singer whose remarkable vision has included us all."[26]

Curiously enough, the best work even in his early years had always emerged from Hall's maternal wellspring, the farm at Eagle Pond; not until he returned to Eagle Pond Farm to live permanently with Jane Kenyon, his second wife and herself a fine poet, did his work hit on its vitality; and, coincidentally, not until then did he make contact at last with Maxine Kumin, who would succeed him as Poet Laureate of New Hampshire in the late 1980s. But in the intervening years the pain and the struggle of his private life, not revealed in his work until years later, most notably in *The One Day* (1988), occasionally peeped out from behind the surface. As William Matthews discerningly wrote, "In a few poems from [the late 1950s and early 1960s] ('Digging,' 'Internal and External Forms,' 'Self-Portrait as a Bear,' and 'The Wives') another [self] begins to try to imagine a form in which it can manifest itself."[27]

In the years after Hall moved back to New Hampshire, his life did not become any less busy, nor his ambition any less intense, but his poetry, after he was fifty, began getting better and better; and in recent years I have had the pleasure and gratification of editing the books in which this spacious and intense poetry appears. I am not sure which of us is the more surprised.

3. Philip Booth

Night Notes on an Old Dream

Like a seal
in broken sleep,
aware of how
cold the moonlight
lies on salt ice,
I let the sea
work. The floodtide
under my skull,
lugged by the full
March moon, under-
cuts the barrier
shelf, folds back, and
opens a lead
to my forehead.
The moon waves in.
Adrift, and washed
by the equinox,
I let the sea
work. Under me
the shelf calves off;
my sleep ebbs East,
offshore. Sure, for
once, I'm neither
mad nor dead, I
dive awake from
the floe where last
night's snowbirds rise;
and I count them,
white and moonstruck,

climbing, beyond
Orion, to the moon
behind my eyes.
WRITTEN *1959*; FROM The Islanders, *1961*

Philip Booth arrived in Boston in 1954 to take a teaching
job at Wellesley, and he remained there until 1961. He
spent his summers in an ancestral home in Castine, Maine,
where his mother's family had lived for generations. He
was born in 1925 in Hanover, New Hampshire. His father
was a professor of English at Dartmouth, and Philip at first
somewhat intermittently attended college there, leaving to
enlist in the Army Air Corps, where he was an aviation
trainee till the end of the war. On his discharge, at twenty-
one, he married Margaret Tillman and returned to Dart-
mouth, obtaining his B.A. degree in 1948, having also
trained in a woodworking shop, where the confident and
shapely handcraft that displays itself in his poems may well
have taken its beginnings. He also spent a good deal of this
time sitting at the feet of Robert Frost, who at this time
spent two seasons a year at Dartmouth. Booth attended
graduate school at Columbia, where he studied under Mark
Van Doren and wrote his master's thesis on Frost's poetry,
attaining his M.A. by 1949, after which he spent two un-
happy years teaching at Bowdoin College but dropped out
of academic life again to return to live across the Con-
necticut River in Norwich, Vermont, and work as assistant
director of admissions at Dartmouth, holding in addition
various jobs connected with woodworking, skiing, tutoring,
while writing poems and working part-time in the English
department. In 1954 he came at last to full-time academic
work at Wellesley College, living at a cautious country dis-
tance from Wellesley in Lincoln (as did Richard Wilbur),
raising three daughters, and making friends very early with
John Holmes.

Booth's lover's quarrel with the academic life must have been associated with his father and Dartmouth: for of all the teachers of poetry in his generation Booth may have been the most devoted to his students.

Wellesley was splendid, it was gorgeous in 1956. It was an education to be part of that department and even to learn Harvardese from other members of the faculty, who were a little skeptical of me, somewhat rightly. Wellesley did not have much to do with poetry for me. The great delight of poetry was that there were good readers coming. Nearly everybody came before I left. Adrienne came to my poetry workshop, as a friend. I cannot remember when I did not know Adrienne. I think it's likely to be through Don Hall, and she and I came to be fairly close to each other through our fondness for Cal Lowell. I can remember having lunch with her a couple of times, and we arranged to meet sort of to talk about how Cal was doing. We talked a lot that way. She was the person to tell me that I could deduct typewriters and things, as a business. And we certainly went to dinner with Alf and Adrienne and they must have come out to Lincoln, but I certainly don't feel that Adrienne and I were "poetry companions." We were friends who happened to be poets. We admired one another's readings, we admired one another's poems. I still think that "Stepping Backward" [in *A Change of World*, 1951] is one of the most remarkable love poems ever to be written by a young poet, when she was nineteen, or something. At Wellesley there were poets like the great Spanish exile, Jorge Guillén; and at Brandeis Pierre Emmanuel, and I knew Stanley Kunitz when he came there. I had written a review of his *Selected*, saying it ought to get the Pulitzer. I was beginning to review about then either for the back of *The Village Voice* or for the *Monitor*. I can remember going to Stanley, and I remember at his invitation I brought some poems, and he looked at one of them and said, "There is one wrong word in this poem. It is a wonderful poem but there's one wrong word." I pointed and said, "Is it this one?" and he said, "Yes."

But John Holmes was still the center for me. He would call up when there was going to be a reading at Tufts, and I can remember going to John Crowe Ransom's reading there. I traded poems with Holmes, casually. But I didn't trade much with other poets. Fundamentally I've always been more of a loner than my colleagues. But I went with John to teach at the New Hampshire Workshop in the summer of 1957, just after my first book, *Letter from a Distant Land*, came out, and I can remember Gregory Corso coming up and saying, "Booth, you're not of the age." Later, in 1958, John signed me on to coach the B team at the Boston Center for Adult Education for one semester, but he never invited me into his reading circle: I was I thought a step ahead, with a book out. And then, I guess, I began to know Maxine well, better than I ever knew Anne Sexton or George Starbuck. I was never much interested in the Poets' Theatre. I remember Bunny Lang's play *I Too Have Lived in Arcadia* but very few others. We were invited to Jack Sweeney's place a number of times, after readings generally, and after Ted Hughes' reading [April 11, 1958] we all went to the Sweeneys'. And that was where I first met Sylvia, on that occasion. My aunt was her doctor at Smith, Marion Booth, the first woman psychiatrist ever appointed to be a college physician anywhere. When Ted and Sylvia moved to Boston we certainly went there once or twice and they came out to the house once or twice, and I think particularly of an evening with John Holmes and Doris. Late in the spring of 1959 we went

out with them to Annisquam, a long day, one of those
cold spring picnics. We had a good time with both of
them. They were in some sense newlyweds; they
seemed very happy, they appreciated each other.[28]

Philip Booth characterizes his Boston years as a "surge,"
thinks of the Boston poets as "having all been on our way
at the same time," but that "we didn't necessarily think we
were good or splendid or trying to make it. I don't have any
particular sense of that except partially with Don. But the
rest of us were not . . . we were there together. In retrospect
it is like saying, Yeah, I was on Guadalcanal. We were there
together."[29]

As these scattered reminiscences suggest, Philip Booth
broke the pattern of his cadre. I remember meeting him at
poetry gatherings—a large party at John Malcolm Brinnin's
for Howard Moss at Thanksgiving 1958; a group of local
poets brought to Harvard to meet an Italian translator
named Roberto Sanesi, when Maxine Kumin and Anne
Sexton, George Starbuck, and Booth and I dined as the
guest of Arthur Freeman, one of those occasions which for
some mysterious reason seems particularly vivid (both to
Booth and to me): it was, I suppose, the first time I had
spoken seriously to either Anne or Maxine. But Phil Booth,
pipe-smoking, handsome, with characteristically slow-
paced New England speech, had a country-gentleman air
about him that was not typical. He always lived, by choice,
in the country; his work was strictly metrical and given to
the natural world—and, like Richard Wilbur's, remained
so—and his domestic life seems to have remained placid,
satisfying, and steady. Like Wilbur and Kumin, he is, as I
write this, still married to his original spouse, and, even
more firmly than most other poets of the Boston group, he
was staunchly grounded in a sense of place. As with Hall,
the maternal homestead drew him back; and, like Hall, he
lives today in the house that sheltered his grandparents in

the nineteenth century. His involvement in the poetry of his time was especially dedicated to his students.

Booth's attention to his own poetry became particularly intense after he fell in with Robert Lowell, thanks to John Holmes again, during 1956 in Boston. Lowell's elderly cousin, Harriet Winslow, was, like the Booths, a summer resident of Castine. Beginning in 1955, Lowell began visiting Castine every summer, living in the Winslow house on the central square, just a few doors away from *Booth's* cousin Harriet's rather grander house and only a few hundred yards from Booth's own family house. Booth, who in 1957 had been away from Castine for six years, was delighted to find Lowell collecting his mail in the post office one June morning. During that first summer, Lowell was attempting to learn everything that could be known about Castine. It would obviously be the younger native to whom he would turn for questions about boats and outboard engines, currents, fishing and nautical information, local customs, fishermen's habits, and anecdotes of the marine life that had always enthralled Lowell since his Nantucket days. Booth wrote, "Cal wants to hear the Maine voice in which I tell stories, or he wants to be taken sailing. . . . For matters practical, Cal has no native talent."[30]

If a *Collected Poems of Robert Lowell* can ever make its way into existence, it could reasonably be entitled, for numerous reasons, *Near the Ocean*, like the Castine volume Lowell would publish in 1967. Booth often visited Lowell's little barn/study right at the water's edge looking out over a weedy cove of Castine Harbor and was invited to show Lowell his poems. "I begin to understand that I am for the first time hearing a master teacher. I listen and listen, reminding myself that when I get home I must write myself notes about everything Cal is saying. . . . I walk along the harbor and home up the hill, stunned by Cal's impact. Nobody before has ever cared so much for my poems: cared to criticize them so brilliantly, cared to demand of them, even in parts so cared to praise them, as Cal has this day."[31]

In spite of this hero worship, Philip Booth, like Lowell and Merwin, was attempting to get back to his native sources in the summer of 1957. *Letter from a Distant Land* had been published as the Lamont selection the previous year, chosen by an all–New England jury consisting of Richard Wilbur, Louise Bogan, John Holmes, Rolfe Humphries, and May Sarton; and it was these poems which Lowell was reading and criticizing for Booth, even though they were already in print. However, as he approached his second book, *The Islanders*, Booth determined to work his immediate surroundings, striving for a more intimate connection with his neighbors, the sort of sensate contact that comes from rowing boats, hoisting sails, hauling trawls, gliding through thick fog over the waters—in short, an effort to re-create the sea-marked country of his motherland, while exploring the ways it touched on his inner world. His mother had some years before become seriously ill and died in a mental hospital,[32] and this summer was the first in his long struggle to mourn her death, as evinced in poems like "Night Notes on an Old Dream." When he returned to Boston after this summer (and, coincident to the sequence of Robert Lowell's breakdowns in 1958 and 1959) Booth would turn to a classical psychoanalysis for three years, five times a week, scuttling in his car from Wellesley between classes and gnawing a sandwich as he drove, to lie on a couch in Waban for a fifty-minute hour and then return to his Wellesley students.

During this three-year period he wrote poems more powerful and poised, but darker, than in his first book: *The Islanders* is preceded by an epigraph from Frost's "The Oven Bird": "The question that he frames in all but words / Is what to make of a diminished thing." More Frost-ian than any of his earlier or later work, these poems do not yet clear the depression that had fogged him in, a depression which gives his work as a whole a sense of great care in the shaping, like a dedicated worker in wood who, by the process of carving it out, stroke by stroke, knows when he has arrived at the end of the day, and, eventually, at the end of the job when he can see it, touch it, hold it. Thus Booth writes about the celebrated boat builder Mace Eaton:

> By late May she takes shape: he hums when he
> pays in the caulking, and jibes back, eyeing
> her lines, as he planes the planked hull.
> His wife died last fall. Time is ebbing
> under the wharf; a fair tide and a last coat
> of gloss on this vessel, he'll launch a yacht.
> Her topsides primed, he touches her, rubbing
> his gut, to draw the line where she'll float.
> As she will, to the last eighth-inch, in any
> sea, designed by his winters of lying
> hove-to in this shop—with her lee-rail
> dry in a gale, like the old *Annie Gott*.[33]

Booth would eventually, on retirement from Syracuse University, to which he moved in 1961, return to Castine full-time, enabling him, without having at any time in his career deliberately chosen to write in a style other than the one he was born with, to deepen his tone, to produce poems that had, as it were, a patina rubbed into them by the years of his life.

6. A New Skin:
Anne Sexton, 1956–1961

For John, Who Begs Me Not to Enquire Further

Not that it was beautiful,
but that, in the end, there was
a certain sense of order there;
something worth learning
in that narrow diary of my mind,
in the commonplaces of the asylum
where the cracked mirror
or my own selfish death
outstared me.
And if I tried
to give you something else,
something outside myself,
you would not know
that the worst of anyone
can be, finally,
an accident of hope.
I tapped my own head;
it was glass, an inverted bowl.
It is a small thing
to rage in your own bowl.
At first it was private.
Then it was more than myself;
it was you, or your house
or your kitchen.
And if you turn away

because there is no lesson here
I will hold my awkward bowl,
with all its cracked stars shining
like a complicated lie,
and fasten a new skin around it
as if I were dressing an orange
or a strange sun.
Not that it was beautiful,
but that I found some order there.
There ought to be something special
for someone
in this kind of hope.
This is something I would never find
in a lovelier place, my dear,
although your fear is anyone's fear,
like an invisible veil between us all . . .
and sometimes in private,
my kitchen, your kitchen,
my face, your face.

WRITTEN FEBRUARY *1959*[1]

I don't recall ever having been with Anne Sexton when she did not require someone to take care of her. The witnesses to her life all agree—and so do her own frequent and voluble letters and interviews and her biography by Diane Middlebrook—that in the usual round of daily life she was more than ordinarily helpless. Once she began writing in 1957, her husband and his mother helped her through her everyday doings, including housekeeping and child-tending; her poetic friends, especially Maxine Kumin, saw to it that Anne reached John Holmes' classes, poetry readings, and other literary functions; and later, when Anne became well enough to strike out on her own, she usually found a friend, a lover, a fellow poet, or an amanuensis to steer her from place to place. Arthur Freeman, a longtime friend, colleague, and fellow poet, recalled that in 1959 "she

151

couldn't cross the street without getting George [Starbuck]'s advice."[2] It seems that the only destination she could locate unaided was her psychiatrist's office.

Her emotional life was preternaturally amplified. I can remember an evening at dinner at Arthur Freeman's house when Sexton, who smoked continuously, struck a match and seared her hand with a fragment of phosphorus. For the next two hours her pain was a presence in the room larger than that of any of the guests: ice was brought, her hand was immersed in a plastic bag full of ice water, her ululations rose and fell, her husband comforted her again and again. The guests tried to speak of other things, but it proved impossible: it was the pain that governed.

Diane Middlebrook's biography[3] has made it abundantly clear just how intimately Sexton's psychic difficulties, and their demanding therapeutic treatment, were intertwined with the development of her poetry. Anne's agony culminated, the day before her twenty-eighth birthday, on November 8, 1956, in the first of numerous suicide attempts. Her life till then had, externally at least, seemed that of an average housewife and mother. Born Anne Gray Harvey in 1928, she came from Yankee roots, growing up in the town of Wellesley and summering on a Maine island, the daughter of well-to-do middle-class parents. She received a relatively casual education without any college training, and eloped at nineteen with Alfred M. ("Kayo") Sexton II, a handsome and charming salesman in the woolen trade, with whom she settled in Newton Lower Falls, Massachusetts, after intervals with her parents near Boston in Weston, and with her husband's parents in Annisquam. Her first daughter was born in 1953; her second, in 1955. Her breakdowns followed hard on the heels of the birth of the second child.

The story of Anne Sexton's emergence as a poet has been simply described: "Suddenly, in 1956, through a cracked surface a buried self emerged and began looking for something to do."[4] Her infant daughter went to Annisquam to be taken care of by Kayo's parents. After her recovery from her birthday suicide attempt, Sexton's psychiatrist, Dr. Martin Orne, suggested she attempt writing, as a means to dispel her sense of worthlessness. ("It is difficult to communicate fully how pervasive Anne's profound lack of self-worth was and how totally unable she was to think of *any* positive abilities or qualities within herself," he would write years later.[5]) She had written verses in high school and a few since, but then, in December 1956, Sexton happened by chance to watch I. A. Richards on public television explaining the sonnet form. She immediately wrote a sonnet herself, and began flooding her psychiatrist with poems. "Among both mental patients and poets she found she felt 'more real, sane'; and it was within the realm of psychotherapy that she discovered and began to develop her talents."[6] The realm of psychotherapy, fantasies of the unconscious, "the commonplaces of the asylum," Oedipal struggles, and, again and again, transference to the psychiatrist, were the subjects that flooded her mind and her poems. The first poem in her first book, written for the Holmes workshop, begins:

> You, Doctor Martin, walk
> from breakfast to madness. Late August,
> I speed through the antiseptic tunnel
> where the moving dead still talk
> of pushing their bones against the thrust
> of cure. And I am queen of this summer hotel . . .[7]

Other poems, from the outset, were just as physical as this in their imagery. Over and over again, Sexton's poems refer to the sensitivity of the skin, of the discomfort of the body inside the skin. To see her with Maxine Kumin, broad-shouldered and dark-haired, athletic, graceful, whose skin fit her body like a panther's, grave and recessive in demeanor but lighting up in response to someone else's remark, contrasted in body language with Anne, whose skin clearly did not fit her. Equally tall and perhaps a bit more glamorous, Anne walked nervously, jittery, feverish, either notably silent or talking a trifle raucously, gesticulating as though through a barrier of fright, always smoking, vivid and uninhibited, with green eyes and careful hairdo.

In January 1957 Sexton entered John Holmes' poetry workshop at the Boston Center for Adult Education and before long was attending regularly with Maxine Kumin, whom she met there, and they began driving in together from Newton. Even considering the complications of Sexton's life—her psychotherapy with Dr. Orne, her family life stretched thin, with Kayo often travelling on business and the two young daughters, one in Newton with her parents and one in Annisquam with her grandparents, and the increasingly demanding poetry workshops and classes—Anne might conceivably have attained a level, workmanlike routine not unlike the one that Maxine Kumin, with comparable family responsibilities, was able to handle; but Sexton was not stable enough to conduct normal life without assistance. Her daughter Joyce ("Joy") remained in her mother-in-law's care for nearly two years. Kumin became the link between Sexton and the poetry community.

Kumin had at first fought shy of Sexton:

I was initially very leery of her because she was so flamboyant. She was so exhibitionistic and confrontational about her psychiatric history. This was the first thing that everyone had to take notice of. . . . I'd had a good friend who had a postpartum depression and killed herself when her baby was about nine months old, only a year and a half before I met Anne, so I was a little hesitant to get involved. But Anne was very seductive. Enormously so. She probably had more personal charisma than anybody I've known since. And I guess I was elected, and I just found it irresistible. I

was I think attracted and appalled by those early
poems. I did give myself points for understanding that
very first poem, "Music Swims Back to Me," when she
came over to my house [in September 1957] and asked
if she could show it to me. I knew I was in the presence
of greatness. It was just an incredible poem, and that
was when I laid down my arms and decided, well, what
will be will be. And we were off and running.[8]

> Wait Mister. Which way is home?
> They turned the light out
> and the dark is moving in the corner.
> There are no sign posts in this room,
> four ladies, over eighty,
> in diapers every one of them.
> La la la, Oh music swims back to me
> and I can feel the tune they played
> the night they left me
> in this private institution on a hill. . . .[9]

When Sexton brought Kumin this poem, she wanted to
know: Did she dare present it in class? Could it be called
a poem? It was her first breakaway from the adolescent
lyrics she had written in rhyming iambic pentameter.[10]
"She knew, she knew," Sexton said later. "She responded!
I had done this crazy thing, written this poem. Always Max-
ine responded to my poetry."[11] This exchange began the
close connection that held them together for the rest of
Anne's life. They went together to poetry readings, includ-
ing W. S. Merwin's at the DeCordova Museum, to hear
Marianne Moore at Wellesley College, to Robert Graves,
to Robert Frost, and to parties after the readings. After the
Holmes workshop resumed, Maxine Kumin and Anne ex-
changed telephone numbers so that they could work to-
gether on their own, and this began what would turn out
to be eighteen years of telephonic consultation about their
poems, reading them aloud to one another in draft, criti-

cizing and praising. In later years this so dominated their household telephones that they installed a special telephone line for the purpose.

In April of 1957 Anne Sexton's mother, Mary Gray Harvey, was diagnosed as having breast cancer, and on May 27 Sexton attempted suicide for the second time. Her recovery was swift enough to enable her to turn over to her mother, at the end of 1957, a folder of thirty-seven poems marked NOT TO BE SEEN, which brought Mary Gray Harvey and her youngest daughter together in the mother's remaining two years of life. But, although Sexton was now writing with increasing energy, her home life was still at sixes and sevens: her younger daughter, Joyce, was still living with Kayo's parents. Anne did not yet feel strong enough to let Joy come home, but in the interim she had been taking an antidepressant drug,[12] writing herself back into strength, and exploring other kinds of power: during the winter and spring of 1958 she began an affair with another member of the Holmes workshop, entirely unknown to her husband or Maxine or anyone else except her psychiatrist. But by April 1958 she had learned enough, and written enough—Middlebrook estimates she had written sixty-five poems by the time the spring class ended[13]—to be able to break off the affair, and to be able to bring Joyce home from her two-year exile at the elder Sextons' house.

For reasons that went beyond her personal life, Sexton was overwhelmed when she first read W. D. Snodgrass' poem to his daughter, "Heart's Needle," in the Hall/Pack/Simpson anthology, New Poets of England and America. In the summer of 1958 Sexton persuaded Ruth Soter, one of her workshop colleagues, to accompany her in enrolling in a summer writers' conference at Antioch College, where Snodgrass was teaching, and he reacted positively to her work, though he thought Soter a more naturally talented poet. Later he said, "It seemed clear that Sexton was a

person so driven that she would go on and do the work.
And indeed that is what happened. At the time she came
to Antioch she had published, I suppose, between four and
six poems. The following year she published in something
like forty different magazines."[14] After her return from An-
tioch Sexton began an intense correspondence with him.
"When I read your poem, that first time, leafing through
the anthology . . . it walked out at me and grew like a bone
inside of my heart."[15]

Joy's return home was a triumph for Anne Sexton despite
the downward course of her mother's terminal cancer, and
now she began the finest poem of her early work, "The
Double Image," a celebration of Joy's return, backlit by
the dread of her mother's illness. It is one of her most
touching and tender poems, and the one that would make
her name. She would work on this poem through the
autumn of 1958, both on her own and in the seminars she
was involved in, and by the time it was done, at Thanks-
giving,[16] she would have achieved one of the finest poems
of her career:

7.

I could not get you back
except for weekends. You came
each time, clutching the picture of a rabbit
that I had sent you. For the last time I unpack
your things. We touch from habit.
The first visit you asked my name.
Now you stay for good. I will forget
how we bumped away from each other like marionettes
on strings. It wasn't the same
as love, letting weekends contain
us. You scrape your knee. You learn my name,
wobbling up the sidewalk, calling and crying.
You call me *mother* and I remember my mother again,
somewhere in greater Boston, dying. . . .[17]

Partly because of Anne Sexton's productivity, John Holmes proposed the more exclusive version of the workshop. This workshop differed from the earlier one. Not only smaller, it met at the five members' houses, circulating from one to the next; for another, drinks and coffee (for Holmes, who as a recovering alcoholic did not drink) were served; and the poets made carbon copies of their work so that they could read their poems aloud themselves instead of leaving the choice to Holmes, who in this workshop was the senior participant, not the leader.

In September 1958, backed by Snodgrass, Sexton also enrolled in the poetry seminar that Robert Lowell was teaching at Boston University. Lowell's course met regularly from 2:00 to 4:00 on Tuesdays. Sexton now found herself at a different level of instruction—less encouraging, perhaps, than the Holmes workshop, but far more intense. Lowell's mere range of learning, to say nothing of his stature on the national poetry scene, far outstripped that of anyone in the Holmes group: his passionate involvement with poetry of all periods and numerous languages enriched his teaching and his students; moreover, at the time he admitted Sexton to his class, he was finishing *Life Studies*, and he responded to her application, "Of course your poems qualify. . . . I am not very familiar with them yet, but have been reading them with a good deal of admiration and envy this morning after combing through pages of fragments of my own unfinished stuff."[18] She responded, "What a fine letter you wrote me. I am considering framing it to prove to all comers that poets are people."[19] And, in October, not long after the class had begun, she wrote Snodgrass, "Lowell just called and says the poets' theater [*sic*] wants you on November 9th. I want to announce that I will be there clapping and also that on November Ninth I will be thirty years old."[20]

She was there, and so were about forty more of us. In the dusty dark upstairs cavern of the Poets' Theatre we listened as Robert Lowell, swaying, hesitating, and stirring the air with his finger, praised his former student in the most elevated terms, explicitly declaring his homage to Snodgrass, and then stepped aside, without reading a single poem from the completed *Life Studies*, as Snodgrass read "Heart's Needle," with its spacious range of reference to the Korean War, to birds, trees, landscapes, and a palette of sense-impressions which combined to enrich the deep emotions the poem conveyed. The poem, in ten sections, each different prosodically, rhyming in diverse stanzas of four, five, six, and eight lines, speaks with an authority which Sexton was still far from reaching, and which Lowell's poems-in-progress would not attain, though their intensity, like Sexton's, was more disturbing, less elegiac. Snodgrass ended the reading, as I recall, with a wonderful piece of self-mockery carrying the refrain "Snodgrass is walking through the universe." It was clear that Lowell had, quite intentionally, administered a benediction. Snodgrass stayed with the Sextons and the Lowells during his Boston visit. Anne and "De" remained friends thereafter: his influence on "The Double Image" is profound.

The Holmes/Kumin/Starbuck/Sexton/Albert meetings, much more combative and leaderless, continued concurrently with the Lowell classes. The new addition was George Starbuck, all knees and elbows, tall as a crane with great shadows under his eyes, and a slow, melancholy, throwaway manner of speaking that penetrated further than the pipe-puffing ruminations of John Holmes. Starbuck, born in Columbus, Ohio, in 1931, had been educated in mathematics at the California Institute of Technology, and at Berkeley. After two years in the Army during the Korean War, he entered graduate study at the University of Chicago, where he helped edit the *Chicago Review* along with Philip Roth, Paul Carroll, and others, and was married to Janice King, a beautiful young woman. Elizabeth Hardwick recalls of Starbuck, "He was strange, droopy. We once went to his place on Beacon Hill and were struck by the hangdog, waiflike children hanging around the room. He seemed pathetic, she seemed pathetic, they seemed pathetic, everything seemed out of sorts."

As Maxine Kumin remembers Starbuck: "We had a very warm family relationship with George while he was at Houghton Mifflin. He used to come out and have dinner with us at least once a week. Danny Kumin has vivid and fond memories of George; he used to give him his bath. I'll never forget George coming to the house with Rolfe Humphries' version of Ovid's *Metamorphoses* in paperback. He read these to Danny, expurgating them a little bit. George was wonderful. He was *so* troubled. . . . Jan and the kids were still on Beacon Hill when George and Anne were lovers, and the kids went to live with Jan's parents; I guess that was in California."[22]

Starbuck had met Sexton and Kumin after a reading that John Holmes had arranged for him to give in early 1958 at the New England Poetry Club. By the time he joined the workshop in September 1958 his marital plight prevented him, for financial and family reasons, from remaining in graduate school. Archibald MacLeish recommended him to Houghton Mifflin Company as an editorial candidate, and he took an office there, concentrating on fiction and poetry. He was living on Pinckney Street on Beacon Hill. His work at Houghton Mifflin involved acquiring new literary writers, and, during his two years in the job, he signed up three first books by authors of permanent importance: Galway Kinnell's *What a Kingdom It Was*, Philip Roth's *Goodbye, Columbus*, and, by May 1959, Anne Sexton's *To Bedlam and Part Way Back*, which over the past months he had seen developing line by line, poem by poem, in the sessions of the Holmes writing group.

Though John Holmes was still the only senior, published, poet in the group, both George Starbuck and Maxine Kumin were disciplined prosodists. Holmes himself wrote in traditional forms. Anne's powerful surges of emotion wanted harnessing, and the critical demurs of both Kumin and Starbuck were welcome to her. From Kumin she learned what to read, to expand her literary background; from Starbuck, who was a virtuoso at metrical devices, she learned something more about syllabics, about rhyme schemes, even about tricks and wordplay, like acrostics, a favorite device of Starbuck's. (At about this time he sent me a poem at *The Atlantic Monthly*, in which the initial letters of whose lines read: "O Ted Weekss head leaks I said Ted Weekss head leaks." Weeks was *The Atlantic Monthly*'s editor-in-chief. I gently suggested George might submit this poem to *Harper's*.) But though Starbuck might decorate a poem's fringes with an acrostic, the poem often engaged serious, even grim, war-torn subject-matter. One long poem, which he labored over night after night in a Harvard Square cafeteria in May of 1959,[23] concealed bawdy versified gibes at the anthologist Oscar Williams within a hundred-line excursus in dactylic monometer on the Normandy invasion, in virtuoso metrics, entitled "A Tapestry for Bayeux."[24] Another, "War Story," described how the official corpse collectors did their work:

> The 4th of July he stormed a nest.
> He won a ribbon but lost his chest.
> We threw his arms across the rest
> And kneed him in the chin.
> (You knee them in the chin
> To drive the dog-tag in. . . .)[25]

The members of the group listened thoughtfully to one another's critiques, but some were a little hesitant about utilizing them; Sexton would devour recommendations of all kinds and incorporate them in her work, as she had done with Snodgrass and as she would soon be doing with Lowell. She could be imperious in rejecting suggestions too, but she might rewrite or write entire new sections into a poem, or even use entire lines volunteered by Starbuck; and the discussions could become quite heated. But Starbuck was a natural teacher, a brilliant editor, and I know from his own later generosity to me how uncannily useful his insights could be. Sexton's excitement, however, had an adverse effect on Holmes, whose Yankee comportment, as well as whose personal experience of his first marriage, made him try to slow her down, an effort which Sexton interpreted as dislike:

Sexton: John found me evil.

Kumin: But I think it should be said, that the reason for John's reaction, we *guess*, is that his first wife had *been* mentally ill, and had killed herself.

Sexton: But I was writing about this subject. He kept saying, no no, too personal, or you mustn't, or anything. Everything he said about my poems was bad, almost altogether. And yet, from the beginning, from the class, from him, I learned. And from Maxine. I must say Maxine, my best teacher—although for a while I was copying Maxine's flaws. . . . Always Maxine responded to my poetry. Not John, but Maxine, although in spite of herself because it was hard for her.

Kumin: Yes, it was hard. Here was my Christian academic daddy saying, stay away from her. She's bad for you.

[Enid] *Showalter* [interviewer]: Did he actually say that?

Sexton: He would write letters saying, she's evil. He did, he said, be careful of her.

Kumin: Oh yes, he would write me letters. He was my patron; he got me a job at Tufts. . . . We were a good group. George was icily cerebral. George would be sitting there counting the syllabics. But I could point to lines that I changed because of George. . . . We were very open and raw and new then. We were all beginners.[26]

Starbuck has said of Sexton: "She did exhaust all of us at times. It wasn't that she wanted to manipulate people and use them for her own advancement, exactly . . . she was just feverish and high energy and had a two-year-old's sense of the passage of time."[27] Sometime in the early months of 1959, George Starbuck and Anne Sexton became lovers as well.[28] Maxine Kumin, who was in on the secret "from the very beginning," says, "It was a very important relationship to both of them, I think, two very needy people coming together. And George was a wonderful critic in our little group and he did mediate disputes between John and Anne all the time. I always felt more comfortable when George was aboard."[29]

Sexton described her other seminar, Robert Lowell's class at Boston University, quite awkwardly, touchingly:

> The class met at Boston University on Tuesdays from two to four. . . . We were not allowed to smoke, but everyone smoked anyhow, using their shoes as ashtrays. Unused to classes of any kind, it seemed slow and uninspired to me. . . . I had never been to college and knew so little about poetry and other poets that I felt grotesquely out of place in Robert Lowell's graduate seminar. It consisted of some twenty students—seventeen graduates, two other housewives . . . and a boy who snuck over from M.I.T. I was the only one in that room who hadn't read *Lord Weary's Castle*. Mr. Lowell was formal in a rather New England sense. His voice was soft and slow. It seems to me that people remember the voice of the teacher they loved long after they have forgotten what he said. . . . At first I felt impatient, packed with ideas and feelings and the desire to interrupt his slow line by line reading of student work. He would read the first line—stop—and then

143

discuss that line at length. I wanted to go through the whole poem quickly and then go back. . . . At that point I wrote Mr. Snodgrass about my impatience and his reply . . . went this way: "Frankly, I used to nod my head at his every statement and he taught me more than a whole gang of scholars could." So I kept my mouth shut. And Snodgrass was right. . . . He didn't teach me what to put into a poem, but what to leave out. What he taught me was taste. Perhaps that's the only thing a poet can be taught.[30]

Meanwhile, the Holmes workshop had been wondering whether Sexton was ready to publish a book of poems which, drawn from a line in "The Double Image," she proposed calling *To Bedlam and Part Way Back*. On February 8 John Holmes, who had been holding himself in, wrote Anne a long letter, which included the words "I distrust the very source and subject of a great many of your poems, namely, all those that describe and dwell on your time in the hospital. . . . It bothers me that you use poetry this way. It's all a release for you, but what is it for anyone else except a spectacle of someone experiencing release? . . . Don't publish it in a book."[31] Anne's response was a letter, written February 12, enclosing one of her most touching poems, "For John, Who Begs Me Not to Enquire Further," and which included the lines "I tapped my own head;/it was glass, an inverted bowl." She would certainly have presented this poem to the Lowell class. (It may be no more than coincidence that Plath's first novel should be entitled *The Bell Jar*, but the two images have an uncanny kinship.) Sexton also gathered her collection of poems together to show to Lowell, who showed them to Stanley Kunitz and to William Alfred and then, without consulting Anne, passed the manuscript along to Harry Ford, who had been responsible for publishing *Heart's Needle* at Knopf in New York.[32] This must have caused confusion to several people, for Anne called Ford to say the book wasn't finished, and asked him to return it.[33] She wrote to Snodgrass, "A friend at Houghton Mifflin is dying to get his hands on it."[34] On February 24 Sexton wrote to Snodgrass that her book was taking shape; she had been at a John Holmes party after Richard Wilbur's reading the week of February 15, along with Robert Lowell, Stanley Kunitz, Philip Booth, John Malcolm Brinnin, Ted Hughes, Sylvia Plath, Isabella Gardner, Maxine Kumin, and, of course, George Starbuck.[35] And, introduced by William Alfred, she gave a reading of her poems at the Poets' Theatre on March 1, along with Maxine, George, and Arthur Freeman, a reading so successful it was repeated a week later. Lowell insisted that she read "The Double Image" in the Boston University seminar.

On March 10 Mary Gray Harvey died after her long metastasized cancer. The dramatic events of 1959 were coming to a head. In April, after the afternoon sessions of Lowell's class, Anne, in one may imagine how calm a frame of mind, had time to kill between the ending of the class and her psychiatrist's appointment. George Starbuck, likewise distraught, began, when he could, to look in on the Lowell class, and the two took themselves, along with Sylvia Plath, to the Ritz bar, parking Anne Sexton's Ford in a loading zone. ("We were only going to get loaded," she quipped.) "I weave with two sweet ladies out of the Ritz," Starbuck would write in a poem. Sexton wrote to Snodgrass on April 8, "[Sylvia Plath] is going to Lowell's class along with George Starbuck (poet) and we three leave the class and go to the Ritz and drink martinis. Very fun. My book is at H.M. now. Tho only in a half way sort of way. I don't think it is ready to be a book quite yet." Sexton wrote to Snodgrass again the next day: "There is a rather nice poet in Boston who is in love with me. I guess I'd better give up and sleep with him."[36] The chances are she already had.

Young Girl

Dear love, as simple as some distant evil
we walk a little drunk up these three flights
where you tacked a Dufy print above your army cot.

The thin apartment doors on the way up will
not tell on us. We are saying, we have *our* rights
and let them see the sandwiches and wine we bought

for we do not explain my husband's insane abuse
and we do not say why your wild-haired wife has fled
or that my father opened like a walnut and then was
dead.
Your palms fold over me like knees. Love is the only
use. . . .

Climbing the dark halls, I ignore their papers and pails,
the twelve coats of rubbish of someone else's dim life.
Tell them need is an excuse for love. Tell them need
prevails.
Tell them I remake and smooth your bed and am your
wife.[37]

Even before these events Sexton had written to Carolyn
Kizer, "I am just not so sure about Lowell. He has been
very kind to me . . . but he is very shy. We hardly speak
when we meet publicly. Then he will call me up and we
will both enjoy a frightfully stilted conversation as he tells
me he has shown some poem of mine to this one or that
one and they concur with his high opinion. . . . It is so
strange that I can't explain it. I think he may like my work
because it is all a little crazy or about being crazy and it
may be that he relates to me and my 'bedlam poetry.' . . .
Though I haven't seen Cal's [new book] I fear it is full
of personal poetry and think that he is either copying me
or that I'm copying him."[38] But the publication of *Life
Studies*, and Lowell's hospitalization in late April, broke up

the class and the equilibrium of the little group within it.

The "triple-martini afternoons" soon ceased: Sylvia Plath wrote, on May 3, that she was typing her new manuscript to submit to Houghton Mifflin but she feared that "A.S. is there ahead of me, with her lover G.S. writing *New Yorker* odes to her and both of them together." And she went on, mysteriously, to refer to "that memorable afternoon at G.'s monastic and miserly room on Pinckney: 'You shouldn't have left us': where is responsibility to lie? I left, yet felt like a brown-winged moth around a rather meager candle flame, drawn. That is over."[39] Though the Ritz revels were made much of by Sexton after Plath's death, a glance at the calendar makes it obvious that there could have been no more than three or four "triple-martini afternoons." I suspect, however, that there was a good deal going on among the three companion/rivals in the spring of 1959, and that we shall never know much more about it than we do now—unless the manuscript journals of Plath at Smith College reveal more when they are opened to the public in 2013 A.D. On May 18, 1959, one week after the publication of *Life Studies*, Houghton Mifflin accepted *To Bedlam and Part Way Back*. In June George Starbuck's book *Bone Thoughts* beat out Plath's and Kumin's manuscripts to win the Yale Series of Younger Poets prize from its new judge, Dudley Fitts. The threesome was by now clearly shattered, especially as Sylvia Plath and Ted Hughes were planning to leave Boston on a three-month cross-country automobile trip, and were anticipating a baby as well.

Sexton was not given much time to rejoice in the acceptance of her book. Her father had by no means fully recovered from the stroke that had felled him the previous November, and his behavior throughout this eventful winter had been trying indeed, actually causing Sexton to seek hospital rest herself. No sooner had she come out, on June 2, than Ralph Harvey died of a second stroke, and it was revealed after his death that his apparent wealth had all disappeared, his interest in the company that bore his name sold to a silent partner, and that Kayo's expectations of inheriting control of the company had vanished into thin air.

Anne had her new editor/lover for solace, and they saw much of one another during the summer, even attending the Bread Loaf Writers' Conference together, where a romantic photograph arranged by the conference shows them sitting with other eager students at the feet of Robert Frost. When Starbuck's *Bone Thoughts* came out, it carried the dedication:

> To the one with her head out the window, drinking the rain.
> To the one who said me a lullaby over the phone.
> To the one who, divining love in this rocky terrain, has made it her own.[40]

In September Sexton had to undergo surgery for what might have been a malignancy in her pelvic area but which turned out to be a benign cyst, and she managed to transform this additional trauma into "The Operation," one of her most striking poems. She was already bristling with poems for her next book, which would be entitled *All My Pretty Ones*, to elegize all those of her family who had died. In the spring of 1960 yet another death struck: Kayo Sexton's father, whose generosity had paid a great many of Anne's hospital bills, was killed in an automobile crash. And in May 1960 she underwent an abortion, suspecting that the child she was carrying was not her husband's. She had suffered three family deaths and two surgical procedures in twelve months, and every one of them would be exploited for poetry. Soon after the affair with Starbuck had faded, the summer of 1960 would find her involved in an intense correspondence-cum-love-affair with James Wright. The pattern of her future was taking shape.

To recollect Anne Sexton's actuality becomes more difficult as the literature about her work and her self-presentation proliferates. To recall Anne's vividness as a person always brings up the correlative impression in the late 1950s of two people devoted to her protection: her likeable husband, Kayo, for her domestic life, and the sensitive and fiercely loyal Maxine Kumin for her life as a poet. My testimony would be incomplete if I relied only on the recollections of others; still, I had met Anne only intermittently, nearly always with Maxine and sometimes with Maxine and George Starbuck, at a poetry reading or at a party, before Tuesday, April 18, 1961, when we set out on a three-day expedition to Cornell, to give readings of our own poetry at Cornell's annual spring arts festival. Early that morning, as news of the Bay of Pigs disaster was beginning to filter into our consciousness, George and I, in my black Volkswagen bug, stopped at 40 Clearwater Road, Newton Lower Falls, to pick Anne up at the house where she lived for the greater part of her married life, and drive, in her larger car, to Cornell. The house was white clapboard, conventional, suburban, low-lying. The children, very young, were on their way to school and Anne hugged them farewell and fussed about her luggage. Once we'd set off on the nine-hour drive to Ithaca, George and Anne and I conversed in a general way about people, poems, and poetry. I already knew George quite well, from his poetry, from mutual friends in Cambridge, from our mutual publishing concerns, and from our spirited weekend softball games, which Harvey Breit had once written up in *The New York Times Book Review* as "the Poets' Softball Team." I had no idea then that there had been anything more than poetic and editorial relations between Anne and George.

When we arrived at Cornell, toward dark, it became apparent that Anne was developing a sprightly case of nerves, fully anticipated by George, about her forthcoming public appearance, despite our dubious support. "Walking into places," she once explained to a friend, "is the worst part," and in her daily life she usually succeeded in finding someone to walk into places with her. That George and I might have our own anxieties (it would be my first public reading of my own work anywhere) did not, it seemed, occur to Anne: she demanded cocktails (keeping for backup a pint of vodka in her bag) and we soon, after being provided with comfortable rooms by our hosts at Telluride House, a sort of honors fraternity, became happily buzzy at the expense of the English department, welcomed by short-story-writer James McConkey, Donald Carne-Ross (the British-born translator of Ariosto), poet David Ray, and Baxter Hathaway, the revered editor of Cornell's literary magazine *Epoch*. Our hosts at dinner were the members of Telluride House, including C. Michael Curtis, editor of *The Trojan Horse*, a student literary magazine in upstart rivalry with *Epoch*.

Anne during this dinner governed the center of the long table like a reigning queen, a vivacious and volatile one, flirting, guffawing, pronouncing, exclaiming; and after dinner, apparently undeterred by nerves, she was ready for more party. Having shared the long drive to Cornell with George, I was tired enough to turn in early, for I had some publishing appointments arranged for the next morning. Anne, however, plunged into the evening revels with undiminished zest. She and Starbuck were now only good friends, and on her return to Boston Anne would boast to her psychiatrist: "I was scared the whole time—ordered double martinis on the rocks with a long straw, and reached for it only with my arm braced. And when I'd light a cigarette, I'd rest my elbow on the chair. . . . [I tried] constantly to have a guardian, and managed not to have an affair with anyone."[41]

Wednesday morning brought a warm spring day, noisy

with the sounds of loudspeakers braying the news from Cuba, and student speakers lamenting their disappointment, even disillusion, with the new Kennedy administration that had so recently declared its hope that the world would become a different kind of place, a place where we would defend freedom, not attack it. It wasn't clear to most of us at Cornell whether our sinking feeling came from our having lost the battle, or having done the deed. Neither had been wanted. Perhaps this moment was, in a spiritual sense, the end of the 1950s: nobody could be trusted, not even the bright new administration.

Before the reading, in the afternoon, there was a panel discussion about publishing to which I contributed in my role as editor. In the evening Anne and I gave our reading, alternating two groups of poems. I was sampling my as yet unfinished first book, and I began with a series of portraits of madmen and madwomen; Anne's first group came from *To Bedlam and Part Way Back*, published the year before, and ended with "The Double Image." My second group ended with "Not Forgotten," the sequence of poems that mourn my mother's death from cancer; and Anne balanced it with a group of poems from the as yet unpublished *All My Pretty Ones*, concluding with "The Operation," written in 1959 at just about the same time as "Not Forgotten." It was an antiphonal experience, hearing her read that great fugue of a poem taking the deaths of her mother, and the other deaths of her dear ones, upon her own skin like drumbeats. The two groups of poems, hers and mine, seemed to mourn the passing of a world, a world of sanity, an Eden of poetry that was about to die into a new world of mere truth, no matter how harsh, no matter how revealing, no matter how self-indulgent. If Maxine Kumin had been warned in college—as I had—not to reveal too much, this was a new aesthetic, as disillusioned as the students chanting on the campus lawn outside.

After the reading there was another party, to which Anne

once more fled as to salvation, but which after a while I deserted. The next morning, leaving George behind to give his reading the next day, Anne and I set off on what would prove to be a nine-hour free-association highway encounter session, with a two-hour indulgence for drinks and lunch at Keeler's in downtown Albany, then the best restaurant at that latitude between Boston and Detroit. Anne's openness, her excitability, her frankness about her suffering and her joys, were infectious and seductive. We found a whole sequence of parallels between our lives and chewed them over thoroughly. Anne wanted to tell me, and wanted me to tell her, all about various poets and editors: *Hudson Review*'s editor Frederick Morgan, who had published my "Not Forgotten" as he had published Anne's "The Double Image"; James Wright, and Anthony Hecht, to whom at this particular moment she was especially drawn. And there was a good deal to say about Sylvia Plath, who even then, when her highest achievements and fame were a long way in the future, aroused vigorous conversation among her friends. By the time we reached Newton Lower Falls, after dark, and Anne was welcomed home by Kayo, Linda, and Joy, I felt I knew more of her intimate life than of anyone I had ever met before, and that she knew more of mine. I came in for a drink before returning to Cambridge, and we had a relaxed and agreeable talk with Kayo, whom I liked on this first meeting, and always thereafter. I departed, somewhat dazed, to return to my own wife and child. It was the only time I ever entered Anne Sexton's house, though I saw her often for the next several years.

The story of Anne Sexton's growth into a poet is among the most familiar of the era, thanks in part to Anne's frequent and uninhibited interviews. Her emotional outspokenness lay at the heart of her poetry; yet her life was full of secrets that she told no one except her eternal psychiatrist. Only in the beginning, when she was just being recognized, was that interaction between poetry and psychiatry a help to her with other poets; later her endless threnody of self-absorption became a bore to all but her newest and her most faithful friends. Of all the poets of this period, Sexton alone can be described as pure "confessional": Plath transmuted her inner demons; Lowell turned his into fables; Snodgrass turned to other modes of poetry; but Anne lurched through her life from breakdown to breakdown, recovering herself and her talent by insisting on candor heaped upon candor, no matter how repetitive or trivial. As Schopenhauer wrote to Goethe—and as Anne wrote to John Holmes to accompany the poem which opens this chapter—"It is the courage to make a clean breast of it in face of every question that makes the philosopher. He must be like Sophocles' Oedipus, who, seeking enlightenment concerning his terrible fate, pursues his indefatigable enquiry, even when he divines that appalling horror awaits him in the answer. But most of us carry in our heart the Jocasta who begs Oedipus for God's sake not to inquire further. . . ."[42]

Her next epigraph was comparable: *All My Pretty Ones*, published in 1962, unrelentingly quoted Kafka: ". . . the books we need are the kind that act upon us like a misfortune, that make us suffer like the death of someone we love more than ourselves, that make us feel as though we were on the verge of suicide, or lost in a forest remote from all human habitation—a book should serve as the ax for the frozen sea within us." This epigraph was very much in tune with the times, but even then it seemed melodramatic to some, as did the rigorous self-exploitation of Sexton's later poetry. In 1965, tiring of it, I wrote a poem of my own, as a sort of citizen's response to Sexton's new swimming pool, constructed with fellowship money from Radcliffe, and I will conclude this chapter with it:

One of the Muses

She sits beside a pool with pen and paper.
" 'A book should serve as an ax,' " she writes,
" 'for the frozen sea within us,' " and she turns
next to poems, chopped into the paper,
driftwood from a torrent, strokes clanging:

"I have taken pains to seek pain through the world.
Cataclysm is your only weather.
They say, the others, take cold but stay alive,
pain's a poor husband, they say delirium
crushes the breasts without caressing them,
death brings no blossoming nor impregnation.
What do they know? The world will turn to ice
if no one keeps the crystals from uniting,
and I am hot to break it up, with bleeding
knuckles if necessary. I must save the world
for the tides to wrestle in, and I shall ride."

She wallows in her howling sea of feeling,
enraptured, impaled on a thrusting mind—
her lonely lover, the last partner alive,
not yet drowned. Around, amid
the chambers of the brain, she dances him
to death, while he must grab and grin
but never shut his eyes for gazing at her.
That is her triumph. Pain gives her her joy,
for only pain will worship her completely
and never never take his girl for granted.

This dance follows no music: the dance
comes first, the music after. By the pool
she listens for the motions of the dance:
receding footsteps, memories of woe,
echoes of servitude. Slaves kneel in chains before her.
Away at the center of the pool is Self,
sinking in weightless silence to the depths,

hauling up to gasp above the surface
till it turns back again with bursting lungs
to thrust itself beneath the alien element
where she will be alone, enclosed, adored.[43]

Arthur Freeman told Anne that I had written this poem about her and, after her first surprise, she told him she liked it. "It's a good poem," she said.

7. Your Day Approaches:
Sylvia Plath, 1957–1959

"A clear blue day in Winthrop. Went to my father's grave, a very depressing sight. . . . Great cramps, stirrings . . . Am I pregnant?"

THE JOURNALS OF SYLVIA PLATH, MARCH 9, 1959

The Colossus

I shall never get you put together entirely,
Pieced, glued, and properly jointed.
Mule-bray, pig-grunt and bawdy cackles
Proceed from your great lips.
It's worse than a barnyard.

Perhaps you consider yourself an oracle,
Mouthpiece of the dead, or of some god or other.
Thirty years now I have labored
To dredge the silt from your throat.
I am none the wiser.

Scaling little ladders with gluepots and pails of Lysol
I crawl like an ant in mourning
Over the weedy acres of your brow
To mend the immense skull-plates and clear
The bald, white tumuli of your eyes.

A blue sky out of the Oresteia
Arches above us. O father, all by yourself
You are pithy and historical as the Roman Forum.
I open my lunch on a hill of black cypress.
Your fluted bones and acanthine hair are littered

In their old anarchy to the horizon-line.
It would take more than a lightning-stroke
To create such a ruin.
Nights, I squat in the cornucopia
Of your left ear, out of the wind,

Counting the red stars and those of plum-color.
The sun rises under the pillar of your tongue.
My hours are married to shadow.
No longer do I listen for the scrape of a keel
On the blank stones of the landing.[1]

The Manor Garden

The fountains are dry and the roses over.
Incense of death. Your day approaches.
The pears fatten like little buddhas.
A blue mist is dragging the lake.

You move through the era of fishes,
The smug centuries of the pig—
Head, toe and finger
Come clear of the shadow. History

Nourishes these broken flutings,
These crowns of acanthus,
And the crow settles her garments.
You inherit white heather, a bee's wing,

Two suicides, the family wolves,
Hours of blankness. Some hard stars
Already yellow the heavens.
The spider on its own string

Crosses the lake. The worms
Quit their usual habitations.
The small birds converge, converge
With their gifts to a difficult borning.[2]

157

The gushing pages of Sylvia Plath's *Letters Home* embody one of the artificial personalities she wore; the self-lacerating pages of *The Journals of Sylvia Plath*, another. The memories and memoirs of those who knew her reflect yet other masks with which this molten, dedicated, ambitious young woman protected herself. Alfred Kazin, her teacher at Smith College in January 1955, described her to me, just before I met her that winter, in words almost identical to those he later used in an autobiographical book. (They may even have found their way into and out of his journals):

> The college's most brilliant literary graduate in years, winner of all its prizes, straight-A girl all the way . . . She was the last in line waiting to get admission to another asinine "creative writing" class. All the girls seemed to be blondes in camel's hair coats. . . . The last girl in line looked like all the others. When she handed over some pages, I had grown so wary that I began to skim, and then became suspicious. The writing was so coolly professional that I scented plagiarism, and said with some bitterness, "These could be published in ———— and ————." "I know," said the girl, "they've already taken them." I read them carefully and turned back to the top sheet to learn her name. "Sylvia Plath . . ."
>
> When we met at home, she was the first to clear the dishes after coffee. She was certainly a "regular" girl, full of smiles. Despite her lonesome need to "talk" at our few lunches in a spaghetti joint on Green Street, she was guarded to an extreme. I knew nothing about her and never expected to know anything. . . . I saw only bleakly skillful stories. . . .

She had tried suicide and had been discovered under a porch just in time. Her manner was "perfect," as Smith College liked to say; the things she indifferently turned out for me were also "perfect." There was not a line, not a thought, not a word that the magazine business would have changed. Sometimes, when she seemed tremulous and on the brink of saying something unusual, I wondered again at the cool professional sheen to anything she wrote. She had tried suicide; she had notoriously been tried, tested, and honored, over and over—their pet achievement—by the nervous English Department. But the words came to my desk any Tuesday at four as if she could write in her sleep.[3]

This was the prose-student Sylvia Plath, the version of herself presented to a revered teacher. Yet another self came out in a girlish letter to a woman poet her own age as she graduated from Smith in June 1955: "fortunately, a very nice assistant editor from harcourt, brace, is conveniently changing his job this month to assistant to director of harvard u. press, and with his coming cambridge locale, I hope to see a bit of him. I love cambridge enormously, and would love to end up with a professor there."[4] In August 1955 what she presented to me in person was quite different: a gushing enthusiasm, a gee-whiz semblance of naiveté, an insatiable curiosity, an athletic and eager eroticism, and behind them all a dedicated regimen of writerly self-education. I have told of my astonishment when she burst out with the terrible story of her earlier suicide attempt, and of my abrupt dismissal. For some years my vanity was sufficiently unhealed to let out its grievances now and then in the form of what Janet Malcolm has lately characterized as "pronounce[ments] on her personality problems,"[5] but I have found myself over the years, despite that difficult personality, growing in gratitude for having known Sylvia when she was young and not fully formed, and remembering all she taught me.

It turns out that during the summer of 1955 Sylvia Plath was conducting four simultaneous love affairs, all of which she attempted to terminate before leaving America for a new life at Cambridge.[6] She sent me a card that September from the Victoria and Albert Museum, on one side a picture of a faun with pan-pipes (a favorite symbol), and on the other the message "Somehow this charming chap reminded me of you," which I did find flattering, not knowing at the time that it was one of her *other* lovers, Richard Sassoon, who really reminded her of a faun. Her early months at Cambridge followed the experience of other American students: excitement, culture shock, overstimulation, followed by depression, compounded, in Sylvia's case, by a new snake's nest of love affairs and an insistently ambitious passion for work. On February 26, 1956, almost the very day when her depression hit bottom, she met Ted Hughes, the most powerful presence yet to enter her life. Her description of these entanglements in her journal for the winter of 1956 came to a climax with their violent first meeting, the famous occasion when, at a drunken literary party, she recited two of Hughes' poems to him from memory, he kissed her in a back room and took her scarf and earrings, and she bit him till the blood ran down his face. The next day she wrote "Pursuit," which begins:

> There is a panther stalks me down:
> One day I'll have my death of him;
> His greed has set the woods aflame,
> He prowls more lordly than the sun. . . .[7]

Despite this melodramatic declaration, she did not know what to make of Hughes or what to do about him, as her journals vividly describe.[8]

At the Easter vacation, en route to a Paris rendezvous,

as she thought, with Richard Sassoon, she encountered Hughes in London, spent what she called "a holocaust of a night" with him, and then dashed off to Paris in search of Sassoon, who had unbeknownst to her made his exit to Spain with another girl. Once she had recovered from that shock, she managed to find consolations; and she then fled to Italy with yet another longtime lover, the unquenchable Gordon Lameyer, with whom she now quarrelled incessantly. Finally she fled once more, on Friday April 13, back into Hughes' arms in London. She announced the outcome to her mother almost at once in letters of high rhetoric and full spate: "I shall tell you now about something most miraculous and thundering and terrifying. . . . It is this man, this poet, this Ted Hughes. . . . He has a health and hugeness. . . . I have never been so exultant, the joy of using all my wit and womanly wisdom is a joy beyond words."[9] To her brother she wrote more levelly: "I have hacked through a hard vacation, shared really only the best parts with mother, not the racking ones (it is so easy to give merely the impression of rich joy here and not the roots of sorrow and hurt from which it comes) and am now coming into the full of my power: I am writing poetry as I never have before; and it is the best, because I am strong in myself and in love with the only man in the world who is my match. . . . His name is Ted Hughes."[10]

They were secretly married in London on June 16— secretly, on the naive but erroneous assumption that Sylvia would lose her Fulbright scholarship if she was married, though the secrecy was perhaps even more complicated by the fact that, though Sylvia's mother flew to England to be at the wedding, none of the Hughes family was present, nor, it appears, had any of them been notified of the event.[11] The couple spent a summer vacation in Spain and only then paid a visit, at last, to the Hughes family in Yorkshire. During these months she began to learn what Ted Hughes had to teach her as a poet—a great deal, to be sure, but some of the results could be almost ventriloquial, as in the avalanche of consonants in "Ode for Ted":

From under crunch of my man's boot
green oat-sprouts jut;
he names a lapwing, starts rabbits in a rout
legging it most nimble
to sprigged hedge of bramble,
stalks red fox, shrewd stoat.[12]

At the end of a productive summer, Sylvia returned alone to Cambridge, where in her mail she found a letter from me telling her of my new job at the Atlantic Monthly Press. *The Atlantic Monthly* had already accepted her poem "Pursuit." Her response to my letter was four jam-packed single-spaced pages describing her first year at Cambridge as a "magnificent madhouse," claiming Paris as her "second home," announcing her plans: "I am spending the year reading like fury, and writing four hours a day: chief projects, getting a volume of poems together to submit to the Yale Younger Poets series . . . and, writing a novel . . . on an American girl in Cambridge . . . called, tentatively, 'Hill of Leopards.' . . . I'd like best to submit it for one of those big publishing house prizes—am I right in thinking the Atlantic Company runs one?" On and on the pages tumbled. She had discovered a marvelous new writer named Ted Hughes. "Unpublished professionally. I became his agent, as it were, in America. . . . *The Atlantic Monthly*, by the way, has had some of his poems for four months . . . children's fables . . . adult fables. . . . I am desperate to know more about copyright laws: both Ted & I will want to . . . keep the TV and movie rights. . . . I would like to keep in close touch with you this coming year. . . . You can really be a terrific help." Finally, toward the bottom of page 4, she added, "I'll be bringing Ted Hughes home in June, too, to be married in Wellesley: we're hoping to get teaching jobs in New England at twin colleges and go on writing like fury."[13] As she wrote this she had, in fact, already been married for three months. In November they settled things happily with the Fulbright people and the authorities at Cambridge, and at Christmas she sent me a card revealing that she and Ted were "now married and living in our own flat."[14]

Her hopes, some of them, were realized. On March 12, 1957, she wrote her mother: "I have just been offered a teaching job for next year! AT SMITH! I got the nicest little letter from blessed R. G. Davis this morning (I know dear, blessed Miss [Mary Ellen] Chase is responsible for this and for my knowing so early.)"[15] ["Dear, blessed Miss Chase," who in 1955 Plath had regarded as "my dearest friend,"[16] would before long be described in the journals of 1959, during Plath's psychotherapy, as one of those "lesbians (what does a woman see in another woman that she doesn't see in a man: tenderness?). I am also afraid of M.E.C.: you must hate her, fear her: you think all old women are magical witches."[17]]

When the Hugheses came to America as a couple in June, 1957, they spent their first summer lolling and writing on Cape Cod. Plath was again girding her loins to become a major writer: "I will be stronger [than Virginia Woolf]: I will write until I begin to speak my deep self, and then have children, and speak still deeper. . . ."[18] There had been a reception for the newlywed couple in Wellesley on June 29, to which I was invited, and which biographers say I attended, but I can remember nothing of it, nor of a lunch which my diary suggests I gave them on July 2. I was in fact moving from one Cambridge apartment to another over that weekend. During their year in Northampton I did not see a lot of them, but there was plenty of correspondence between us, regarding submissions by both poets to *The Atlantic Monthly*. Plath's published journal, once the Smith 1957–1958 academic year began, is full of woeful complaints about the difficulty of teaching, the horrors of aca-

demic life, and some of the difficulties of marriage, though
it expresses little enough of the friendships that were begun
in Northampton, except the deep relations with Leonard
and Esther Baskin that commenced toward the end of their
stay, and the vexed connections with Paul and Clarissa
Roche. Little is said of Anthony Hecht, Daniel and Janet
Aaron, George Gibian, and others. Plath's difficulties, how-
ever, had more to do with the agonies of unfulfillment as
a writer, frustrated by her tutelary duties, as she records
in her journals. Some of her faculty colleagues, Maureen
Howard for example, have spoken of her nervousness and
self-consciousness as a teacher,[19] but Daniel Aaron, pro-
fessor of American literature, who was deputized to look in
on her classes and evaluate them from time to time, reports
that she was surprisingly good, surprisingly adept, rather
schoolmarmy, prim and neat, and she ran her classes very
effectively and well.[20] Aaron also remembers how very def-
erential she was to her husband, how it was very important
to Plath that Hughes should be included in everything. The
Smith year wore on, with both husband and wife developing
a distaste for the academic life and vowing to live as in-
dependent writers.

For Sylvia Plath to return to the scene of her student
triumphs could not have been likely to assist her in becom-
ing a writer, not the conflicted daughter of two teachers, a
self-doubting success-chaser "who so wanted to be a Smith
woman," especially since she had an English husband in
tow who found himself unable to land a decent academic
job in spite of his rapidly burgeoning reputation as a poet.
Anne Stevenson's account of the seesaw year in Northamp-
ton describes with particular acuity Sylvia Plath's internal
conflicts. Hughes' first book, *The Hawk in the Rain*, which
Sylvia, acting for him, had entered in a publication contest
juried by W. H. Auden, Stephen Spender, and Marianne
Moore, and sponsored by the Poetry Center at the YMHA

in New York, was chosen out of 387 entries and published in October 1957.

The book's reception was extraordinary and changed the couple's life. W. S. Merwin, in *The New York Times Book Review*, was perhaps the first to single Hughes out. Philip Booth praised *The Hawk in the Rain* in *The Saturday Review*; and, most authoritatively, Edwin Muir, the great Orcadian poet, translator of Kafka, and recently Charles Eliot Norton Professor at Harvard, wrote in *The New Statesman*: "Mr. Ted Hughes is clearly a remarkable poet and seems to be quite outside the currents of his time. His distinguishing power is sensuous, verbal and imaginative; at his best the three are fused together. His images have an admirable violence."[21] Such welcomes on both sides of the ocean produced immediate effects, one of which was to get Hughes a teaching job at the University of Massachusetts in Amherst effective in January 1958; another was John L. Sweeney's invitation to Hughes and Plath to dine in Boston with William and Dido Merwin in November, and for Hughes to read his poems at Harvard in April. I have alluded in chapter 3 to the first meetings between the Hugheses and the Merwins in Boston, meetings that changed the young couple's minds about their future in the academic life.[22]

Over Christmas Sylvia, as a consequence of overstrain and overwork, came down with viral pneumonia and fled to her mother's house in Wellesley, where the decision came to a head, under Mrs. Plath's anxious eyes, to leave Smith at the end of the academic year. Also, symbolically enough, Sylvia visited her childhood neighborhood in Winthrop. "We must fight to return to that early mind. . . ."[23] Sylvia notified the Smith English department on January 5, 1958, that she would not return for the second year of her instructorship and promptly sank into a depression that she might have anticipated, having cast off her academic moorings after so many years of riding at them.

As she returned after vacation to what would be the hostility, real or imagined, of her colleagues at Smith and undertook her last semester of classes, she picked up the newly published *New Poets of England and America* and, reading through it, burst into a rage: "Jealous one I am, green-eyed, spite-seething. Read the six women poets. . . . Dull, turgid. Except for May Swenson and Adrienne Rich, not one better or more-published than me."[24] She was quite right: reflecting the poetic climate of the time, the anthology contained thirty American male poets and fifteen British: only seven of them women, three of them talented, were included from either side of the ocean. But it makes an interesting, and symptomatic, contrast that, while Anne Sexton read this anthology and found her way to W. D. Snodgrass' "Heart's Needle," Plath had eyes for the women only, at once identifying her living "rivals": Edith Sitwell, Marianne Moore, May Swenson, Isabella Gardner, "and, most close, Adrienne Cecile Rich."[25]

Almost at once Plath began expanding her ambitions for her poetry, revising and retitling the work she had on hand for offer to publishers. The young couple began arranging to find a flat in Boston, visiting the Merwins but rejecting the Merwins' offer of their apartment, with its long view of the water. On March 30, 1958, they came to have tea in my treetop apartment in Cambridge, where I gave Ted a copy of Jung's *The Undiscovered Self*, which quickly found its way into his work: "The Jung is splendid—one of the basic notions of my play, curiously enough."[26] And, as the April 11 date for Hughes' reading approached, Plath herself burst into productivity, writing eight poems during the spring holiday, including the important "The Disquieting Muses," on a painting of De Chirico.

At the Harvard reading on April 11, recorded in ecstatic detail in Plath's journal, I remember an audience rapt by the emphatic consonant-crunching of Hughes' voice, which emphasized his nouns and underplayed the verbs; and a slog afterward through the sleety dusk to a reception on Kirkland Street, where the Harvard/Boston literary contingent gathered around: Jack Sweeney, who had performed the gracious introduction; Mr. and Mrs. I. A. Richards, who devotedly attended all readings; W. J. Bate, who stood in as head of the English department; Philip Booth ("handsome and strangely nice-guy innocent-looking," wrote Sylvia, "Hope to meet again") and "Adrienne Cecile Rich: little, round and stumpy, all vibrant short black hair, great sparkling black eyes and a tulip-red umbrella: honest, frank, forthright and even opinionated."[27] The evening ended with the Sweeneys entertaining Sylvia, Ted, Adrienne, and her husband, Alfred Conrad, at a restaurant in the Italian North End of Boston, and with Sweeney's invitation to Sylvia to record her poetry for Harvard on Friday June 13. The only literary friends missing were the Merwins, who had returned to Europe at the end of March.

On May 5, back in Northampton, Sylvia put on her "white pleated wool skirt and deep lovely median blue jersey with the square neck to hear Robert Lowell this afternoon: read some of his poems last night and had oddly a similar reaction . . . as when I first read Ted's poems . . . : taste the phrases: tough, knotty, blazing with color and fury, most eminently sayable."[28] No female rival would ever be vouchsafed that degree of praise.

As the moving day approached for Sylvia to return to her hometown, Plath noticed her mother's anxiety: "Queer mother—stiff about helping us come to Boston. . . . Her guarded praise at our getting poems published, as if this were one more nail in the coffin of our resolve to drown as poets and refuse all 'secure' teaching work. Another title for my book: *Full Fathom Five*." And she went straight on from the notion of drowning into flaying and digging, seeking the most vivid tropes of self-punishment for the act of poetry: "Oh, only left to myself, what a poet I will flay myself into. . . . Digging into the reaches of my deep submerged

head, 'and it's old and old it's sad and old it's sad and weary
I go back to you, my cold father, my cold mad father, my
cold mad feary father . . .'—so Joyce says, so the river flows
to the paternal source of godhead."[29] One could hardly ask
for a more Oedipal prediction.

The biographers and the journals all testify to a *tsunami*
of rage that now began to overwhelm Sylvia Plath, even in
her relations with her husband, over the late spring and
summer in Northampton, even after a tiny but "ideal"
apartment had been located and leased on Beacon Hill, the
sixth floor of 9 Willow Street, two blocks from the Sweeneys'
apartment, a stone's throw from Louisburg Square, for $115
a month. The actual arrival in Boston on September 1 was
exciting: the unpublished journals and letters to friends
speak of the cheerful but unaccustomed noise of the city,
church bells and fire engines, and describe tours of the back
streets, the Public Garden, waterfront taverns, and the
open-air stalls in Haymarket, where the Hugheses would
go for their food shopping. But this little honeymoon soon
wore off, and Sylvia, without a place in which to be admired,
without a position in the Smith world, without a position
of any kind, found the depression growing deeper. By Sep-
tember 11 she was restlessly combing the classified ads,
looking for a job.

On September 16, when, at their invitation, I went to
have tea at Willow Street with Ted and Sylvia, she seemed
wary, tense and withdrawn, while Ted responded helpfully
to the novice poems I brought them to look at. On Sep-
tember 28 Ted and Sylvia Hughes seem to have given a
reading at the Poets' Theatre,[30] and Ted, in a letter to
me, inquired whether a Poets' Theatre grant might be avail-
able to help him finish the play he was working on. I saw
them again, at the house of Marcia Brown Plumer, on Oc-
tober 1, the day after Sylvia, whose loneliness and distress
had reached bottom, had been interviewed for a job at Mas-

a week to put in his part-time teaching stint at Brande[s] University, Ted and Sylvia got into the custom of calling a[t] his temporary apartment at 1200 Massachusetts Avenue, in Cambridge. In Kunitz' words,

They made a point of stopping by my apartment on a Thursday or Friday evening, and it became a sort of ritual, but it was very strange because we weren't seeing the same people so far as I could gather, nobody had much to talk about personally. It was like a formal visit, paying a call. It was serious talk about poetry, and I know that Ted had a feeling about my poems, and I had a good strong feeling about his. Ted did all of the talking. Sylvia—I noticed this was almost ritual—Sylvia would always take a chair a little behind him, so that it was as though Ted and I had front stage, and she was back there, listening, very attentively, being very adoring, as she heard him talking, and very mousy. She scarcely opened her mouth. Not that Ted was very voluble, he was slow. Sylvia usually had tea and I don't recall whether Ted had a drink with me or not. It was not intimate. It was serious talk. And it was always pleasant, I was always happy to see them, but I didn't feel it had any deep connections.[37]

In late January the Lowells had gone to dinner with the Fassetts at the Hughes' apartment, Sylvia sedulously preparing for the event by reading not only Lowell's poems but Hardwick's stories at the library, while worrying about how to prepare a supper all in one dish, given the tiny table space available in their apartment. (Elizabeth Hardwick has no memory of this event, recalling only visits the Hugheses paid to her Marlborough Street house.) Nonetheless, by February Plath was sitting in on the Lowell seminar at Boston University and calling it "a great disappointment. Lowell good in his mildly feminine ineffectual fashion. Felt a regression. The main thing is hearing the other students'

sachusetts General Hospital. And I saw them again on November 16, when they came to my apartment in Cambridge to meet Robert Frost, as I have already described (see pages 51–52).

Sylvia began work on October 7 in the psychiatric clinic of Massachusetts General Hospital, transcribing the records of mental patients in a process that enabled her not only to defuse her own seething angers and frustrations, but to find in the recorded fantasies of others a way of expressing, in fiction at least, a way to write about her own accelerating confrontations with "the Panic Bird." She soon wrote the finest piece of fiction of her career, "Johnny Panic and the Bible of Dreams," one of the few of her writings in which her own pain reaches out to melt into a sympathy with others:

I've a dream of my own. My one dream. A dream of dreams.

In this dream there's a great half-transparent lake stretching away in every direction, too big for me to see the shores of it, if there are any shores, and I'm hanging over it, looking down from the glass belly of some helicopter. . . . It's into this lake people's minds run at night, brooks and gutter trickles to one borderless common reservoir. . . . Call the water what you will, Lake Nightmare, Bog of Madness, it's here the sleeping people lie and toss together among the props of their worst dreams, one great brotherhood, though each of them, waking, thinks himself singular, utterly apart.[31]

The narrator takes it as an act of dedication to copy out these dreams, one by one, example after example, in the dead of night, in honor of Johnny Panic, the panic-god: "Johnny Panic injects a poetic element in this business you don't often find elsewhere. And for that he has my eternal gratitude."[32] But at the 4:00 a.m. height of her dedication in copying out the dreams of others into her "bible," the narrator is caught at it, led away by the clinic director, laid down on a white cot, robed in "sheets virginal as the first snow. . . . The crown of wire is placed on my head, the wafer of forgetfulness on my tongue. . . . I am shaken like a leaf in the teeth of glory. . . . The air crackles with blue-tongued lightning-haloed angels. His love is the twenty-story leap, the rope at the throat, the knife at the heart. He forgets not his own."[33]

Not only did these 4:00 a.m. encounters strangely predict the "dawn poems in blood" of October 1962, but Plath's electric memory took her back to the depths of her previous suicidal breakdown in 1953. Unbeknownst to her husband or her mother,[34] she sought out the psychiatrist Ruth Beuscher, who had treated her five years before, at McLean Hospital in Belmont, and who was willing to take her back as a patient. Beuscher (whose maiden name had been Barnhouse, which she resumed after her 1962 divorce; she eventually joined the ministry) had a large number of children and was the daughter of a Protestant evangelical family. Plath went to see her for the first time on Wednesday December 10, and for the next six months, Plath would see her once or twice a week. The psychiatric work routinely revived memories of Sylvia's childhood in Winthrop, a streetcar suburb north of the Boston airport, where she spent most of her first eight years, before her father, a professor at Boston University and an expert on bumblebees, had died of diabetic gangrene, after which her mother had moved her two young children to Wellesley. Soon Sylvia took Ted to visit these childhood haunts, and her poetic imagination also turned to the past, not only in such regressive gestures as acquiring a kitten named Sappho, but in writing such poems as "Full Fathom Five," "Green Rock, Winthrop Bay," in late 1958, and "Point Shirley," finished before January 20, 1959, recalling her grand-

mother, which she would get up the courage to record for Stephen Fassett in February:

> She is dead,
> Whose laundry snapped and froze here, who
> Kept house against
> What the sluttish rutted sea could do.[35]

On January 20, 1959, the same day she called this poem "oddly powerful," she described in her journal a call on the Lowells at 239 Marlborough Street: "A moment with Elizabeth Hardwick and Robert Lowell: she charming and high-strung, mimicking their subnormal Irish house girl, whom they have at last let go, he kissing her tenderly before leaving, calling her he would be late, and all the winsome fondnesses of a devoted husband. . . . Lowell's half-whisper and sliding glance." She declared in the same entry, "We decided to live in England. I really want this. Ted will be his best there."[36]

As Plath began to come out of herself, she also began to move with her husband among the poetry circles of Boston. From the beginning of their stay they had been hospitably treated by the Sweeneys; and, ever since Plath's recordings with Stephen Fassett for the Harvard Library collection (one in June 1958 and a second scheduled for February of 1959), she had become closer to and fonder of these near neighbors, only half a block away on Beacon Hill. In February, after Richard Wilbur's Harvard reading, they met Stanley Kunitz at a party at John and Doris Holmes' house. Clearly some sort of friendship was struck up. Kunitz, who admired Hughes' work, would be one of the warmest reviewers of *Lupercal* in *Harper's*, but, more important, his *Selected Poems*, 1928–1958, recently published by the Atlantic Monthly Press, was the book of the season, and Hughes and Plath clearly found much to chew on in these poems. Though Kunitz was in Boston only one or two nights

poems and his reaction to mine."[38] She recorded her poems on February 22; probably attended, either on March 1 or March 8, the joint reading by Anne Sexton, George Starbuck, and Maxine Kumin at the Poets' Theatre; and kept going to her sessions with Dr. Beuscher, which take up a great deal of space and sound in her journals.

She was also studying the work of her "rivals," notably Adrienne Cecile Rich: "Finished her book of poems [*The Diamond Cutters*] in half an hour: they stimulate me: they are easy, yet professional, full of infelicities and numb gesturings at something, but instinct with 'philosophy,' what I need. . . . Must try poems. DO NOT SHOW ANY TO TED. I sometimes feel a paralysis come over me: his opinion is so important to me. . . . Am happy about living in England."[39] And, three weeks later, "I must get philosophy in. Until I do I shall lag behind A.C.R. A fury of frustration, some inhibition keeping me from writing what I really feel."[40] The "jam-up of feeling behind a glass-dam fancy-facade of numb dumb wordage,"[41] which would continue to stand between her ambition and her achievement for most of the next three years, needed some breaching, and on March 9 she and Ted Hughes took a subway-and-trolley journey to Winthrop to visit her father's grave, "to prove he existed and really was dead." Within a few days she was, in characteristic creative fashion, complaining: "Yesterday a nadir of sorts. . . . Cramps. Pregnant I thought. Not, such luck. . . . What good does talking about my father do? . . . I cry at everything. . . . Finished two poems, a long one, 'Electra on Azalea Path.' . . . They are never perfect, but I think have goodnesses. Criticism of 4 of my poems in Lowell's class: criticism of rhetoric. He sets me up with Anne Sexton, an honor, I suppose. Well, about time. She has very good things, and they get better."[42]

So much of Sylvia Plath's capacity to capture our imagination as a creative figure lies in this tangled conflict of motives: the wish to excel, to triumph over others; the hope

173

to find a simple way of doing it (putting in more "philosophy"!); the deeply ambivalent desire to find out more about the depths in herself and the concomitant fear of doing so—was her father really dead? Not if she could bring him to life! How was a poet to face that terrifying possibility? And, finally, the burning wish to be recognized, by Lowell, by "A.C.R.," by her peers, by her husband. The dreams and visions of deformed and tortured people would keep surfacing in poem after poem, some of them among her greatest, like "Berck-Plage," "The Applicant," "Cut," "Lady Lazarus," "Purdah," all but the very last poems of transcendence written in the final weeks of her life in early 1963. She would, in fact, never find a way to stop such dreams and poems—but she would find a way, and very soon now, to get some of the howling into her poetry.

"Electra on Azalea Path" was one of the first, after "The Disquieting Muses," and yet, within a few weeks of finishing "Electra on Azalea Path," with its violent exhumation of her father's body and its anagrams on the name of Aurelia Plath, she would pull back, understandably enough, and decide for reasons of either squeamishness or, more likely, simple mercy, to omit it from the manuscript of the book she was writing:

It was the gangrene ate you to the bone
My mother said; you died like any man.
How shall I age into that state of mind?
I am the ghost of an infamous suicide,
My own blue razor rusting in my throat.
O pardon the one who knocks for pardon at
Your gate, father—your hound-bitch, daughter, friend.
It was my love that did us both to death.[43]

But there was more to Plath's inner life than this struggle in the vicinity of death with Oedipal forces: she had at last found some companions in the art of poetry beside her

husband. As she wrote to a friend two days after her grave-
yard visit:

> We have seen a little of Philip Booth, who is now trying
> to write at home on his Guggenheim with his wife and
> beautiful daughters & sounding as if it were starvation
> pay. [Plath would not have known of Booth's psycho-
> analysis—or the concomitant fees.—P.D.] Also have
> seen a good bit of Robert Lowell whom I admire im-
> mensely as a poet, and his wife, who writes stories for
> the New Yorker. I have been auditing a poetry course
> he gives at BU with some bright young visiting poets,
> George Starbuck, who is an editor at Houghton Mifflin,
> & has published everywhere, and Anne Sexton, an-
> other mental hospital graduate, who Lowell thinks is
> marvelous. She is having about 300 lines coming out
> in the Hudson, published in the Partisan, New Yorker,
> etc., without ever having gone to college. I like one of
> her long poems, about a very female subject: grand-
> mother, mother, daughter, hag trilogy ["The Double
> Image"—P.D.], and some of her shorter ones. She has
> the marvelous enviable casualness of the person who
> is suddenly writing and never thought or dreamed of
> herself as a born writer: no inhibitions. Perhaps our
> best friends are these Fassetts around the corner: Aga-
> tha's book on Bartók's American Years is magnificent.
> I have never heard her play the piano, but evidently
> she is accomplished as only a Hungarian can be; or
> something of the sort.[44]

The Lowell course did indeed develop a certain esprit
de corps. "She used to drop in on my poetry seminar at
Boston University," Lowell wrote in his foreword to *Ariel*
in 1966. "I see her dim against the bright sky of a high
window.... She was willowy, long-waisted, sharp-elbowed,
nervous, giggly, gracious—a brilliant tense presence em-
barrassed by restraint. Her humility and willingness to ac-

cept what was admired seemed at times to give her an air of maddening docility that hid her unfashionable patience and boldness. . . . I sensed her abashment and distinction, and never guessed her later appalling and triumphant fulfillment."[45] Anne Sexton and George Starbuck found it pleasant and even convenient to take Sylvia along when they went, a few times in April and May, to the Ritz bar for a drink after Lowell's classes. The nature of this triad was a trifle unfathomable, given the unhappiness, as well as the productivity, of all three poets, steeped, as each was, in mourning and sadness (Sexton's mother had died on March 10, and Starbuck's marriage had crumbled, his children sent to California to be cared for by their grandparents) and the struggles that both Sexton and Plath were undergoing in psychotherapy.

Sexton, always the professional suicide, has claimed in a rollicking, slightly saccharine tribute written after Plath's death, that the two women exchanged suicide stories: "It's a wonder we didn't depress George with our egocentricity," Sexton said. Starbuck's version differs a bit: "I guess that's as close as I'll ever come to feeling like what they used to call a *cavalier servente*, giving these two talkative ladies an escort while they had their drinks at the Ritz. *Not* martinis. Anne drank stingers at the time—awful stuff—I don't remember what Sylvia drank. They had these hilarious conversations comparing their suicides and talking about their psychiatrists. . . . It didn't quite cross my mind that Sylvia's episodes had been as severe as they came out in her writing. She was playful but not flamboyant. Her journals indicate that she was wary of me."[46] As Diane Middlebrook writes, "Sexton's life every Tuesday proposed to the wickedly parodic Plath the plot of one or two ladies' magazine stories: seminar with famous poet, martinis at the Ritz, love in the afternoon, and an appointment with her psychiatrist in the evening."[47]

Moreover, even if no hint of flirtation entered into the

relations between Plath and Starbuck, Plath's competitive instincts were at work: both she and Starbuck, as well as Maxine Kumin, had entered their new books in the Yale Series of Younger Poets competition. Plath wanted to submit her book to Houghton Mifflin as well, but it became clear that Anne Sexton had the edge, with Starbuck as editor. Plath's journal at this time is loud with the gnashing of teeth: "How few of my superiors do I respect the opinions of anyhow? Lowell a case in point. How few, if any, will see what I am working at, overcoming? How ironic, that all my work to overcome my easy poeticisms merely convinces them that I am rough, antipoetic, unpoetic. My God."[48] On the other hand, Sexton's view of Plath contained unease in its rivalry: "I told Mr. Lowell that I felt she dodged the point and did so perhaps because of her preoccupation with form. . . . Sylvia hadn't then found a form that belonged to her. Those early poems were all in a cage (and not even her own cage at that). I felt she hadn't found a voice of her own, wasn't, in truth, free to be herself. . . . She gave me and Robert Lowell . . . credit for our breakthrough into the personal in poetry. . . . Perhaps she influenced Robert Lowell too. . . . but . . . if one feels compelled to name an influence then let us begin with Theodore Roethke."[49]

Sylvia Plath was desperate to become pregnant. Month after month had gone by without the desired result. The Hugheses attended a reading Stanley Kunitz gave at Tufts on May 12, with a party afterward at the house of John and Doris Holmes, the day after the announcement that Kunitz' *Selected Poems* had won the Pulitzer Prize. On May 20, just after Plath learned that her book for the Yale competition had failed "by a whisper" to win Dudley Fitts' selection for the Yale Series of Younger Poets, Ted and Sylvia accompanied Philip and Margaret Booth for an expedition to the seaside at Annisquam, which is commemorated by a charming but typical snapshot of Ted and Sylvia at this period, he looming, with a grin, in the foreground, the bulk of his body partly concealing Sylvia, smiling behind him on the rocks at Cape Ann. But the Booths always enjoyed themselves with the Hugheses. "We found ourselves not talking to one or the other, but to both of them equally."[50]

On May 31, the day Sylvia came to dinner at my house for the last time, she wrote of "A heavenly, clear, cool Sunday. . . . I feel that this month I have conquered my Panic Bird. I am a calm, happy, and serene writer." But by June 20, after she had learned that George Starbuck's book *Bone Thoughts* had won the Yale Series of Younger Poets prize, that Maxine Kumin's *Halfway* had been accepted by Holt, and had also learned that she was apparently not yet pregnant, she was able to rage and rant ("Everything has gone barren. I am part of the world's ash. . . . How can I keep Ted wedded to a barren woman?"[51]) and plan to write a wicked story about George Starbuck, his wife, Anne Sexton, and George's children. These violent mood swings have, in a persuasive article by Catherine Thompson,[52] been plausibly attributed to the likelihood that Plath suffered from "a severe form of the hormonal disorder now recognized as premenstrual syndrome, or PMS," and that, not only this spring, but in past and future years, her most extreme outbursts, "the periodic fits of vituperative rage familiar to women with PMS," coincided with the push and pull of her menstrual cycle. The couple attended, in mid-June, a party the Lowells gave after his release from the mental hospital, a party attended by Adrienne Rich and Anne Sexton, their spouses, and others, but, as it happened, by the time Ted and Sylvia departed from Boston in early July for their long-planned coast-to-coast automobile trip, she was in fact pregnant. Her day was approaching.

The automobile journey is known to us almost entirely from the remarks and descriptions of Ted Hughes, from a poem or two that Plath wrote about it later on, and from a rather sinister story, "The Fifty-Ninth Bear," in which a marauding bear in Yellowstone Park raids the food supplies of a couple very much like Ted and Sylvia Hughes (as one in fact did, breaking into their car), and kills the husband. This dire fictional ending suggests that perhaps the journey was not all bear and skittles, but by September 10 the Hugheses were nestled in Yaddo for the last phase of their American adventure. Yaddo, a nineteenth-century tycoon's summer estate, had been transformed in the 1920s into an artists' colony, a cluster of houses, outbuildings, and studios surrounding a large mansion (open only in the summer season), set in four hundred acres of mixed woodland with a chain of lakes, formal rose gardens, and a staff of cooks, maids, housekeepers, and grounds keepers. Yaddo has sheltered and nurtured the work of some of the most notable American writers, composers, sculptors, and painters of our century. During the time Ted and Sylvia stayed there, after the mansion was shut down for the winter, they were housed in a secondary but luxurious residence named West House and attended to by the longtime director, Elizabeth Ames, and, in later weeks, by her assistant, the poet Pauline Hanson. Their fellow guests included Malcolm Cowley, May Swenson, Charles Bell the novelist, and composers Gordon Binkerd and Chou Wen-chung, with whom Ted struck up a friendship, frequently went fishing in the Yaddo lakes, and discussed collaboration, never completed, on an opera based on the Tibetan Book of the Dead. Hughes did, however, finish a play based on the *Bacchae*, and Sylvia expressed the hope that it might be presented or read at the Poets' Theatre.

She embarked on a reading and writing spree, making her way through the books of a number of female writers who had been Yaddo residents—Eudora Welty, Jean Stafford, Katherine Anne Porter, Mavis Gallant (who had published a novel about a mother-daughter conflict, culminating in the daughter's suicide)—but her reading of fiction, though it gave her pleasure, did not much affect her continuing frustrations with her own fiction: "The glaze again. Prohibiting the density of feeling getting in. I must be so over-conscious of markets and places to send things that I can write nothing honest and really satisfying. . . . I write as if an eye were upon me."[53]

She also read the poems of Ezra Pound and was "rapt. . . . I would have him as a master,"[54] but she learned to her disappointment that Henry Holt and Company had declined her book, just as they were accepting Maxine Kumin's *Halfway*. She suspected, as her unpublished journals suggest, that Robert Frost took a part in this refusal. She was reading her "rivals" Elizabeth Bishop and May Swenson and admired them, and was particularly fascinated by May Swenson ("Several poems I liked. . . . Elegant and clever sound effects, vivid images . . ."[55]), who was due to come to Yaddo in November: and, most important of all, she was reading C. G. Jung's *Symbols of Transformation*, Theodore Roethke's *The Waking*, and Paul Radin's *African Folktales*, books which can be found in West House to this day. The imagery she gleaned from these books made its way directly into the poems she wrote on October 19, in her tower studio, where, for the first time since her marriage, she worked physically apart from her husband.

Sylvia Plath's studio looked out into a swath of tall white pines, beyond which lay a huge vegetable garden that, before it was grassed over in later years, helped furnish the tables for the artist guests. Gardeners stored the keepables for the coming winter in the greenhouse, which she liked to visit after reading the greenhouse poems of Theodore Roethke: "Watering cans," she wrote, "gourds and squashes and pumpkins. Beheaded cabbages inverted from the rafters, wormy purple outer leaves. Tools: rakes, hoes, brooms, shovels. The superb identity, selfhood of things."[56]

Yaddo was the tuning fork by which the poet, suspended between the ghost of her buried father and the spectre of her unborn child during the fourth and fifth months of her pregnancy, first found the true pitch in her poetry, during ten weeks between September and November. It was the most intensely productive time in her writing life prior to the conflagration that overtook her three years later, at the same season of the year, October and November 1962.

In "The Manor Garden" the body of the unborn embryo, as in the poems of Roethke, is assembling itself: "You move through the era of fishes,/The smug centuries of the pig—/Head, toe and finger/Come clear of the shadow."[57] In "The Colossus" chaos and frustration overcome the opening lines: "I shall never get you put together entirely,/ Pieced, glued, and properly jointed./ Mule-bray, pig-grunt and bawdy cackles/Proceed from your great lips./It's worse than a barnyard. . . ."[58] This fragmentation of the body yearned for reassemblage. Finally, in "The Stones," the last section of "Poem for a Birthday," in which the speaker has divided herself into a half-dozen personalities, she goes forward to take her body apart piece by piece: the stomach, the belly, the head-stone, the mouth-hole, the paps, the food tubes.

> The jewelmaster drives his chisel to pry
> Open one stone eye . . .
> . . . the chamber
> Of the ear . . .
> . . . the flint lip . . .
> . . . a pink torso.
> The storerooms are full of hearts.
> This is the city of spare parts.
>
> . . . legs and arms . . .
> . . . heads, or any limb.
> On Fridays the little children come

To trade their hooks for hands.
Dead men leave eyes for others.
Love is the uniform of my bald nurse.

Love is the bone and sinew of my curse. . . .
Ten fingers shape a bowl for shadows.
My mendings itch. There is nothing to do.
I shall be as good as new.[59]

In this poem Plath established the imagery of the poems for her next two and a half years: butchered bodies, blind stone eyes, bones scattered among stone landscapes, colors that cannot be taken in, ears that cannot hear, limbs that cannot move, would populate the poems Sylvia Plath wrote[60]: "Waving and crutchless, half their old size./The lines of the eye, scalded by these bald surfaces . . ."[61] Only after the birth of her son, Nicholas, in January 1962, and the undermining of her marriage in the summer and fall of 1962, would the poems, hissing and burning, begin to reassemble the parts of the body:

Do you wear
A glass eye, false teeth or a crutch,
A brace or a hook,
Rubber breasts or a rubber crotch,

Stitches to show something's missing? . . .

You have a hole, it's a poultice.
You have an eye, it's an image.
My boy, it's your last resort.
Will you marry it, marry it, marry it.[62]

In the appalling struggle of the *Ariel* poems the body would gradually arise from the desert in a dance of death, resurrected, whole again, in an apocalyptic orgy ("Your dark/ Amputations crawl and appall"[63]); and as Plath's sensibility expanded into the last poems, written in early 1963, the body has been healed, the spirit annealed, wholeness tragically accepted: "Once one has been seized up//Without a part left over,/Not a toe, not a finger, and used,/ Used utterly . . .//The heart has not stopped."[64] "The blood jet is poetry./ There is no stopping it./You hand me two children, two roses."[65] "She has folded//Them back into her body as petals/Of a rose close when the garden//Stiffens and odors bleed/From the sweet, deep throats of the night flower.// The moon has nothing to be sad about. . . ."[66]

The year 1959, as it drew to its close for her at Yaddo, was for Sylvia Plath, as it was for other poets of the enclave, the year in which her voice was found and her real work began. Her husband saw it and heard it happening; but he was not the only one. May Swenson, who came to Yaddo in November, was watching Sylvia and her husband very carefully, as scrupulously as she described the Yaddo scene in her journal:

> When I got up this morning there was white frost decorating everything. And out walking I stepped through a lot of "window-panes" in the ruts—frozen-over puddles. At the waterfall at the lower lake fantastic ice-shapes had been sculptured on the fallen limbs that the spray of the fall keeps wet . . . temperature has really fallen. I was teaching Sylvia to play chess last. night . . .[67]

The two women were very unlike—Swenson much smaller, older by nearly twenty years, and a poet of natural and erotic lucidity, gazing narrow-eyed into her surroundings like a cat, and watching the young couple as silently and carefully as they were watching her. Sylvia, big-boned, heavily pregnant, suspended between aching visions of sterility and blindness and the embryology that was operating within her, was wary of Swenson, but fascinated. Something of a triangular field of force began to operate. "Dangerous to be so close to Ted day in day out. . . . May Swenson in the other room: freckled, in herself, a tough little nut. Independent, self-possessed M. S. Ageless. Bird-watching before breakfast. What does she find for herself? Chess games. My old admiration for the strong, if lesbian, woman."[68] "If only I could break through my numb cold glibness . . . my Boston experience. If only I can go deep enough. A party at Agatha's, Starbuck's wife. . . ."[69] And so, life went on. "The fountains are dry and the roses over./Incense of death. Your day approaches."

When Sylvia Plath left Yaddo she had in hand all the poems she would need to make up her first book, *The Colossus*, which she typed up for publishers over Christmas in Yorkshire and sent out to James Michie, the poet/editor at William Heinemann Ltd., in January 1960. In February Plath wrote her mother, "The first British publisher I sent my new collection of poems to (almost one-third written at Yaddo; 48 poems in all, after countless weedings and re-weedings) wrote back within the week accepting them!"[70] It was a reassuring welcome from her husband's country after having her poems declined over and over again by American publishers—but no American publisher had laid eyes on this book; and even after *The Colossus* was published in England in 1960, it took a while to find an American publisher for it. I was one of the editors who read the book, in late 1960, for the Atlantic Monthly Press, and painfully declined it: it seemed to me still dead, still cold, still disassembled, and even now I read it without the sense of marvel that the best of Plath's late poems supply. *The Colossus*, wrote A. Alvarez, "was the culmination of her apprenticeship in the craft of poetry. . . . Now all that was behind her. . . . In the light of her subsequent work, and, more persuasively, her subsequent death, *The Colossus* has been overrated."[71] Even Knopf had trouble bringing themselves to accept the book, and it was barely noticed during Plath's lifetime. Stanley Kunitz reported to me:

Now a curious thing happened. They were back in England, and I had a letter from Judith Jones at Knopf, saying that they were interested in publishing Sylvia's book: they would like me to read it for them, so I said I'll be happy to do that . . . without payment. And I was impressed, but I did recommend that a certain poem that was so obviously imitative of Roethke should come out. It threw the book out of balance and would open her to the challenge of being a slave to Roethke's influence. It was one long poem, as I remember, "Poem for a Birthday." Judith agreed with me, and they took the poem out.[72]

Or so Stanley thought. But Sylvia restored two of its parts, "Flute Notes from a Reedy Pond" and "The Stones"—and she was right. They were the very poems Ted Hughes had recognized as catching the first tones of her true voice: "It was as if a dumb person finally spoke."[73]

8. More Merciless to Herself Than History: Adrienne Rich, 1955–1960

FROM *Snapshots of a Daughter-in-Law*

2.

Banging the coffee-pot into the sink
she hears the angels chiding, and looks out
past the raked gardens to the sloppy sky.
Only a week since They said: *Have no patience.*

The next time it was: *Be insatiable.*
Then: *Save yourself; others you cannot save.*
Sometimes she's let the tapstream scald her arm,
a match burn to her thumbnail,

or held her hand above the kettle's snout
right in the woolly steam. They are probably angels,
since nothing hurts her anymore, except
each morning's grit blowing into her eyes.

3.

A thinking woman sleeps with monsters.
The beak that grips her, she becomes. . . .

4.

. . . Reading while waiting
for the iron to heat,

Solano/Napa Partners
Benicia Public Library
4/26/2003 1:36:19 PM

- PATRON RECEIPT -
- RENEWALS -

ID: 27240000019365
NAME: WONACOTT JOAN T

1: Item Number: 31177013757884
   Title: The brave Bostonians
   Renewed Until: 5/24/2003

2: Item Number: 37045000068496
   Title: Letters of a loyalis
   Renewed Until: 5/27/2003

3: Item Number: 37240000808252
   Title: Boston
   Renewed Until: 5/24/2003

4: Item Number: 37240000503788
   Title: Boston
   Renewed Until: 5/24/2003

5: Item Number: 37045000404725
   Title: The fading smile : p
   Renewed Until: 5/27/2003

------- Please Keep this Slip -------

writing, *My Life had stood—a Loaded Gun—*
in that Amherst pantry while the jellies boil and scum,
or, more often,
iron-eyed and beaked and purposed as a bird,
dusting everything on the whatnot every day of life.

5.

Dulce ridens, dulce loquens,
she shaves her legs until they gleam
like petrified mammoth-tusk.

6.

When to her lute Corinna sings
neither words nor music are her own;
only the long hair dipping
over her cheek, only the song
of silk against her knees
and these
adjusted in reflections of an eye. . . .
. . . has Nature shown
her household books to you, daughter-in-law,
that her sons never saw?

7.

"To have in this uncertain world some stay
which cannot be undermined, is
of the utmost consequence."
                                    Thus wrote
a woman, partly brave and partly good,
who fought with what she partly understood.
Few men about her would or could do more,
hence she was labeled harpy, shrew and whore. . . .

9.

. . . Sigh no more, ladies.

Time is male

and in his cups drinks to the fair.
Bemused by gallantry, we hear
our mediocrities over-praised,
indolence read as abnegation,
slattern thought styled intuition,
every lapse forgiven, our crime
only to cast too bold a shadow
or smash the mold straight off. . . .

10.

. . . she's long about her coming, who must be
more merciless to herself than history.
Her mind full to the wind, I see her plunge
breasted and glancing through the currents,
taking the light upon her
at least as beautiful as any boy
or helicopter,

poised, still coming,
her fine blades making the air wince

but her cargo
no promise then:
delivered
palpable
ours.

WRITTEN *1958–1960*[1]

Adrienne Rich has been endowed from the start with tremendous natural gifts, a precocity which, from a very early age, seemed to make for enviable poetic achievement. She played the sedulous ape to her grand seniors, Frost, Yeats, Auden, Stevens; she was roundly praised by the generation ahead of her, chosen at twenty-one for the Yale Series of Younger Poets by Auden himself, whose praise took on an irritating paternalism: "The poems a reader will encounter in this book are neatly and modestly dressed, speak quietly but do not mumble, respect their elders but are not cowed by them, and do not tell fibs."[2] She was praised in honeyed terms by Randall Jarrell: "Adrienne Rich is an enchanting poet; everybody seems to admit it; and this seems only right. . . . The poet whom we see behind the clarity and gravity of Miss Rich's poems cannot help seeming to us a sort of princess in a fairy tale. . . . It seems to me that she herself is, often, a good poet who is all too good—one who can afford to be wild tomorrow; meanwhile, today, she is also an endearing and delightful poet, one who deserves Shakespeare's favorite adjective, *sweet*."[3] Richard Wilbur, a faculty member at Harvard when Rich was a student, recalls, "My picture of her . . . was of a very young and daughterly student at the elbow of Ted Morrison, who had been helping her with her poems, which were very Frostlike at that time. . . . Ted had sent some of her poems to me to look at, and I can remember the pleasure of complimenting Adrienne together with Ted somewhere in a sunny corner of Harvard Yard. So I think of her as an extremely gifted, really prodigiously gifted undergraduate poet. Well, she's never done anything not touched with talent."[4]

It's not surprising, perhaps, that this sort of praise began to drive Adrienne Rich wild. "I'd always gotten good reviews on the basis of being a dutiful daughter, doing my craft right. . . . The first 'feminist' poem I ever wrote was around 1958, 1959: 'Snapshots of a Daughter-in-Law.' "[5] After that she regarded herself increasingly as an outcast from conventional society: she complained that she "was told, in print, that this work was 'bitter,' 'personal'; that I had sacrificed the sweetly flowing measures of my earlier books for a ragged line and a coarsened voice."[6] What a fate for the fairy-tale princess of Cambridge and Boston!

Born in Baltimore on May 16, 1929, Adrienne Cecile Rich was the daughter of an Ashkenazic Jewish father from Birmingham, and a Protestant mother, a musician, "with white gentile roots in Virginia, North Carolina."[7] Her father turned his back on Judaism before attending the University of Virginia, declaring himself a freethinker, and eventually became a distinguished pathologist at the Johns Hopkins Medical School. Rich has described her highly charged family situation in detail in a series of intensely written prose essays, the most recent of which reads:

This is the child we needed and deserved, my mother writes in a notebook when I'm three. My parents require a perfectly developing child, evidence of their intelligence and culture. I'm kept from school, taught at home till the age of nine. My mother, once an aspiring pianist and composer who earned her living as a piano teacher, need not—and must not—work for money after marriage. Within this bubble of class privilege, the child can be educated at home, taught to play Mozart on the piano at four years old. She develops facial tics, eczema under her elbows and knees, hay fever. She is prohibited confusion: her lessons, accomplishments, must follow a clear trajectory. For her parents she is living proof. A Black woman cleans the apartment, cooks, takes care of the child when the child isn't being "educated."[8]

I was sent to the Episcopal church, baptized and

confirmed, and attended it for about five years. . . .
Neither of my parents ever entered that church, and
my father would not enter any church for any reason
—wedding or funeral. . . . My father was an amateur
musician, read poetry, adored encyclopedic knowl-
edge. He prowled and pounced over my school papers,
insisting I use "grown-up" sources; he criticized my
poems for faulty technique and gave me books on
rhyme and meter and form. His investment in my in-
tellect and talent was egotistical, tyrannical, opinion-
ated, and terribly wearing. . . . He made me feel, at a
very young age, the power of language and that I could
share in it. . . .[9]

Rich's memoirs strike readers as uncomfortably contra-
dictory in their description of a childhood both "impover-
ished" and lavish, a childhood from which the poet
inherited a passion for the centrality of poetry, and a deep
suspicion of hypocrisy. The conflict between these elements
produced an insatiable fury which, at first suppressed, be-
gan in her post-college years to break out. "I was a young
white woman who had never known hunger or homeless-
ness, growing up in the suburbs of a deeply segregated city
in which neighborhoods were also dictated along religious
lines: Christian and Jewish. I lived sixteen years of my life
secure in the belief that though cities could be bombed and
civilian populations killed, the earth stood in its old inde-
structible way. . . . And a recurrent theme in much poetry
I read was the indestructibility of poetry, the poem as a
vehicle for personal immortality."[10]

Those aspects of the history of her time which her con-
temporaries could not help, she could not help being in-
furiated by. But she played by the rules prevalent in her
youth: though she and I shared Jewish ancestry, mine from
Memphis, hers from Birmingham and Vicksburg, we had

both turned—or been turned—to Episcopalianism. Her parents sent her to the neighborhood Episcopalian church for social reasons.

When she graduated from Roland Park Country School in Baltimore in 1947, "I went on to Radcliffe, congratulating myself that now I would have great men as my teachers. From 1947 to 1951, when I graduated, I never saw a single woman on a lecture platform, or in front of a class. . . . Harvard's message to women was an elite mystification. . . ."[11] "In the universe of the masculine paradigm, I naturally absorbed ideas about women, sexuality, power, from the subjectivity of male poets—Yeats not least among them. The dissonance between these images and the daily events of my own life demanded a constant footwork of imagination, a kind of perpetual translation, and an unconscious fragmentation of identity: woman from poet."[12] But she did discover that poetry was actually connected to events in the outside world. Of the gifted literati of her Harvard generation, along with John Updike and L. E. Sissman, she was one of the few who did not study with Archibald MacLeish. "I enrolled in his big poetry course when he first came to Harvard," she writes, "but dropped out because I thought him insufferably sonorous and self-consciously good-looking and because, as I remember telling a friend, 'he thinks he's as important as Yeats.' "[13]

Soon after that Rich was writing the poems which, before she had graduated from Radcliffe, would be published in her first book. She also began to immerse herself in works of a different stripe than Yeats': the prose of Mary Wollstonecraft, and later Simone de Beauvoir (*The Second Sex* was published in the U.S. in 1953), and James Baldwin's *Notes of a Native Son* (1955). She rejected Eliot as a model and adopted Stevens. She began to "resist the apparent splitting of poet from woman, thinker from woman, and to write what I feared was political poetry. And in this I had very little encouragement from the literary people I knew, but I did find courage and vindication in words like Baldwin's: 'Any real change implies the breakup of the world as one has always known it, the loss of all that gave one an identity, the end of safety.' "[14]

But even after her graduation, Rich's friendships were mainly with men; and her first poems dealt with traditional relationships, as in "An Unsaid Word":

> She who has power to call her man
> From that estranged intensity
> Where his mind forages alone,
> Yet keeps her peace and leaves him free,
> And when his thoughts to her return
> Stands where he left her, still his own,
> Knows this the hardest thing to learn.[15]

The shadow of Yeats can be felt here, as the shadow of Matthew Arnold would fall across the poems of *The Diamond Cutters* in the early fifties, a book which the author herself has described as "poems of tourism."[16] After travels to England and the Continent on a Guggenheim Fellowship in her early twenties, even Cambridge—where, in 1953, she married Alfred H. Conrad, a charming and outgoing economist in Harvard's Economics Department and Wassily Leontief's Institute for Economic Research—became a topic of tourism. Listen to the ending of "A Walk by the Charles":

> O lovers, let the bridge of your two hands
> Be broken, like the mirrored bridge that bends
> And shivers on the surface of the stream.
> Young oarsmen, who in timeless gesture seem
> Continuous, united with the tide,
> Leave off your bending to the oar, and glide
> Past innocence, beyond these aging bricks
> To where the Charles flows in to join the Styx.[17]

Such poems have not yet evoked Nature's "household books
. . . that her sons never saw." Rich's poetic consorts, like
her husband, were at this stage entirely male. She turned
mainly, in the early 1950s, to Donald Hall, W. S. Merwin,
Philip Booth, then I. A. Richards, and Robert Lowell—with
his wife, Elizabeth Hardwick. Lowell's interest in her work
helped validate her as a poet, for, she says, he treated her
as a poetic colleague; but he rarely understood what she
was doing in individual poems.

After five years of marriage, two children, and two pub-
lished books, Rich was ready in 1958 to cross the moun-
tains. "Snapshots of a Daughter-in-Law" would mark the
continental divide in her life and work. Taken alone as a
poem, it conveys the sense of a courageous, mettlesome,
learned, suffering climber dragging herself to the crest with-
out the mental endurance or clarity of destination to cross
into the valley beyond, but brandishing her learning as a
token of her métier. In retrospect the poem, and what led
up to it, became mythic in Rich's own copious writings on
the subject; but those who knew Adrienne Rich prior to
"Snapshots" speak of her in ways that sound very different
from the ways she later spoke of herself, e.g., "I could
remember little except anxiety, physical weariness, self-
blame, boredom, and division within myself: a division
made more acute by the moments of passionate love, delight
in my children's spirited bodies and minds, amazement at
how they went on loving me in spite of my failures to love
them wholly and selflessly."[18] This was not the amiable
woman we saw from the outside, nor the woman who was
expressed in her ingratiating early poems.

I for one remember her as pixyish and charming, witty
in person as her written work seldom is, though her con-
versation never lacked a slight sharpness of edge. After
reading *The Diamond Cutters*, I took her to lunch, perhaps
in 1957, at a basement restaurant in Harvard Square. She

was agreeable indeed, easy to talk to, though wary, since I came to her as an admiring editor, surely not the first, hoping to publish her future work. Her attitude toward her own poetry, however, puzzled me: she was clearly as glad as anyone to be admired, but she was holding something back, not only her own consent to the work she had finished, but her commitment to the work she was yet to create. When I praised her work she looked at me quizzically, as though there were something she (or I) did not understand.

During the late 1950s I saw her from time to time, since we had close friends in common, outside the world of poetry. And my last view of her before she left Cambridge came in 1963, a few days after the death of Robert Frost, when she and I, with William Meredith, were called to elegize Frost's work on television, and I was surprised, given the extent of Frost's influence on her earlier poetry, at the asperity Rich brought to the discussion. She had been his ardent imitator as a young girl, his near neighbor in Cambridge in his last years, and her mentor, Theodore Morrison, showed Frost her poems, which he praised as having "a lot of mind in them," but she was one of those who could not abide his public persona.[19] "Frost was *not* what I needed."[20]

In the early 1950s, before her transformation, those who knew Adrienne Rich, either as a fellow student, or as a fellow poet, or as the wife of Harvard economist Alfred Conrad, remember her as winsome, witty, pretty, intelligent, with all the charms that a female of that era would take pride in—and which the Adrienne Rich of a later phase would strenuously renounce. The contrast between those eyewitnesses and Rich's self-presentation is sufficiently dramatic—and significant to the watershed between the 1950s and the 1960s—to justify extensive quotation.

One of the most interesting male views of Adrienne Rich comes from Donald Hall:

The first I ever heard about Adrienne Rich was from Robert Bly, coming back from Radcliffe on a jolly-hop, saying, "I met a girl from Baltimore, surgeon's daughter [Rich's father was actually a pathologist—P.D.], knows all about modern poetry." Indeed she did know all about modern poetry. Bly and I double-dated a couple of times. . . . I was Adrienne's date. We sat in Cronin's and drank beer. Adrienne was a very conventional Radcliffe girl. We all sat and read poems, three of us. I took Adrienne home in a taxi. I tried to kiss her and she wouldn't let me.

My second year at Oxford I got married, lived out of town, and Adrienne, who had a Guggenheim, at the age of twenty-three, lived in a hotel in Oxford most of that year. I used to see her a lot, and that's when we became friends. She was in a difficult time because she was in love with Alf Conrad, and her father was screaming and yelling. I remember calling on her one day, she was in a flood of tears. She had had a letter from her father. I formed a terrible opinion of him though I never met him. He may have been anti-Semitic, but, correctly or not, I have the feeling he would have found something to yell about whoever it was. We became close that year, we became affectionate. We worked together on poems, we handed each other poems. These would have been early poems from *The Diamond Cutters*, and mine would have been, oh, *Exiles and Marriages*. I remember her asking whether she should send poems to *The New Yorker*, and she did send her first poems to *The New Yorker* from Oxford, I believe.

That was 1952–1953; the next year I spent at Stanford, on a writing fellowship. She went back to Cambridge and married Alf ["I was married in 1953 at Hillel House at Harvard, under a portrait of Albert Einstein," Rich wrote later. "My parents refused to come.

I was marrying a Jew of the 'wrong kind.' . . ."[21]], and that year, while I was at Stanford and she was in Cambridge, we corresponded very heavily. At that time we were talking word by word about poems. We were both writing every day all day: she had not yet had children. And once a week, pretty much, we exchanged bundles of poems and criticisms of poems, and as I recall, when she sent me a bundle, I would say, Aha! you've been reading Auden again this week, or Lowell, or Frost, Auden, Lowell, Frost. She was still, at the time of *The Diamond Cutters*, she was terribly in thrall to others. And she would always say, "Oh damn, you're right." She helped me a great deal. She was infinitely more shrewd and proficient than I was.

In 1954–1957 I was a Junior Fellow, living in Cambridge, and later [1956–1957] out in Lexington. Adrienne and I saw a great deal of one another [in 1954–1955]. My son Andrew was born on April 15, 1954, out at Stanford. When I came back, Adrienne was newly pregnant with her first son. That first year of the junior fellowship I did a lot of baby-sitting. Kirby had left Radcliffe after her junior year to marry me, and so when we came back to Cambridge, she spent a year taking three courses. She would leave the house about eight-thirty and come back about one o'clock, when she would take over and I would go off. I would finish up breakfast at eight-thirty and clean up, give him his morning bath and put him down for his morning nap. I was an early housefather for twelve months, five days a week or six, during exams and so on. But Adrienne and I spent a morning together in 1954 about once a week from nine to one. I would hold the baby, carry him around and feed him, and read each other's poems and talk about them. She was pregnant, getting bigger and bigger, and nervous about it, like anybody else, no more than anybody else. [Years later] she said,

"Don, you taught me how to bathe a baby." We worked together on poems, but incidentally there was a course in child care going on. Between us there was an affection which I think was considerable. I'm not using any euphemisms, you understand, it wasn't love. But I had more fun talking to her about poems than anyone else in Cambridge at that time.

And then she had her baby, and she disappeared. And it seemed I didn't see her again, for many many years. I felt very hurt. A lot of people felt hurt. I'm not sure she saw anybody for a while there.

Of course she was ahead of me, she was ahead of all of us in her precocity. But I suppose she took pains not to rub our faces in it. There was not the sort of rivalry there was among the males. The men were the most competitive. Adrienne is *really* competitive and always was determined to be the best. But she was determined not to let it spoil her friendships.[22]

Philip Booth remembers:

I cannot remember when I did not know Adrienne. I think it's likely to be through Don Hall. We had young children together, we had picnics together. We came to be fairly close to each other through our fondness for Cal, so that I can remember having lunch with her a couple of times and we arranged to meet sort of to talk about how Cal was doing, at quite probably the Dreyfus. And you know people met not only at the Grolier Book Store but at the Mandrake Book Store in its old location, and I can remember buying a first, before the publication date, of *Doctor Zhivago*, then. We talked a lot that way. She was the person to tell me that I could deduct typewriters and things, as a business. And we certainly went to dinner with Alf and Adrienne and they certainly must have come out to Lincoln. I certainly don't feel that Adrienne and I were "poetry companions." . . . We were friends who happened to be poets. We admired one another's readings, we admired one another's poems. I still think that "Stepping Backward" is one of the most remarkable love poems ever to be written by a young poet. She wrote that when she was nineteen, or something. It was incredible.[23]

William Alfred describes her relationship with Robert Lowell: "Oh, often we'd go to Alf and Adrienne's for dinner, Cal and I would go. She was never a student of mine, she was Ted Morrison's. Then 'Snapshots of a Daughter-in-Law'—that savage, those first attacks. Then came that awful period that everyone had, writing tendentious poems about Vietnam, and then she came into her own again. Yes, Ivor and Dorothea Richards were very very important. I'd see Ivor and Dorothea at Cal's all the time and I'd see Cal and Elizabeth there, and Adrienne and Alf. And of course Adrienne would show him her poetry all the time."[24]

W. S. Merwin has said:

We saw a fair amount of each other [in 1956–1958]. I had dinner at her house with Al a few times, and she had dinner at West Cedar Street, and we met in coffee shops. More than that, I was for years devotedly and warmly fond of Adrienne, and I still am. She was very confused about children and all that. She advised Sylvia very strongly not to have children. Sylvia told Dido that they had discussed that. I met her first at Don Hall's. I can't remember who else was there, but I also remember that Adrienne and I of all strange things had a flaming argument that first night because I said something to the detraction of Hemingway, and she rose to the defense of Hemingway—now isn't this amazing? I am sure that if you quote this she will hotly deny it. I have never liked Hemingway, ever since I was an undergraduate. I find that dyed-in-the-wool

199

machismo suspect and unpleasant, and I find the tone
so offensive. I think I said that it seemed to me pre-
posterous that people should link Faulkner and Hem-
ingway together, because Faulkner was a great writer
and that Hemingway was a semi-lightweight. So Adri-
enne rose to his defense, and I thought, isn't she en-
chanting, isn't she wonderful. None of which I think
she would like at this point. She had such sparkle and
verve. And I respect the impulse behind the poems so
much.[25]

The persona who appears in the prose books and in the
later poems differs so widely from the woman whom these
people remember, and from the Adrienne Rich who speaks
in person about these days, that it is hard to reconcile the
later figure with the earlier one. Moreover, Rich has written
at length—more than any other poet of her generation—
about the period of her life between 1955 and 1960, when,
after publishing her first two books, she turned to bearing
children, in 1955, 1957, and 1959; and to facing the enig-
mas of female existence, of the "patriarchal society," of
racism, and of lesbianism. It was during this time that she
felt constrained to turn toward poetry as prophecy, poetry
as a form of social and political criticism, and the conflict
between her early training and her postpartum existence
struck her so hard that it had the force of a religious con-
version. In later years she would describe the experience of
this transfiguration over and over again, beginning with the
searing *Of Woman Born* (1976) and in half a dozen addi-
tional prose books.

Sylvia Plath, with characteristic shrewdness, noted, in
1958, that Rich might be "opinionated," and envied the
presence in Rich's work of "philosophy." Neither Plath nor
Sexton, neither now nor later, could claim to be a mainline
feminist, but, as the most precocious and prized of "girl
poets" in her youth, Rich powerfully altered herself to attain

full bloom as a poet and thinker aspiring to take her place as a radical feminist by the side of Elizabeth Cady Stanton, Susan B. Anthony, Margaret Fuller, Simone de Beauvoir, or Mary Daly, and who became capable of writing, at her most extreme, in 1976, that "the ancient, continuing envy, awe, and dread of the male for the female capacity to create life has repeatedly taken the form of hatred for every other female aspect of creativity."[26]

It is perhaps not surprising that the male poets who have survived since Rich's early years give little evidence of having read her feminist prose; but Donald Hall's puzzlement at their estrangement after the birth of her first child in 1955 might have dissolved if he had read *Of Woman Born*, in which the following passage appears:

Two days before my first son was born [in 1955], I broke out in a rash which was tentatively diagnosed as measles, and was admitted to a hospital for contagious diseases, to await the onset of labor. I felt for the first time a great deal of conscious fear, and guilt toward my unborn child, for having "failed" him with my body in this way. In rooms near mine were patients with polio [the last great Boston epidemic of polio, before the release of the Salk vaccine, took place during 1955.—P.D.]; no one was allowed to enter my room except in a hospital gown and mask. If during pregnancy I had felt in any vague command of my situation, I felt now totally dependent on my obstetrician, a huge, vigorous, paternal man, abounding with optimism and assurance, and given to pinching my cheek. . . . My second book of poems was in press, but I had stopped writing poetry. . . . I felt myself perceived by the world simply as a pregnant woman, and it seemed easier, less disturbing, to perceive myself so. After my child was born, the "measles" were diagnosed as an allergic reaction to pregnancy.

Within two years, I was pregnant again, and writing in a notebook: "Of late I've felt, toward poetry—both reading and writing it—nothing but boredom and indifference. . . . I have been dissatisfied with myself, my work, for a long time. . . . [November 1956]" I had never really given up on poetry, nor on gaining some control of my existence. The life of a Cambridge tenement backyard swarming with children, the repetitious cycles of laundry, the night-wakings, the interrupted moments of peace or of engagement with ideas, the ludicrous dinner parties at which young wives, some with advanced degrees, all seriously and intelligently dedicated to their children's welfare and their husbands' careers, attempted to reproduce the amenities of Brahmin Boston, amid French recipes and the pretense of effortlessness—above all, the ultimate lack of seriousness with which women were regarded in that world—all of this defied analysis at that time, but I *knew* I had to remake my own life. . . . By July of 1958 I was again pregnant. The new life of my third—and, I determined, my last—child, was a kind of turning for me. . . . By the time I knew I was pregnant with him, I was not sleepwalking any more. . . . I knew I was fighting for my life through, against, and with the lives of my children, though very little else was clear to me. I had been trying to give birth to myself.[27]

Rich's third child was born in March 1959, at the vortex of the period, just prior to Robert Lowell's publication of *Life Studies*. Rich was perhaps in her most intimate relationship to the Lowell family at this moment. As Kathleen Spivack wrote,

Adrienne Rich was a poet whom Cal admired greatly. . . . She was a classical poet, with restrained feeling, and clearly, he felt, his intellectual equal. He spoke of her highly and arranged for me to meet her. Her work had a clear, noble, crystalline quality, and she had a strong, opinionated way of looking at poetry. I sat in her kitchen, drinking tea, and listening to her beautifully intelligent sentences while her children puttered about upstairs, and she seemed to me outstanding not only in her promise, but in her achievements at that time. . . . Only years later did I realize at what a cost such grace and control were obtained. . . . In the face of her articulateness, I felt my own clumsy, inarticulate intuitions about poetry groping and painful; my brain was slow, I could not think fast enough to be the least bit interesting to Adrienne as a poet or a person. I was afraid to show her my poems.[28]

When the Lowells, after his release from McLean Hospital in mid-June 1959, gave a party, the guests included Rich and her husband, Alfred Conrad. As Elizabeth Hardwick has said, "Adrienne was a witty, intelligent, charming, outgoing person when I knew her. We used to see each other all the time, even as much as every Sunday, when the two families would get together with the children at one or the other house or on a picnic and then shoo the children away so that they could all talk. Adrienne was so alert, so intelligent, so witty. We were great friends, but that all changed later on."[29] At the Lowell party Anne Sexton took second place only to the host himself. *Life Studies* had been published in May, and the reviews were coming out everywhere. But the new girl in town was Anne Sexton. This was perhaps the only time the two women met, and, as Rich later told Sexton's biographer, "I remember feeling that suddenly there was this *woman* whom Lowell and people around Cambridge were talking about, this woman who was going to publish a book called *To Bedlam and Part Way Back*. I would never have acknowledged it at the time, but I felt threatened, very competitive with her. There was little support for the idea that another woman poet could be a source of strength or mutual engagement. I think I suspected—and not because of some profound character defect in me—that if she was going to take up space, then I was not going to have that space."[30] Moreover, Rich may have felt particularly threatened by a poet who, like Sexton, could successfully realize anger in her poetry. Rich felt no such rivalry, and even a certain sympathy, in her several very brief meetings with Plath, despite Plath's careful eyeing of her "rival" "A.C.R."—perhaps because at this stage Plath was still a long way from releasing *her* anger. Plath asked Rich if she felt that one could be a poet and a mother, both at the same time. Rich answered something like, "It can be done, but you'd better think about it really hard." "What I wanted to tell her was 'Don't try,' because I was in such despondency: I'd just had my third child, I was thirty, and I felt that in many ways my life was over, that I would never write again."[31]

Rich's ambition must have added fuel to her despair. At this stage Rich and Maxine Kumin—also Jewish, also a committed feminist—had not met, and of the female poets in Boston Rich truly admired only May Sarton, whom she found dazzlingly beautiful, wearing a black velvet pantsuit and a creamy white jabot, reading rather theatrically with one elbow on the mantelpiece at a Beacon Hill meeting of the New England Poetry Club, where Sarton's style and thrilling voice had impressed the younger woman.[32] Not until the end of the decade, when she drew close to Denise Levertov, did Rich strike up her first friendship with a woman poet of her own generation.

"I have a sense that women didn't talk to each other much in the fifties—not about their secret emptinesses, their frustrations. . . . If there were doubts, if there were periods of null depression or active despairing, these could only mean that I was ungrateful, insatiable, perhaps a monster. About the time my third child was born, I felt that I had either to consider myself a failed woman and a failed poet, or to try to find . . . what was happening to me."[33]

Her close relationship with Lowell might even have made her covet the escape into madness, though no such escape was possible for her. She thought of herself more as a monster than as a madwoman. *A thinking woman sleeps with monsters./ The beak that grips her, she becomes.* There was nobody to whom she could talk about her poetry, or her difficulty in writing the poetry she had to write. Lowell set the agenda in their conversations about poetry, but it was well known that there was no woman poet who would ever equal Elizabeth Bishop in his esteem. "And then, he was crazy so much of that time: I'd be in the kitchen with my and several other children, and Cal would phone from McLean to tell me he was re-writing Milton's Sonnets— 'but only the best.' . . . I felt very wary of him. . . . Elizabeth and I were having babies at about the same time. . . . She lent me her maternity clothes after Harriet was born, they used to visit us on Sundays when their nurse was off-duty."[34] John L. Sweeney seemed to offer Adrienne Rich the sort of kindness and support that she yearned for: she has often spoken of his fatherly generosity to her and to other young poets. "He knew in some way that good poets come from everywhere." He arranged for her to use the Harvard Poetry Room at a time when women weren't allowed in the Lamont Library—he had her come up a secret staircase.

In the foreword to *The Fact of a Doorframe* (1984) she expressed her dilemma most clearly: "One task for the nineteen- or twenty-year-old poet who wrote the earliest poems . . . was to learn that she was neither unique nor universal, but a person in history, a woman and not a man, a white and also Jewish inheritor of a particular Western consciousness, from the making of which most women have been excluded. The learning of poetic craft was much easier than knowing what to do with it. . . ."[35] Notice how here, as in "Snapshots" itself, and even in some of her memoirs, she found herself unable to use the first person. She was, it seems, searching for ways to convey shared experience, and her relations with Robert Lowell's poetry, especially after the first-person revelations of *Life Studies*, helped her "recall herself to a sense of the language," as she says in an unpublished interview with Diane Middlebrook.[36] In another place she recounts her initial difficulties in writing in a woman's voice: "I have a much, much earlier poem that deals with a relationship with a woman. It was written while I was in college and it's in my first book. It's called 'Stepping Backward.' It's about acknowledging one's true feelings to another person. It's a very guarded, carefully wrought poem . . . addressed to a woman whom I was close to in my late teens, and whom I really fled from—I fled from my feelings about her." Not until the late 1950s was she "able to write, for the first time, directly about experiencing myself as a woman. . . . The poem was jotted in fragments during children's naps, brief hours in a library, or at 3:00 a.m. after rising with a wakeful child. Over two years I wrote a ten-part poem called 'Snapshots of a Daughter-in-Law.' "[37]

The poem that gradually emerged from these fragments was the first of Rich's poems to abandon formal verse. ("In those years," she would write later on, "formalism was part of the strategy—like asbestos gloves, it allowed me to handle materials I couldn't pick up bare-handed."[38]) It was also the first to submit hints of what would become one of her dominant themes, the woman struggling to shoulder aside the oppressive language of patriarchal civilization. Yet she has also recalled that in her college years she, like most others, was overwhelmed by Eliot's language, though she struggled to shake it off. But, significantly, in "Snapshots of a Daughter-in-Law," the patriarchal outlook is made to take on the stylistic desiccations of *The Waste Land*, employing T. S. Eliot's rhythms, allusions, and trademark devices: unidentified quotations from foreign languages and allusions to literary sources of all sorts, from Horace to Shakespeare, Baudelaire to Diderot, Dr. Johnson to Cicero and Emily Dickinson. The stylistic irony is no doubt ironic: as Alicia Ostriker writes, "For Rich and for the many writers who have been influenced by her, the inherited language is what history was for Stephen Dedalus: a nightmare from which they are trying to escape."[39]

On the other hand, the woman, the "daughter-in-law" (by which term Rich means a daughter subject to the law, one dominated by men, a fellow subject as oppressed as her southern musician mother), cannot bring herself to speak in the first person. It is a poem which has summoned up the courage to rebel, but not yet the courage to strike the first blow on her own behalf. Note the repeated symbolic appearances in the poem of *angels* and *laundry*, those two characteristic images of the 1950s, recoverable in the work of Wilbur, Plath, Merwin, Kumin, Sexton, and others—as though the patriarchal perfect woman were an angel bent over a laundry tub, or a woman scalding her arm over a stove.

Yet the voice of the angels is overtaken by another, demonic hiss in the ear: "A thinking woman sleeps with monsters. . . ." *Have no patience. . . . Be insatiable. . . . Save yourself; others you cannot save.* Though the music be Eliot's, the furious light shines through from *The Second Sex*, from whom the images of the lovely boy and the helicopter at the end of the poem are drawn, and without whom I suspect this poem would have been unthinkable. But, once written, it began to give Adrienne Rich heart again, and her poetry began to grow and deepen into its own rich, solemn, humorless, accusatory voice, in which she pointed to the ills of society, the oppression of the weak, the domination of the male, the self-sacrifice of the female. Taking herself with implacable seriousness, she went on, in prose and verse, to help lead a sort of revolution, and to write the poetry that would lead, fifteen years later, to the book that still, to this reader, conveys her deepest and most poignant understanding—that joyful paean to same-sex love, *The Dream of a Common Language*. The youth of Adrienne Rich, though it furnished every privilege, seemed to offer little to rejoice in except her commitment to poetry; and it was not until the crucial year of 1959, where everywhere voices were modulating from the full-throated songs of spring to the harsher notes of high summer and the grim silences of early autumn, that she began to heed Rilke's admonition to *change her life*, and found her way, as woman, as radical, and as poet, to the common language she had so long been dreaming of. She was at her most touching, though perhaps not at her most prescient, when she wrote in 1974:

> The woman who cherished
> her suffering is dead. I am her descendant.
> I love the scar-tissue she handed on to me,
> but I want to go on from here with you
> fighting the temptation to make a career of pain.[40]

She may have fought that temptation, but her work of the last twenty years suggests that it was a losing battle. Though no poet of this period expended more agony on the will to change, others may well have more completely succeeded.

9. Mark Time:
L. E. Sissman, 1956–1963

The Museum of Comparative Zoology

Struck dumb by love among the walruses
And whales, the off-white polar bear with stuffing
Missing, the mastodons like muddy busses,
I sniff the mothproof air and lack for nothing.

A general grant enabled the erection,
Brick upon brick, of this amazing building.
Today, in spite of natural selection,
It still survives an orphan age of gilding.

Unvarnished floors tickle the nose with dust
Sweeter than any girls' gymnasium's;
Stove polish dulls the cast-iron catwalk's rust;
The soot outside would make rival museums

Blanch to the lintels. So would the collection.
A taxidermist has gone ape. The cases
Bulging with birds whose differences defy detection
Under the dirt are legion. Master races

Of beetles lie extinguished in glass tables:
Stag, deathwatch, ox, dung, diving, darkling, May.
Over the Kelmscott lettering of their labels,
Skeleton crews of sharks mark time all day.

Mark time: these groaning boards that staged a feast
Of love for art and science, since divorced,
Still scantily support the perishing least
Bittern and all his kin. Days, do your worst:

No more of you can come between me and
This place from which I issue and which I
Grow old along with, an unpromised land
Of all unpromising things that live and die.

This brick ark packed with variant animals—
All dead—by some progressive-party member
Steams on to nowhere, all the manuals
Of its calliope untouched, toward December.

Struck dumb by love among the walruses
And whales, the off-white polar bear with stuffing
Missing, the mastodons like muddy busses,
I sniff the mothproof air and lack for nothing.

UNDATED, WRITTEN PROBABLY *1959* OR *1960*[1]

Sissman's algebra of poetry, in this early, amusing, and characteristic poem with its political references to "progressive-party members" and literary allusions to Browning's "Grow old along with me!" ("from which I issue and which I/Grow old along with, an unpromised land . . ."), ticks and tocks its way backward and forward between the alive and the dead, between the past and the present, between the old and the new. No other poet of his era (I almost wrote "with his ear") dedicated himself so intensively to an attempt to preserve the decorum of past time in evoking it. The reasons were, in fact, not far to seek, though Sissman, one of the most secretive of poets, hid his tracks well.

Though Louis Edward Sissman and I eventually became good enough friends for him to make me his literary executor, and I edited all his four published books of poetry, one of them posthumous, I never knew him at Harvard, where we were contemporaries in education as we were in age, nor in Boston until 1965. All during those years when Starbuck and Merwin and Plath had been strutting their stuff, Sissman too had been tucked away in cheap lodgings on Beacon Hill. But he, unlike them, had been learning the advertising business, scribbling poems which, compared to those he had written in the past and would write in the future, were halfhearted indeed, while tending a first wife who herself had poetic ambitions. Not until 1958, when he moved forty miles to Harvard, Massachusetts, and married for a second time, did he in fact begin writing true poems again after all the years of muttering, of evasion, of tosspot poems scrawled with his left hand; and not until about 1959 did he permit this hand, formerly the hand of Louis, to become the hand of Edward. It seems clear that the left hand was the dreamer; but Sissman's mind was of a different cast from that of the other poets.

Louis Edward Sissman was born in Detroit on January 1, 1928. His mother, Marie Anderson Shannon, of Irish-English stock from Ontario, after a brief career on the vaudeville stage, had borne at seventeen a son, Winfield Shannon, who became an itinerant farm worker, was a trifle lawless, and did not live with the Sissman family. Marie's husband, three years younger than herself, was a designer for the automobile industry. Edward J. Sissman had been born in the Odessa region of Russia to an educated Jewish family—one of his brothers was an orchestral conductor—and he worked his way through Carnegie Tech and took work as a designer at Studebaker, moving later on to Packard. The three Sissmans settled into the automotive community of Detroit, though somewhat eccentrically. Not for them the luxuries of Grosse Pointe or Birmingham Hills: the Sissmans preferred rental studio space and living quarters in the heart of downtown Detroit. "My parents were constitutionally opposed to the idea of private property, fearing its potential stranglehold on their freedom."[2] Their politics were far to the left of General Motors; in fact, they were ardent socialists.[3] In later years they moved from city to city, usually in Texas, never settling in a single identifiable location, but involved themselves in collecting, buying, and selling antiques. Their son needed a place to send down a taproot.

Young Louis Sissman was tutored assiduously at home by his mother, later attending dame school. His mother's intrusive tutelage, buttressed by his father's critical discipline, pressed him to keep up to the intellectual competition, and, beginning at age ten, he learned to win mental competitions. In 1941, he won the National Spelling Bee and would have been presented in person with a plaque at the White House by President Roosevelt had the president not been distracted by the difficulties of getting the Lend-Lease program through Congress. But the more important effect of this honor was to gain his admittance to the fashionable Detroit Country Day School, where he seems to have undergone a bit of hazing, whether for his precocity, for his oddness of appearance, or even for his uneasily carried Judaic heritage, it is by now impossible to know. Eventually, Sissman was summoned to appear on the radio as a Quiz Kid, in a scene which he describes mournfully:

Exterior: Long shot: the Masonic Temple in Detroit on a damp and chilling night in the fall of 1943. Decrepit Turret-Top Oldsmobiles, Torpedo-Body Pontiacs, and pontoon-fendered Terraplanes stop, squealing, to let shabby crowds of pedestrians cross Cass Avenue to the almost windowless twelve-story Crusader-Gothic monolith of the Temple. Interior: the Auditorium . . . Out onto the platform, where a gleaming walnut conference-room table waits unadorned except for microphones, troops a tiny queue of undersized mock-scholars in black gowns and mortarboards, its rear brought up by an oversized mock-scholar, me. The

Quiz Kids take their seats . . . and, at eight o'clock straight up, the Blue Network and its affiliates carry the program to a waiting nation, coast to coast.

How did I, at fifteen, six-three, and a rather flabby 195, get myself into this? You may well ask. Probably mostly because, for a long time now, American children have been treated as extensions of their parents; the teachers' frustrated drives for power and glory. . . . Partly too because I, like many of these children—the child stars, the infant tap dancers, the tiny, tail-coated piano prodigies—had discovered that the way to an adult's heart, and the perquisites that flowed therefrom, was through the exercise of my trick intellect. . . . When it became apparent to my parents and teachers that I was glibber than most in parroting things back . . . I was loudly encouraged, not to say coerced, to become a competition winner. . . . My main reaction to all this was to lose my lunch more frequently than usual, a long-standing symptom of my revulsion to performing in public, and to conceive a lifelong hatred for the exploitation of the young. . . . Longer term, my small ordeals soured me for life on the veracity of teachers and the validity of their desires for me, a sourness which led to my getting kicked out of Harvard for a couple of years after the war.[4]

But first he had to be admitted, which, with his intellectual record, seemed to present no difficulty. When he arrived at Harvard in 1944 he was sixteen years old, cross-eyed, ambidextrous, six feet four, and two hundred pounds. He wrote later that he began to feel at home in Boston for the first time in his life, mainly through the contrasting friendships of a Boston-Brahmin roommate and a Boston-Irish cleaning woman. He was also in precociously full cry in pursuit of girls: his poems written later on—which chronicle in infinitesimal detail his college and post-college years—testify to ribaldry, carousing, intellectual curiosity and emotional instability: while his meagre family records show his father, in 1946, writing to his mother, who doted on him, to inveigh about his son's "nervousness," and complain that her son might be consorting with "the wrong kind of people." (Were the wrong people political radicals or Jews or both? Edward J. Sissman, though himself both, would have found it hard to countenance either. It is not to meet the wrong kind of people that bright young sons are sent to Harvard.)

But Louis Sissman did so, in spades. He caroused with his school friends from Detroit; he explored the bohemian side of Harvard, and he wrote poems of remarkable balance and maturity, but he disdained study. He had a higher ambition, which involved both literature and personal style. One of his closest college friends says Sissman was as interested in the ads in *The New Yorker* as he was in the writing.[5] He was, in fact, booted from Harvard in 1946, for reasons he never clearly specified, but which his first wife attributes to "bad grades and insolence. One of the deans said, 'We have no room at Harvard for geniuses.' He was pretty irritated over things that had been said to him."[6] The exile took a room on West Brookline Street in the South End of Boston, landed a job as a stack boy at the Boston Public Library, lugged armloads of bound *New Yorker*s home at night,[7] and, in addition to hanging around with his college friends in Harvard Square, fell in with a new group of friends in Boston, "eccentrics of a broad and gaudy stripe not often met with on American shores."[8] One, he claimed, was a hunchbacked dwarf, said to have been conceived in the lower berth of a Pullman on a through train to Chicago, named Slim. "His voice was that of Stentor, and when he played his own compositions on the piano, he threw himself at the keys like a left tackle."[9] Slim composed a ballet suite based on a long-unfinished piano concerto and staged it "with the help of two other members of the circle: Llewellyn (or Lulu) Bowditch, a tall, blue-faced poet who was both a schizophrenic and a hashish addict, and Morrie Fields, a tiny but nobly muscled ballet dancer with burning black eyes and no discernible mentality whatever. . . . [It] was to be a hymn to hash, a testimonial from a satisfied user. . . . On opening night, I read a poem or two as curtain-raiser; I'm sure my dense, clotted, intentionally obscure verse of that period could have meant nothing to those furred and stolid ladies . . . a group of serious and respectable Christian Science ladies who devoted their widowhood to dabbling in the arts . . . known grandly as the Salon de Boston."[10]

At a social evening at the Harvard Foreign Student Center, Sissman, not yet nineteen, met Barbara Gertrude Klauer, from Bolton, Massachusetts, a hardworking scholarship student at Boston University, the poetry editor of the Boston University *Beacon*, and two years his senior. Barbara, who was independent of mind, frequented the center in order to meet Indian students, who held a powerful attraction for her. She "was stunned by Sissman's unusual appearance, a tall gawky guy with glasses, dressed in the correct way with a grey suit, and by his brilliance."[11] He pursued her, she retreated, until finally, after he had returned to good standing as a Harvard undergraduate, his importunities prevailed one evening in February 1948 at Boston's most elegant dining place of the day, the Hotel Vendôme Restaurant, where he proposed marriage, while (as she remembers) a grey mouse peeped around a corner. The engagement was a stormy one, marred by a depressive breakdown which left Barbara dejected and confused for months; but on November 11, 1948, they were married, against her parents' wishes, and took up residence that spring at 42 Grove Street on Beacon Hill while they both finished their undergraduate degrees.[12] Sissman continued to devote his weekends, with his wife's help, to selling Fuller brushes in the darker reaches of Cambridge even as he was

finishing his honors thesis on Tennyson, which was typed
for him by Alison Lurie, whom we have met as the chron-
icler of V. R. Lang and the Poets' Theatre, and the wife of
then graduate student Jonathan Bishop, who makes an ap-
pearance in the following poem, written some years later:

East Cambridge, 1949

Behind the stacked extent of Kendall Square
There is a little slum; I'll take you there,
Laden with my black brush-filled salesman's case,
Perhaps a mop or two, and, on my face,
The first sweat of the day. This is the place
We start: a neat tan toy house, gingerbread
Proud of its peaky eaves. The lady's in.
She's German, tiny, old, respectable,
Not buying anything. Next door, a tall
Blue tenement hangs open. In its hall,
The fumes of urine and the fractured wall
Don't augur well for brush men. That's all wrong.
Up the length—gaslit, railless—of the long
And aging stairwell live star customers:
Draggled and pregnant girls who fumble coins
Among contending children; pensioners,
Dressed in a skeletal state of readiness,
Who welcome all intruders bearing news
Of the last act of the world; lone, stubbled young
Men who change babies while the wife's at work.
I write the orders in my little book,
Take a deposit, promise delivery
A week from Saturday. At noon I lunch
On tonic and a Hostess Apple Pie
At Aly's Spa in Portland Street. At night,
I leave the last room with a Sacred Heart
And Kroehler furniture for my rendezvous
With Jonathan, a breath of Harvard Square

9. *Mark Time: L. E. Sissman, 1956–1963*

In his black '36 Ford coupe, his bare
Feet on the pedals. We abscond from there.[13]

Sissman's return to Harvard in the winter of 1948 was
not without honor. Although his social life was somewhat
reduced in scope by his married responsibilities and anx-
ieties, he entered writing classes with Theodore Morrison
and John Ciardi. Ciardi, who had been the first to spot the
poetic talent of the would-be musician Frank O'Hara, es-
pecially relished Sissman's poetry, and covered his class
submissions with shrewd and encouraging comments.[14] In
the spring of 1948 Donald Hall shared Theodore Morri-
son's course with Sissman. "I remember him very well. I
thought he was five to ten years older. He acted old, and
he was condescending, extremely condescending to other
people in the class. He was the star. He was the best, and
Morrison knew it. I didn't like him very much, but I admired
him. I never knew him when he was grown up, only when
we were both twenty years old."[15] Sissman was of course
aware of the other poets who shared his undergraduate
years—Ashbery, O'Hara, Koch, Hall, Bly—but he was
never of the *Harvard Advocate* group, which had gathered
together in about 1947, while Sissman was out of college
and ineligible. His friends included Jonathan and Alison
(Lurie) Bishop, Albert Cook, Norman Wexler, a brilliant
but erratic friend from Detroit, and A. K. Donoghue, a
flamboyant model for J. P. Donleavy's *The Ginger Man*.
Indeed, in addition to carrying a huge course load, Sissman
founded, with Albert Cook and Aaron Rosen, a quarterly
magazine called *Halcyon*, which entered boldly but not very
successfully into rivalry with *Wake*, another "creative" mag-
azine edited by John Hawkes and Seymour Lawrence.

Halcyon, whose first issue (Winter 1948) included con-
tributions from E. E. Cummings, Marya Zaturenska, James
Merrill, Oscar Williams, Richmond Lattimore, Howard
Nemerov, Stanley Moss, Harry Brown, and Albert Cook,

also of course included three pages of poetry by L. E. Sissman. *Halcyon* was, alas, unable to survive beyond its second issue, which included poems by Wallace Stevens and William Abrahams, and paintings by Morris Graves, as well as an outrageously irreverent review of the poems of Richard Eberhart by Sissman. Its rival, *Wake*, continued, on an irregular publication schedule, for nearly ten years longer. (My own allegiance was to *Wake*, to which I was a contributor only in a minor financial sense.)

Sissman's undergraduate poetry was, as he himself described it, dense and clotted, but it was accomplished enough to win Harvard's Garrison Medal in poetry (which Kenneth Koch would win the year before him, and Donald Hall the year after), but his work also included such deftly turned pieces as this parodic villanelle tweaking William Empson's disdain for the Auden school of poetry:

Just a Whack at Empson

We rot and rot and rot and rot and rot.
Why not cut badinages to the bone?
Alas, cockchafers cuddle. We cannot.

We recognise the hand upon our twat;
Unfortunately X is always known.
We rot and rot and rot and rot and rot.

Unfortunately X is always not
Quite what we had in mind to end our moan.
Alas, cockchafers cuddle. We cannot.

Why must we be contained within our pot
Of message which we have so long outgrown?
We rot and rot and rot and rot and rot.

Your physic beauty made my inwards hot
Whilst talking to you on the telephone.
Alas, cockchafers cuddle. We cannot.

Each greening apple has its browning spot:
"The rank of every poet is well-known."
We rot and rot and rot and rot and rot.
Alas, cockchafers cuddle. We cannot.[16]

Despite their wit and ingenuity, Sissman's early poems gasped at the deeper emotions, which other Harvard/Radcliffe poets of the time also found difficult to handle, and which the tutelage of the time, as so many poets young in the 1940s, e.g., Maxine Kumin, Adrienne Rich, and I, would later note, tended to disparage. When Sissman's early poems made the major move they tended to become grandiose, formal, elaborate, portentous, as in "Canzone: Aubade," the poem that nonetheless won him the Garrison prize, $160, and a silver medal:

I cannot think of you at all at noon
As my late lover whose long body still
I punctuate with exclamations. Noon—
The rigid, brazen upright arm of noon—
Casts a long shadow between now and night
Where intervened the tortuous forenoon:
The twice-told tale of snaillike afternoon,
That we know better than we need to know. . . .[17]

But Sissman's ambitions, though they never abandoned poetry altogether, were now turning toward making a living in book publishing; and by the summer of 1949, while living on Upland Road, in Cambridge, he had got the first of several jobs in that field, at Addison-Wesley, a newly founded technical publishing company, still headquartered in Cambridge; and his wife, Barbara, got work as children's librarian and storyteller at the Boston Public Library.

But at the end of the year they followed their star to New York, where they found a one-room cold-water flat on East Eighth Street above a funeral home.

December 29, 1949

The Hotel Storia ascends
Above me and my new wife; ends
Eight stories of decline, despair,
Iron beds and hand-washed underwear
Above us and our leatherette
Chattels, still grounded on the wet
Grey tessellated lobby floor.
Soon, through a dingy, numbered door,
We'll enter into our new home,
Provincials in Imperial Rome
To seek their fortune, or, at least,
To find a job. The wedding feast,
Digested and metabolized,
Diminishes in idealized
Group photographs, and hard today
Shunts us together and at bay.
Outside the soot-webbed window, sleet
Scourges the vista of Eighth Street;
Inside, the radiators clack
And talk and tell us to go back
Where we came from. A lone pecan
Falls from our lunch, a sticky bun,
And bounces on the trampoline
Of the torn bedspread. In the mean
Distance of winter, a man sighs,
A bedstead creaks, a woman cries.[18]

Louis Sissman worked as a copywriter and copy editor at
Prentice-Hall, and Barbara got a children's library job at
the East Houston Street Branch, where she was sent be-
cause, she says, with a name like Sissman, the librarians
assumed that she must know Yiddish. Barbara, who at first
enjoyed the company of Sissman's literary friends—Albert
Cook, Saul Touster, Stanley Moss, Aaron Rosen—at the
San Remo in the East Village, found New York cramped

and ugly, and after nine months returned to Boston to work in a bookshop.

Sissman, dissatisfied with Prentice-Hall, managed to buy a Buick, to get a different editorial job, undesirable and underpaid, with A. A. Wyn, a now-defunct publisher, and he persuaded Barbara to rejoin him in New York if they might live somewhere outside the city. They found a flat in an old brick building in Pearl River, in Orange County, New York, whence they commuted to work together, he to the Fifty-seventh Street area, and she to a job at the Irving Trust at One Wall Street. One day, while the Sissmans were having lunch together in the gallery district, "an interesting guy came up to him. He was In Shoes, and he tried to sell Ed some of his pictures. Warhol was a Polish guy from Pittsburgh, and very nice to talk to."[19] But this balance did not last more than a year or two. Barbara was "overwhelmed with world problems, the bomb threat." Sissman was fired from his job, and his wife went into another psychic depression. They moved permanently to Boston in 1952, where she began long-term psychiatric psychotherapy and he got work as a paid campaign aide in John F. Kennedy's senatorial campaign. But his wife descended further into depression.

Though for a while Sissman was obliged to supplement his income by selling vacuum cleaners door-to-door in the byways of Vermont on weekends, he found a job in Boston with the Copley advertising agency, at a starting salary of sixty dollars a week. He would find advertising—eventually he worked for four successive agencies—a pleasure for the rest of his life. Yet the other circumstances of his life still seemed to interfere with the writing of poetry. His correspondence of the time is full of plans to write fiction and to edit unfounded magazines; but the few actual manuscripts that survive from the 1950s are at best mediocre. It is as though his poetic talent went into hibernation, continuing to breathe and function but at an extremely reduced metabolic level. He enjoyed the advertising business because he liked writing copy for print and radio and television, and he liked the salaries, higher than publishing. He said to his wife, "Let's stay married and get rich." Mrs. Sissman was reluctant to have children, but she too entered advertising, taking his place at the Copley advertising agency when, in January 1954, Sissman—now, significantly, having adopted his middle name, Ed (the same as his father's) and abjuring the "Lou" that he had carried through college and New York, went to work for the John P. Dowd advertising agency. After a siege on Pinckney Street, the young couple took up residence at 35 Anderson Street, on the "wrong" side of Beacon Hill.

Sissman's change of name was dramatic to those who had known him as Lou, though his wife had always called him Ed or "Eddo." Old friends were now specifically asked to call him Ed. The marriage wound down: Barbara spent years in absorbing, and successful, psychiatric psychotherapy, and Sissman, through his friendship with John P. Dowd, Jr., displaced some of his marital animus into sports-car racing and rallies, travelling to Sebring, to Watkins Glen, to Pebble Beach. But in 1956 he left the Dowd agency to join Kenyon and Eckhart, "casting and filming a series of T.V. commercials for H. P. Hood, working on Underwood Deviled Ham, W. R. Grace, and other accounts."[20]

Still there was no new poetry; but one has to imagine, knowing what was to come, that Sissman's "trick intellect" was storing up a treasure of memory and incident for use in the future. His archives contain a certain number of rather careless notes and drafts, and the beginnings of two distinctly unfinished novels; but this man possessed so remarkable a memory that when I knew him he never needed to write down a telephone number, and if there were poems forming in his head, he didn't need to record them to keep them from escaping. In fact, the surviving drafts of his later poems seldom betray a blotted line. Though his silence of some years seems nearly absolute, it is far from unique in the annals of poetry: Valéry kept silent for twenty years, Wallace Stevens for seven; and Robert Lowell, during these same early 1950s, for five. The mystery of a precocious poet who wrote no decent poems between the ages of twenty-one and thirty-five is not perhaps easily soluble, but it does not altogether elude explanation. I think it has to do more with the dissonance of his marital situation and his place of residence than anything so crude as his involvement with the advertising business.

In a last effort to save the marriage Barbara and Ed Sissman moved first to Cambridge; and then, having failed, Sissman moved alone back to Beacon Hill, this time to 58 Anderson Street, in order to be nearer his advertising work, and to a new source of attraction. He was divorced on October 31, 1957. At this time Beacon Hill was swarming with poets—Merwin, Starbuck, Sweeney, with Plath on the horizon—but Sissman knew none of them. His friends included E. A. Muir and Will Davenport, both advertising men with an interest in poetry, but although they exchanged manuscripts from time to time and talked about them over lunch, the poems he wrote now were not good. Not until, on one of his trips to New York, Sissman showed some of his older poems to his New York poet/friend, Saul Touster, was there a breakthrough. Touster, on his own initiative, sent "Just a Whack at Empson," written in Sissman's Harvard days, to *The Review* in Oxford, and to the delight of poet and friend alike it was published, along with a poem of Touster's and an essay by Christopher Ricks.[21]

For nearly a decade Sissman's path had taken him away from poetry. He had tried to write, but without success, perhaps partly owing to the doting dominance of his mother and the slightly competitive concern of his first wife, both of whom took an intense interest in poetry and, perhaps, not a truly supportive attitude toward Sissman's. Over the years, Sissman had become close to Barbara's half-brother,

Andreas Paul Klauer, and his wife, Anne, who lived nearby
on Beacon Hill. The marriage between Anne and Andreas
Paul also began to break up at this time. After her divorce
in 1957 Anne Klauer moved into a flat at 63 West Cedar
Street, across the street from the building where W. S.
Merwin was living. Sissman began to court her, but, despite
their long friendship, Anne resisted a permanent relation-
ship, partly because she was self-conscious about being
seven years older than her lover. But he wrote love poems
to Anne, and she did not try to rewrite them. And they
determined to move to the country, just as Wilbur and Booth
had done. In the spring of 1958, when Anne's Beacon Hill
lease expired (and, coincidentally, at just the time the Mer-
wins were leaving Boston), the couple bought property in
Still River, Massachusetts, near the town of Harvard, some
forty miles to the west of Boston, and set up the first real
house Sissman had ever had, on the side of a country road,
with a long view down across the valley toward Fort Devens.
Then came marriage:

We arise
At seven in our tiny country house—
The center of November, and the point
Of no return to cities, with their sour
Remarks on ruinous first marriages—
Eat eggs, dress in dark clothes, get in our black
Jaguar roadster, and in dusting snow—
The season's first, greasing the roads—we go
Across the line to Nashua, where, in
A blank room of dun office furniture,
We say our vows before a registrar
In rimless glasses, and, as witnesses,
Flower girls, trainbearers, maids of honor, two
Gum-chewing, French-accented typists . . . lunch alone
In a decrepit tearoom; to come home

To a new, mutual aloneness in
Our little house as winter enters in.[22]

Documents surviving from 1958 and 1959 show signs, despite what he claimed in after years—that he was in fact already beginning to come back to life as a poet. The new marriage, and its new pattern of life, offering him new sources of emotion—a marriage full of unstinting love and support, an esteemed profession at a distance from his home, and a countryside full of natural impressions— seemed to release something in Sissman's highly trained, inhibited, and long-suppressed talent. But, though, like most other contemporary Boston poets, he found a new way to write poetry in 1959, his was entirely different from theirs. His preference was for highly formal verse, either rhymed or blank. And, although some of the first new poems he wrote were pastorals, like "The Tree Warden," the principal work of his second poetic period found him scanning back over the years of his youth, those years in which poetry had turned its back, to recover the feelings and outrages, the iniquities, errors, and peccadilloes of his college years, his sieges in Boston and New York.

No other poet of his time would set out to create such a chronology—few poets of any time would regard poetry as a way of recording personal history. No one has ever alluded to Sissman as a "confessional" poet, but in literal fact, his poetry, written in the early 1960s, was as chronologically autobiographical as that of any poet of his time; and, once he had been diagnosed in 1965 with Hodgkin's disease, then regarded, as he said, as "routinely fatal," he had a more powerful motive than ever to record, with the powerful tool of his astounding memory, the days of a life that he had good reason to fear would soon come to an end. He was daring enough, when his first book was published in 1968, to entitle it *Dying: An Introduction*, as though his whole life had served as a mere introduction; and then, as the disease closed in on him, he published copiously: 51 poems and 45 book reviews for his long-beloved *The New Yorker*, 108 monthly columns for *The Atlantic Monthly* under the rubric of "Innocent Bystander," as well as 13 poems. He published two more volumes of verse, *Scattered Returns* (1969) and *Pursuit of Honor* (1971) during his lifetime. Between 1965 and 1974 he wrote as many as 50 poems a year worthy of publication, and he continued writing with alarming facility and skill until, as his health failed in 1974, two years before his death, the poems would no longer come. Consequently he sought the counsel, unavailing insofar as his poetry was concerned, of the psychiatrist Robert Coles. "The muse has departed the body—looking back on its quickening decline," Sissman mused ironically to Coles in one of their conversations.[23] In a final poem entitled "Tras Os Montes," after his half-brother and both his parents had died, his mother in 1973 and his father in 1974, he could see no way forward except across the mountains to describe not only the approach of his own death on March 6, 1976, but (with uncanny prescience) the details of his own funeral, and the destination that lay beyond.

Though it was not published until the late 1960s, "A War Requiem" forms his most literally autobiographical poem, and in its sequences he wrote his own version of his return from the worlds of advertising, auto racing, the pursuit of women and the pursuit of honor, to the great world of poetry. Whether the date in the title is legendary or authentic, no one can now testify.

Writing, 1963

For years he was cross-eyed, the right eye turning in
Shyly, and he, shyly ducking his head
To hide the inturning, failed to notice the eyes
Of all the others, also in hiding from
The eyes of others, as in a painting of

The subway by Charles Harbutt. Self-denying
Can get you something if, behind the blank,
Unwindowed wall, you don't become a blank,
Unfurnished person. He was lucky. In
The dark of those bare rooms to let, there stirred
Something: a tattered arras woven with
A silent motto, as Eliot said. A word
Now, in his thirty-sixth summer, surfaces, leading
A train of thought, a manifest freight, up to
The metalled road of light—for the first time
In ten disused, interior years—along
The rusted, weed-flagged lines. And so the raid
On the inarticulate, as Eliot said,
Begins again. Square-bashing awkward squads
Of words turn right about under the sun,
Form ragged quatrains in the quiet room
Under the eaves, where his pen cuts its first
Orders in ages, and the detail moves off
The page, not quite in step, to anywhere.[24]

Curious, perhaps, that the metaphor L. E. Sissman should adopt for the marshalling of poetry should be a military one. Perhaps it was the propinquity of Fort Devens when he wrote "A War Requiem" in the late 1960s, during the worst of the Vietnam War, hearkening to Benjamin Britten's music, and sitting where he could see and hear artillery practice from his own windows; perhaps it was the echo of the childhood discipline that had enabled him to garner success with the adult world through the exercise of his "trick intellect"; perhaps it was merely the fact that love, that poetry, that nature, were all threatened by the fading smile that ends in death. But it is true of him as it was only of Kunitz and Merwin in the Boston enclave that he did it without the protection of patrons or universities, as a professional poet who wrote for print, and whose work, under the sponsorship of *The New Yorker*'s Howard Moss and *The*

Atlantic Monthly's Robert Manning, found its way to an audience quite different from and, in the short run at least, considerably larger than that of other poets. After his death it was John Updike who most warmly praised his poetry, and Elizabeth Hardwick who, though she did not know him, strove on his behalf to see that his last, death-haunted, posthumously published cancer poems contained in his last book, *Hello, Darkness*, won the National Book Critics Circle Award in 1979, three years after his death.[25] While in a military sense he had marked time during his youth, he chronicled the middle-class life of Boston and New York in the years between 1945 and 1970 as no other poet has. Like Lowell and Kunitz, though unlike them in many other ways, he was ambitious to recover for poetry what had been usurped by fiction.

10. Be Patient with My Wound: Stanley Kunitz, 1958–1959

Robin Redbreast

It was the dingiest bird
you ever saw, all the color
washed from him, as if
he had been standing in the rain,
friendless and stiff and cold,
since Eden went wrong.
In the house marked For Sale,
where nobody made a sound,
in the room where I lived
with an empty page, I had heard
the squawking of the jays
under the wild persimmons
tormenting him.
So I scooped him up
after they knocked him down,
in league with that ounce of heart
pounding in my palm,
that dumb beak gaping.
Poor thing! Poor foolish life!
without sense enough to stop
running in desperate circles,
needing my lucky help
to toss him back into his element.
But when I held him high,
fear clutched my hand,

for through the hole in his head,
cut whistle-clean . . .
through the old dried wound
between his eyes
where the hunter's brand
had tunneled out his wits . . .
I caught the cold flash of the blue
unappeasable sky.

WRITTEN 1959[1]

When Stanley Kunitz, at fifty-three, arrived in Cambridge in the fall of 1958 to teach two days a week at Brandeis University, his poetic reputation was still obscure, though it was about to brighten. Like his juniors Elizabeth Bishop and Charles Olson, Kunitz was born in Worcester, in 1905. His parents, both immigrants from Lithuania via the sweatshops of New York, were partners in a dress-manufacturing business, which, while Stanley, their third child, lay in the womb, went bankrupt. His father, Solomon Kunitz, committed a desperate suicide by ingesting carbolic acid six weeks before Stanley's birth. His mother, Yetta Helen Jasspon, was so embittered by the act and its circumstances ("My mother never forgave my father/for killing himself,/ especially at such an awkward time/and in a public park,/ that spring/when I was waiting to be born"[2]) that she forbade any mention of his name in her presence. The child was brought up "like Dionysus, in the company of women —mother and two older sisters."[3] "The terror of oblivion haunted my childhood. I dreaded falling asleep at night because of the fear of losing consciousness. I'm sure that affected my biological rhythm because, to this day, I hate going to sleep and fight it off as long as I can. I practically never go to bed before three or four in the morning."[4]

One day, when the boy, rummaging in the attic, found a picture of his father and brought it to his mother,

she ripped it into shreds
without a single word
and slapped me hard.
In my sixty-fourth year
I can feel my cheek
still burning.[5]

When Kunitz was eight, his mother, having dauntlessly and successfully revived the dressmaking business, married again to "a gentle and scholarly man who was no help at all to my mother in her business, but who showed me the ways of tenderness and affection. His death six years later left me desolate. Both my sisters married and died young. My mother survived these onslaughts, as well as another bankruptcy . . . and lived alertly to the age of eighty-six, articulate to the last on the errors of capitalism and the tragedy of existence."[6] She gave her young son over to the charge of nursemaids, kept a considerable library in her house, and encouraged him in his learning, which was also nurtured by teachers and librarians who introduced him to the poetry of Blake, Donne, Keats, and Wordsworth. He played the violin. He haunted the public library and the Worcester Art Museum. "My religious upbringing was negligible. What influenced me most was the secular Jewish tradition, with its ethical emphasis. Socialist theory and liberal principles in general left their permanent mark on me. I am drawn to religious mythology of any persuasion, but resist and fear institutional religion."[7]

After a childhood of rich and varied experience in a succession of houses in and outside Worcester (roaming the woods, working as a lamplighter, stealing off to the movies on school days, climbing ledges, fishing in the reservoir, planting trees, hurling stones, devouring the books available in the public library), especially in the countryside which he has beautifully chronicled in the poems of his old age,

Kunitz went on to Harvard in 1923, where he made a brilliant record as a student, with rooms next door to J. Robert Oppenheimer. In his last year he persuaded Alfred North Whitehead to admit him into an advanced course in the nature of the universe, while, in his literary studies, he discovered—on his own, not in courses—the poetry of George Herbert, Hopkins, Yeats, and Eliot, and studied prosody under Robert Hillyer (whose class he remembers my father visiting as a lecturer in 1927). He won the Garrison Medal in poetry, as Kenneth Koch, L. E. Sissman, and Donald Hall would do subsequently.

On his graduation, *summa cum laude* in 1926, followed by a master's degree in 1927, he looked to a possible future at Harvard as a member of the faculty, but

> I did not stay on; I was told indirectly through the head of the English department that Anglo-Saxons would resent being taught English by a Jew, even by a Jew with a *summa cum laude*. That shook my world. It seemed to me such a cruel and wanton rejection that I turned away from academic life completely. After I left Harvard I had no real contact with universities for almost twenty years. . . .[8] My principle has been never to accept tenure. I have always operated on a year-to-year contract and usually as part-time faculty. . . . If you're on the payroll for life tenure, you may as well admit that you're a subject of the academic state.[9]

Cowed and furious, Kunitz retreated to Worcester to devote himself to his poems, while taking full-time employment as a reporter and night-editor on the *Worcester Daily Telegram*, where he had been doing summer work during his Harvard vacations. After writing some special features on Robert H. Goddard, the father of rocketry, he became immersed in the Sacco-Vanzetti case, which so obsessed him that he went to New York in 1928 to try to get Vanzetti's letters published, without success. However, he found employment with the H. W. Wilson Company, a publisher of reference books for libraries, founding and editing the *Wilson Library Bulletin* and also working on biographical reference books for the company. In 1929 he was able to spend most of a year in Europe, through the good graces of H. W. Wilson, who was willing to continue Kunitz' work on the *Library Bulletin* through the mails.[10] The European trip, as well as a short visit to Yaddo in 1928 (where Kunitz met his first wife, Helen Pearce, "a great beauty"), was undertaken in the interests of his poetry, but it was a solitary journey.

The poets of Kunitz' generation, unlike the next, were scattered, disparate, isolated from one another, and he found himself writing for himself alone. The giants of the older generation—Frost, Stevens, Eliot, Pound—were far outside his ken and seemed to him totally unreachable. He felt a need for communication with other poets, "persons who shared my passions and convictions. That search for a community has been one of the dominant drives of my life,"[11] and was the magnet that drew him at first to New York.

In these years he was writing poems that were highly formal, stretched, intent, and relentlessly truthful. In his poetry Kunitz was torn, like other poets, between the actualities of his life and the difficulties of rendering these in a language that did them justice. His father's suicide, his mother's apparent coldness to him, his mishaps in marriage, his struggle to be heard as a poet, his intelligence and learning—all these wrestled with the angel of poetry. He drew at first on the contemporary poetic language of Eliot and Stevens and of the metaphysical poets, and persisted in a determination to encompass feeling inside strict forms—but, yearning for prophecy according to the intentions of Blake, he produced a kind of poetry that at worst repelled by its formidability and, at best, thundered with self-contained power. Louise Glück has shrewdly described these as poems in which "great tasks are undertaken, forests planted; the poems are full of difficult commissions, of hard and patient labor, a zeal to replenish, to restore, to *do* right . . . [and spoken in] the diction of overt mastery, dense, opulent—faceted language, more brilliant than lustrous."[12] A characteristic example of the early work is "Poem," which begins:

> O Heart: this is a dream I had, or not a dream.
> Lovingly, lovingly, I wept, but my tears did not rhyme.
>
> In the year of my mother's blood, when I was born,
> She buried my innocent head in a field, because the earth
>
> Was sleepy with the winter. And I spoke the corn,
> And I cried the clover up, with the dewy mouth of my mirth.[13]

Back in New York in 1929, he sent his first book, written entirely between the ages of twenty-three and twenty-five, off to Doubleday Doran Publishers simply because they were the biggest in New York, and perhaps to his surprise got a phone call two weeks later from Ogden Nash, the poetry editor at the time, accepting it.[14] *Intellectual Things* was published in 1930 in an edition of five hundred copies. Kunitz, imagining himself on easy street, married Helen Pearce, resumed and expanded his work as a free-lance editor for the H. W. Wilson Company, bringing out *Living Authors: A Book of Biographies* and *Authors Today and Yesterday* (with Howard Haycraft and Wilbur Hadden) in 1933, the earliest in a series of reference books on contemporary authors, involving the writing of scores of portraits of their lives and work in two-thousand-word essays. However, he could not abide New York as a residence. ("I'm not really an urban creature. I need to be working the land to come fully alive. I need some green."[15])

In 1930 I was 25, trying to survive in the midst of the Depression on a 100-acre farm in Connecticut that I had bought for $3,000, with a $500 down payment— a fair price then, considering the condition of the property and the state of the economy. With a yoke of white oxen I cultivated the stony fields on top of Wormwood Hill, raising food and forage for domestic use and herbs for the market. Freelancing helped me pay the mortgage, but it was a struggle. Although my first collection of poems had been favorably reviewed on publication, I was cut off from the literary world. And I was going through the trials of a first marriage that was doomed to fail.[16]

After that marriage ended, in 1937, and the 1938 hurricane wiped out all his sugar maples, he shifted headquarters in 1939 to an old stone house with fifteen acres of land in New Hope, Pennsylvania, and, having married again, to Eleanor Evans ("a good marriage, to a fine person, though it ended in divorce"[17]), he settled in to raise chickens and plant trees, having by now not only continued to edit the *Bulletin* but, in addition, edited five reference books for the Wilson Company, and commuting to New York when he was not farming and writing in Pennsylvania.

One night there was a knock on his door, and, filling the doorway, a bearlike man—Theodore Roethke.

My recollection is of a traditionally battered jalopy from which a perfectly tremendous raccoon coat emerged, with my first book of poems tucked under its left paw. The introductory mumble that followed could be construed as a compliment. . . . The image that never left me was of a blond, smooth, shambling giant, irrevocably Teutonic, with a cold pudding of a face, somehow contradicted by the sullen downturn of the mouth and the pale furious eyes. . . . He had come to talk about poetry, and talk we did over a jug grandly and vehemently all through the night. . . . In the proper season, when conversation became dangerous, we would fight it out on the courts for what we liked to boast, with a bow to Joyce, was the lawn tennyson championship of the poetic world. . . .[18]

At last I had found a friend who was as mad about poetry as I was! We were two outsiders, and we needed each other.[19]

Theodore Roethke, even though three years younger and not yet published, already enjoyed a wider acquaintance in literary circles than Kunitz, whose innate shyness and reticence and country preoccupations kept him from acquaintance with poets. But Kunitz carried a certainty in his work that Roethke would not attain for some years to come. Roethke admired this certainty and bowed to it; "I sensed he needed me," Kunitz said afterward, "even more than I needed him."[20] Both poets were lonely, but Roethke sought out such allies as Louise Bogan, Léonie Adams, Rolfe Humphries, W. H. Auden, and John Holmes, and did what he deemed useful to advance his career. He did not, however, introduce them to Kunitz: their friendship flourished on its own, and in their conversations. The two poets agreed that T. S. Eliot and his influence had been baneful: "Eliot's premise, that there was no significant connection between the life of the poet and the work of his imagination, was treated as literary gospel. . . . Overnight, subjective poetry fell out of fashion. I couldn't understand why a theory so obviously false could be taken so seriously."[21]

In the early summer of 1943, Kunitz, just before his thirty-eighth birthday, was conscripted into the U.S. Army, "as a non-affiliated pacifist, with moral scruples against bearing arms."[22] In routine Army fashion, the official papers specifying the limitation on his service never caught up with him, and he spent most of his two-year Army career on KP, digging latrines, and, in fact, catching a variety of ailments; but, while he was still in the service in 1944, his second book, *Passport to the War*, was published by Henry Holt. The 1930s had not been a cheerful or nourishing atmosphere in which to write, nor had the past decade cheered his muse. *Passport to the War*, which Robert Hass has called "a book full of oblique, tormented poems about guilt and waste and failure,"[23] seethes with rage at the world which had created wars, and at the wounds and griefs which had given him poetic birth and plunged him into solitude; yet it contains some of his most powerful poems, especially those which, like "Father and Son," dealt with that central theme in his life and work, the unhealed wound of his father's suicide, or "Open the Gates," which settles on the unopened door as a striking symbol of both life and death. In later years he liked to say that a poem should close both like a door and a window, and it was his genius to create such translucent conclusions. "Father and Son" integrates the intensely personal yearning for the absent father with a rhetoric that T. S. Eliot or Wallace Stevens would not have dared dip a toe into: this was a poetry of the agonized soul that, written in the 1940s, would not be fully appreciated till twenty years later:

Now in the suburbs and the falling light
I followed him, and now down sandy road
Whiter than bone-dust, through the sweet
Curdle of fields, where the plums
Dropped with their load of ripeness, one by one.
Mile after mile I followed, with skimming feet,
After the secret master of my blood,
Him, steeped in the odor of ponds, whose indomitable love
Kept me in chains. Strode years; stretched into bird;
Raced through the sleeping country where I was young,
The silence unrolling before me as I came,
The night nailed like an orange to my brow. . . .

This powerful journey to the interior brings to American poetry a new kind of personal exploration which has nothing to do with confession, nothing to do with symbolism, but which draws on the resonances of archetypal myth and the complexities of natural imagery, as well as the eternal agonies of struggle between the deepest inner forces. The poem goes on for two prayerful stanzas as the son pleads with the father for forgiveness, for instruction, for reparation of his loss, for the restoration of innocence, and concludes with the most bland and terrifying of closings:

> Among the turtles and the lilies he turned to me
> The white ignorant hollow of his face.[24]

This was the sort of poetry that gave heart to Theodore Roethke in his progress toward the filial outcries of *The Lost Son*, and that would echo down the years for poets of my generation and the generation after it, for it turned back to ancient myths, primeval events like the writing on the wall in the Book of Daniel or the great choruses of Sophocles, while reaching out for compassion: "O teach me how to work and keep me kind." This was the poetic parallel to Freud's notion of maturity as learning to love, learning to work.

Thus *Passport to the War* differs from *Intellectual Things* in stretching toward human individual concerns, in conjuring up recognizable figures like members of the poet's own family and figures in history, by reaching further into the field of natural imagery; and it chronicles, indirectly, the dissolution of his first marriage—though it does not blurt out much about his second. Kunitz has never been a "confessional" poet: "I want poems that don't tell secrets, but are full of them."[25] The book did not make an enormous public splash in 1944, though Mark Schorer, in *The New York Times*, wrote of it, "Stanley Kunitz now enters the small group of the very best poets writing in America." Nonetheless, by the time Kunitz was discharged from the

Army in 1945, *Passport* was already out of print. He would not publish another volume for another fourteen years.[26] On his discharge, Kunitz found that he had been awarded a Guggenheim Fellowship—for which he had not even applied—through the good offices of Marianne Moore, whom he did not know. He also received a letter from the president of Bennington College offering him a teaching position for which likewise he had not applied: Theodore Roethke had undergone a severe manic attack while teaching at Bennington, locked himself into a cottage, and refused to come out or submit to hospitalization unless Kunitz was hired in his place. The friendship remained staunch as long as Roethke lived (he died in 1963), and Kunitz spoke out in 1949 when Roethke hit his major stride as a poet: "With *The Lost Son*, Theodore Roethke confirms what some of us have long suspected: that he stands among the original and powerful contemporary poets."[27]

Thus began Stanley Kunitz' long teaching career, starting at Bennington, 1946–1949, though he continued to perform his work on *Twentieth Century Authors* in between teaching poetry workshops at the New School for Social Research in New York City and at Potsdam, New York, in the summers. In 1950 his daughter and only child, Gretchen, was born. His mother died in 1952. In this altered phase of his life, between Bennington, New Hope, and New York, his second marriage began to fail, as echoed in a later poem, "River Road," and in 1951 in New York he first met the beautiful, incantatory, sexually ambiguous poet Jean Garrigue, with whom he would become increasingly, painfully, and intensely entangled for several years, partly spent on an Amy Lowell Traveling Fellowship in Europe.[28] During this period he wrote many of the poems that comprise the section of new poems, "This Garland, Danger," in his *Selected Poems*, poems which, as Gregory Orr says, revolve around a "beloved muse/figure . . . the muse/mistress with whom the poet grapples in a manner both sexual and spiritual and

in a way that is capable of yielding what is most fervently
desired: transformation."[29]

> She taunted me, who was all music's tongue,
> Philosophy's and wilderness's breed,
> Of shifting shape, half jungle-cat, half-dancer,
> Night's woman-petaled, lion-scented rose,
> To whom I gave, out of a hero's need,
> The dolor of my thrust, my riddling answer,
> Whose force no lesser mortal knows. Dangerous?
> Yes, as nervous oracles foretold
> Who could not guess the secret taste of her:
>   ... On the royal road to Thebes
> I had my luck, I met a lovely monster,
> And the story's this: I made the monster me.[30]

Although by the middle of 1953 Kunitz' second marriage
was crumbling, it did not officially terminate until 1957.
When Kunitz returned from Europe, the relationship with
Jean Garrigue was over, and the ties with Eleanor Evans
and his daughter, Gretchen, remained; yet his new teaching
career now called him, in 1955, to Seattle, where Theodore
Roethke was due for a much-needed sabbatical and Kunitz
once again filled his place. There he first met Allen Gins-
berg and Gary Snyder, and read *Howl* for the first time.
And there he encountered, among his students, the poets
James Wright, Carolyn Kizer, David Wagoner, and Jack
Gilbert.[31] These were ties which would remain as long as
life did.

When he returned to New York in 1956, his mode of life
would alter profoundly: he was making friendships with
painters like Mark Rothko, Franz Kline, James Brooks,
Philip Guston, Giorgio Cavallon, Robert Motherwell, and
other members of the first generation of abstract expres-
sionist painters; but the once-treasured setting in New Hope
had not survived the changes in his interior life. One of his
most dramatic poems, a poem included in the new section

of *Selected Poems, 1928–1958,* beginning, prophetically, with a flight of geese, turns on an incident that probably occurred in the autumn of 1953.

End of Summer

An agitation of the air,
A perturbation of the light
Admonished me the unloved year
Would turn on its hinge that night.

I stood in the disenchanted field
Amid the stubble and the stones,
Amazed, while a small worm lisped to me
The song of my marrow-bones.

Blue poured into summer blue,
A hawk broke from his cloudless tower,
The roof of the silo blazed, and I knew
That part of my life was over.

Already the iron door of the north
Clangs open: birds, leaves, snows
Order their populations forth,
And a cruel wind blows.[32]

Though in a written discussion of this poem[33] Kunitz retains his customary reticence about personal content, he does aver that it began in the field behind his house in New Hope on an afternoon in late September in the 1950s, and that, while it began as a descriptive poem, he realized after five nights' work that "it was the disturbance of the heart that really concerned me and that insisted on a language." The poem ordered its population forth. The silo, he adds, was an intrusion from an earlier stage of his life, perhaps Wormwood Hill, another farm, another marriage, a still earlier life. He was undergoing his transformations.

After his return from the West in 1956, to take up teaching again at the New School in New York, Kunitz met Elise

Asher, originally from Chicago, who had begun as a poet but turned to painting as well. She, like Kunitz, was recovering from a failed marriage; she had lost her mother to cancer at an early age; she, like him, had one young daughter and enjoyed a wide friendship among painters. A new kind of joyful compatibility arose between them. They began the next year to join their lives, and they were married, after both had divorced, on June 21, 1958. They settled in New York, but they concurred in settling also in Provincetown, where for several years he and Elise would summer in a shack on the beach among the painters, until in 1962 he was able to buy the house at 32 Commercial Street where he would found his garden and become one of the famous presences of the town as he grubbed and delved by daylight, but, out of eyeshot, worked by night at his poems.

His relationship with Elise Asher coincided with the readiness, in 1957, of a selected volume covering the work of the last thirty years and including thirty-two poems written since World War II. His *Selected Poems, 1928–1958* was published in 1958 by the Atlantic Monthly Press, at the suggestion, as I have recounted, of Richard Wilbur.

It was not easy for me, having begun my relation to Kunitz' poetry with a powerful alteration in my acceptance of myself, my father, and my attitude toward the language, to get to know the man himself. Not at first. Kunitz in those days seemed a little distant, with his European moustache, his way of carrying his head with his prominent nose held high, and his lithe, almost athletic walk. He dressed more formally then than in later years, and in conversation he listened alertly—sometimes to the speaker but sometimes to something distant that seemed outside hearing. When he spoke his voice was high, often excited, a little nasal, and his conversation could range from the most intricate of poetic gossip to the most general of political and aesthetic subjects. Though in later years he would suffer from arthritis and more than one life-threatening disease, he recovered from every ailment and became, in his great old age, a better-looking man than in his middle years, as though the changes in his soul had tailored his body for a better fit. But now, in 1959, one got the sense of a man explicitly in mid-life, neither young nor old, a dedicated poet with unapolo-getically prophetic intentions, whose work one valued as one did that of his peers; there was something in those moments of absence, of absentmindedness, that suggested his mind had its own involvements with the past and with the future—and so it would prove to be.

At about the time of publication of his *Selected Poems* Kunitz took up residence in September 1958 at 1200 Mas-sachusetts Avenue, a rather stark apartment house of quasi-Spanish mien opposite Harvard Yard and Widener Library. He had been sponsored as a visiting professor at Brandeis University by J. V. Cunningham, joining a literary faculty which also included Irving Howe and Philip Rahv. He taught a poetry workshop and a course in fiction, concen-trating on the novella form. He didn't know many people in Boston, and his literary associations were in any case still fairly limited. "I had been out of circulation for a long time."[34] But his first introductions to the literary network of Boston came quickly enough. Though Kunitz, with his well-grounded suspicion of Harvard, did not have the good luck to know John L. Sweeney at this time, John Holmes, who had been a novice instructor with Roethke at Lafayette years before, soon made Kunitz welcome: he invited the visitor to his house several times, usually in a crowd. There he met Philip Booth, George Starbuck, Anne Sexton, Ted Hughes, and Sylvia Plath. These encounters, as I have told (see pages 171–72), led to the ritual weekly call that Plath and Hughes began to pay on Kunitz at his Cambridge apart-ment. And on May 12, 1959, Kunitz gave a reading, intro-duced by Holmes, at Tufts University, which happened to occur on the day after the announcement that he had won the Pulitzer Prize in poetry for *Selected Poems*—and, co-incidentally, on the day after the publication of *Life Studies*. There was a large party at Holmes' house afterward. This moment in Boston erased Kunitz' early obscurity as he describes it:

Well, remember, I had come through, out of years in the margins, and suddenly, with the publication of the *Selected Poems*, became alive again, and it was an astonishing sea change for me. I had been so much an outsider; I was suddenly in the center of things. And back in New York, where I had been teaching at the New School because I couldn't get a university job and was living on a pittance really, I was still doing *Contemporary Authors* as a consultant. What happened to me was that when I'd got into this whole dismal breakup of my marriage, my involvement with Jean Garrigue, and all the poems that came out of that, which were in the *Selected* volume, all sorts of opportunities opened up for me and I became somebody near the center of that world, and I was elected to the Academy and to the Academy of American Poets, and so on.

Every time I have published a book I have a sense of a chapter closing and the need for a revolution. What happened to me right after the *Selected Poems* was the beginning of what I consider to be my whole last phase, and I began moving toward that. Elise and I started going up to the Cape in 1957, in a little shack on the beach there, and so the first poems I began working on were all involved as I see them now with that change in my life and with the sense that these were poems of my age rather than of my youth or my middle years and their association with Elise and my entry into the world of the visual arts. Of course, I was writing a good many essays then too.

"Robin Redbreast" was about that time. That's going

244

back to an episode some years before. I would say the earliest poems out of this period would have been "Robin Redbreast" and "After the Last Dynasty." I think questions of mortality become clearly more dominant, and you have a sense of on the one hand the waning of the body and the other hand the sense of renewal that I had both in my life and my activity in the garden. The garden [begun in 1962] was central, it had to do with the life pulsing there, and the sea, but as I think also there is much more serenity, not ever completely serene, a diminishing of what in the earlier poems emerges as a kind of rage against the world.

And now I began remaking in particular the old legend of my mother, whom I had felt alienated from in my earlier poems and whom I had begun to understand as I grew older and really how supportive she had been despite our differences. But the style I was moving toward had already been formulated before 1959, where the poems, even going back to the *Selected Poems*, "Revolving Meditation" for example, anticipate that whole loosening of the form and the openness of speech and also that three-beat line that I became most happy with. *There was a sense then that a new era was about to begin, which we don't have now.* [Italics mine.][35]

To this day one of the few distinctions that has eluded Stanley Kunitz is an honorary degree from his alma mater; and although Yale would invite him to edit—with great effect—the Yale Series of Younger Poets, and Columbia would give him a position for many years at its School of the Arts, Harvard seldom invited him to give so much as a reading. In 1958, however, Kunitz was made very welcome in Boston, if not entirely at Harvard. Emily Morison Beck soon brought Kunitz and Robert Lowell together for the first time, in the fall of 1958, at lunch at a red-checked-tablecloth restaurant, possibly Durgin-Park, the noted but noisy marketplace/dining room. ("I suppose it could have been there," William Alfred commented. "Cal had a rubber palate.")

Thus began the second important poetic friendship of Kunitz' life. Lowell had already read Kunitz' *Selected* in manuscript, and was quoted on its jacket: "I admire Mr. Kunitz' savage, symbolic drive. He has been one of the masters for years, and yet so unrecognized that his *Selected Poems* make him the poet of the hour." Kunitz' first impressions of that meeting are still vivid:

> He was certainly very articulate! He drank a lot and spoke a lot and was very complimentary about my book. We obviously had a lot to talk about. And he talked to me about *Life Studies*, which he was still working on, but it wasn't yet in final form. The first time I came to see Cal on Marlborough Street he produced the manuscript of *Life Studies* and asked me to look at it, see what I thought of it. That was my first encounter with Cal's whole process of working on a manuscript. I remember in particular "Beyond the Alps": he was still working on that, revising, though like so many of those poems it had a lot of history. I know we worked together on that. It was terribly cluttered, and in fact I think so obscure you could never figure out quite what was going on, in fact I don't think anybody has ever. . . .[36]

Kunitz has described with amused affection the atmosphere of a conversation with Lowell: "As Lowell talks, slumped in his chair until he is practically sitting on his spine, he knits his brow in the effort to concentrate and stirs an invisible broth with his right index finger. The troubled blue eyes, intense and roving behind the thick glasses, rarely come to rest. . . . The sensitive curved mouth contrasts with the jutting, fleshy chin; the nose is small, with wide circular nostrils; he is articulate, informed, and positive, but his gestures are vague and rather endearingly awkward."[37] The friendship between them grew over later years, and Kunitz would eventually speak of *Life Studies* as "one of the watersheds of modern literature."[38]

> His method of composition was uniquely collaborative. He made his friends, willy-nilly, partners in his act by showering them with early drafts of his poems, often so fragmentary and shapeless that it was no great trick to suggest improvements. Sometimes you saw a poem in half a dozen successive versions, each new version ampler and bolder than the last. You would recognize your own suggestions embedded in the text—a phrase here and there, a shift in the order of the lines—and you might wonder how many other hands had been involved in the process. It did not seem to matter much, for the end-product always presented itself as infallibly, unmistakably Lowellian."[39]

Of course, it was not all work, not all manuscript-shuffling, this sort of friendship. Kunitz and the Lowells (when Lowell was not ill) undertook expeditions, lunches, dinners, with Adrienne and Alfred Conrad, with William Alfred, with Philip and Margaret Booth, talk of merry or wild intention. One such meeting that winter brought about Kunitz' first meeting with Robert Frost:

> One day Cal proposed that we have lunch together in Cambridge, and so we did, in Harvard Square. He was I could see in an incipient manic phase, and, of course, we had drinks, and there was a lot to talk about, and he was rattling on, it was a real volley of conversation, and we were both pretty high, and hours passed. It must have been three in the afternoon when Cal said, "Oh my God, I'm supposed to visit Robert Frost, and we're over an hour and a half late," and he dashed to the phone, and I could hear him apologize. He said

that Frost had said, Bring him along, Come right over.
We walked away over to Brewster Street, and he was
alone and sitting there, and he was looking a little dour.
I don't blame him, and it was pretty stiff going for a
while. As you know he liked to dominate a room, and
finally he did offer us a drink, which we didn't need,
but which we accepted, and he poured a big slug for
himself, and then things opened up. But between them.
I had very little to say. I was watching.[40]

Kunitz' friendship with Lowell was, after Roethke, the
second great poetic friendship of his life; and, not only with
the manuscript of the poems of *Life Studies*, but from this
stage of Lowell's life forward, it was to Kunitz (and Eliz-
abeth Bishop) that Lowell would turn increasingly—though
far from exclusively—for advice about his poems. To seek
the turning point in both their poetic lives one must examine
those months of 1958–1959 in Boston.

The next chapter will shift to Lowell's viewpoint; but
Kunitz has stated that 1959 "was certainly a crossroads year
for me."[41] Not only did he gain wide acceptance by the
public and attain peer status in the world of poetry, but he
struck out, like so many in 1959, in a new direction in his
poetry, a direction which would lead from change to
change, from deepening to deepening ("It is necessary to
go/through dark and deeper dark/and not to turn"[42]), and
leave Kunitz, in his late eighties, the senior and most in-
dependent of American poets, still not turning away from
the dark, still brave enough to change, still searching deeper
in the materials of poetry, still leaving poems through a
door that is also a window, as in his 1993 poem "Proteus":
"He heard barbaric voices crying, 'Prophesy!' "[43]

11. Out of Bounds:
Robert Lowell, 1955–1960

For the Union Dead

RELINQUUNT OMNIA SERVARE REM PUBLICAM.

The old South Boston Aquarium stands
in a Sahara of snow now. Its broken windows are
   boarded.
The bronze weathervane cod has lost half its scales.
The airy tanks are dry.

Once my nose crawled like a snail on the glass;
my hand tingled
to burst the bubbles,
drifting from the noses of the cowed, compliant fish.

My hand draws back. I often sigh still
for the dark downward and vegetating kingdom
of the fish and reptile. One morning last March,
I pressed against the new barbed and galvanized

fence on the Boston Common. Behind their cage,
yellow dinosaur steam shovels were grunting
as they cropped up tons of mush and grass
to gouge their underworld garage.

Parking lots luxuriate like civic
sand piles in the heart of Boston.
A girdle of orange, Puritan-pumpkin-colored girders
braces the tingling Statehouse, shaking

over the excavations, as it faces Colonel Shaw
and his bell-cheeked Negro infantry
on St. Gaudens' shaking Civil War relief,
propped by a plank splint against the garage's
    earthquake.

Two months after marching through Boston,
half the regiment was dead;
at the dedication,
William James could almost hear the bronze Negroes
    breathe.

The monument sticks like a fishbone
in the city's throat.
Its colonel is as lean
as a compass needle.

He has an angry wrenlike vigilance,
a greyhound's gentle tautness;
he seems to wince at pleasure
and suffocate for privacy.

He is out of bounds. He rejoices in man's lovely,
peculiar power to choose life and die—
when he leads his black soldiers to death,
he cannot bend his back.

On a thousand small-town New England greens,
the old white churches hold their air
of sparse, sincere rebellion; frayed flags
quilt the graveyards of the Grand Army of the Republic.

The stone statues of the abstract Union Soldier
grow slimmer and younger each year—
wasp-waisted, they doze over muskets,
and muse through their sideburns.

Shaw's father wanted no monument
except the ditch,
where his son's body was thrown
and lost with his "niggers."

The ditch is nearer.
There are no statues for the last war here;
on Boylston Street, a commercial photograph
showed Hiroshima boiling

over a Mosler safe, the "Rock of Ages,"
that survived the blast. Space is nearer.
When I crouch to my television set,
the drained faces of Negro school children rise like
    balloons.

Colonel Shaw
is riding on his bubble,
he waits
for the blessed break.

The Aquarium is gone. Everywhere,
giant finned cars nose forward like fish;
a savage servility
slides by on grease.

WRITTEN *1960*; AS PUBLISHED IN *The Atlantic Monthly*,
NOVEMBER *1960*[1]

Robert Lowell's unmistakable voice—weary, nasal, hesitant, whining, mumbling, a curiously hybrid blend of Yankee and Confederate intonations that descended from both family and literary sources—seems in retrospect to dominate the poetic harmony of the late 1950s in Boston. He was audible everywhere: reading, writing, teaching, socializing, translating—and dramatizing his own suffering in semi-public agony. For his sheer presence and talent no poet attracted more attention from the literati of Boston and Cambridge than Robert Lowell, between his return to residence in Boston in 1955 and his departure in September 1960.

For one thing, he was so completely *Bostonian*. This flawed titan of the famed Lowell family, with two poets in his father's ancestry, was born in his grandfather Winslow's (his mother's father's) house on March 1, 1917, on Chestnut Street, the most beautiful street in Boston, at number 18, near the top of Beacon Hill, across from the former residence of Julia Ward Howe and from that of Ralph Adams Cram; one long block from where his great-granduncle James Russell Lowell had lived and from the former residence of Francis Parkman; and three blocks from the Massachusetts State House and the site, opposite, of Saint-Gaudens' noble monument to Robert Gould Shaw (another remote kinsman) and his Civil War Negro regiment. Lowell's mother, half northern, half southern, was the dominant, and the baleful, influence on his early life.

I never knew I was a Lowell till I was twenty. The ancestors known to my family were James Russell Lowell, a poet pedestaled for oblivion, and no asset to his grandnephew among the rich athletes at boarding school. Another, my great-grandfather, James Russell's brother, had been headmaster of my boarding school [St. Mark's], and left a memory of scholarly aloofness. He wrote an ironic Trollopian *roman à clef* about the school. There was Amy Lowell, big and a scandal, as if Mae West were a cousin. And there were rich Lowells, but none as rich as my classmates' grandfathers in New York. . . . Ours was an old family. It stood—just. Its last eminence was Lawrence, Amy's brother, and president of Harvard, for millennia a grand *fin de siècle* president, a species long dead in America. He was cultured in the culture of 1900—very deaf, very sprightly, in his eighties. He was unique in our family for being able to read certain kinds of good poetry. I used to spend evenings with him, and go home to college at four in the morning.[2]

When this youngest Lowell, after years of wandering, came back after twenty years to settle in Boston in 1955, having survived two severe psychotic episodes and hospitalizations since his mother's death in Rapallo on February 14, 1954 (his father had died in 1950, a year after his marriage to Elizabeth Hardwick), he was already, at thirty-eight, famous throughout literary America not only for the power of his lines but for the agonies and scandals of his private life. Yet poetry for him was central to everything. As Stanley Kunitz once wrote, "Fame did not modify his nature—he always expected to be famous. Money and family gave him advantages, of which he was well aware, but one of his differences from other poets was that he worked harder at his poems than anybody else did. Every day of his life was a day for poetry."[3]

He was also a larger-than-life presence, whether he was sane or mad. I had been made aware of him as a child, in 1937, when Ford Madox Ford and his "wife," Janice Biala, were staying in my family's house in Boulder during the annual Colorado writers' conference. The twenty-year-old Lowell kept presenting himself for every social occasion, though uninvited, and with manic heedlessness paid few of the appropriate courtesies to his hostess. It was in our house that he met Jean Stafford, my father's student and assistant, who would become his first wife. One night, when he routinely presented himself at the door for dinner, my mother turned him away, saying, "I'm sorry, Mr. Lowell. You can't come in. I don't like your manners." Later, in 1949, I had been one of the avid young student/tourists who visited old George Santayana in his last refuge in the Convent of the Blue Nuns in Rome, and he inquired what I could tell him about a young poet named Robert Lowell, whom he did not know, but who had lately (during one of his worst seizures) been writing him some letters he found strange. I passed along the gossip, which as usual had travelled fast, about Lowell's current severe breakdown (he was at the time a patient in the Payne Whitney Clinic in New York), but this clearly did not interfere with the prompt flowering of a Lowell/Santayana in-person friendship the following year. During my first actual conversation with Lowell, in 1956, after a Harvard public reading which included not only his poem on Santayana but his "Ford Madox Ford," he said to me, sadly and sweetly, after I had introduced myself, "I'm afraid I was very rude to your parents in Boulder."

Still, I could not, even in the face of this endearing and graceful apology, wipe out a different sort of memory: a 1954 morning in New York, when the office atmosphere at Harcourt, Brace was shattered by wild laughter as two young men, talking very loudly, strode past the receptionist and struck a wavering course along the aisles. With them, their usher in a cape, scurried Catharine Carver, the assiduous editor who shared my cubicle, attempting to steer Robert Lowell and John Berryman toward their friend Robert Giroux' office. The two poets had been making a night of it, and both, on this morning after, looked seedy and sounded strident. Lowell's nasal whine carried well enough, but not so effectively as Berryman's hollering, until the door of the editorial sanctum closed behind them. (This would be close to the time of Lowell's mother's death.)

I had my own reasons for being frightened of drunken men; but my reaction to this apparition went deeper than genteel anxiety: it aroused my fear of the wildness at the heart of poetry. Later meetings with Lowell during his Boston period were invariably agreeable and almost invariably cordial—except when I had reviewed one of his later books without total surrender—yet he could indeed be a delicious companion. Still, like Adrienne Rich and W. S. Merwin, I could not help feeling wary of him, especially after the one time I encountered him in the throes of a manic surge. His gentleness and humor on ordinary occasions were quite charming, and he was nothing if not generous to those whom he need not regard as competitors. When I wrote him compliments on a newly published poem, he replied, politely, "You say very gratefyingly [sic] everything I could have hoped for or intended. . . . I liked your selection in *A Controversy of Poets* [a current anthology in which we both had poems]. We struggle with the same themes and material."[4] Though his friend William Alfred said of Lowell and his wife, Elizabeth Hardwick, "I'd never talked to people who really cared that much about words. It was absolutely electric," he also said,

> You know when Cal was really manic, it may have been my imagination, but he looked really big, like a bear. When he would get sick he would tease me all the time, mischievous, blasphemous, that sort of thing. Once Cal when he was very sick—and the heartbreaking thing about anyone who is very sick is that there are moments when the sane person looks out from the mad face and asks for some kind of collaboration— and I thought, he's starting to needle me again. And he said, "Now, what do you really think the needle in

the flesh in St. Paul refers to?" I said, "Well, it's gen-
erally talked about as concupiscence." "No," he said.
And then his eyes looked the way they always did, and
he said, "It's ambition." It was heartbreaking.[5]

Alfred had met the Lowells on their initial sortie to Boston
in the fall of 1954, after they had bought a house in Dux-
bury, Massachusetts, at long distance from Cincinnati,
choosing to locate themselves south of Boston in order not
to be dangerously close to Charlotte Lowell; but their arrival
was delayed by her illness and death and by Lowell's sub-
sequent breakdowns and hospitalization, and they found,
after a summer in Duxbury and a winter in a rented apart-
ment on Commonwealth Avenue, that life in the old city
suited them better. In addition Lowell inherited the use of
a house in Castine, Maine, from his mother's cousin Harriet
Winslow, who had grown too infirm to use it herself. With
the lovely house in Castine available in summers, along
with a seaside barn for a studio, the country house in Dux-
bury no longer served any purpose, so they sold it and,
rather than move into the haunted Lowell house at 270
Marlborough Street, bought, in 1955, a spacious house at
239 Marlborough Street, only one block away. Lowell was
already the beneficiary of a trust fund, but his mother's
death had increased his income substantially, and enlarged
his available capital by $50,000 as well.[6]

In 1955 Lowell's mood was relatively peaceful, if rather
muted, after the frenzies of the previous year. The re-entry
to Boston was pleasing to both husband and wife, and a
new social life was blooming around them, both a city life
in Boston and a summer life in Castine. Lowell, having left
the Catholic church, was received back into the Episcopal
church by Father Whitney Hale of the Church of the Ad-
vent, who was also authorized to consecrate his second mar-
riage. Elizabeth Hardwick wrote in April 1955: "Everyone
seems to come here, and so we feel rather more in the

literary world than usual. We've had the Sitwells, Spender, John Crowe Ransom at Harvard last night, Lillian Hellman, and then magazine writers from Everywhere. T. S. Eliot is expected soon. Here in Boston we are somehow expected to do our part and so we are always giving luncheons and cocktails for the visitors and actually enjoying it all."[7] Lowell was frequently called upon to join the endless panels on the future of poetry that furnished one of the principal university delights of the time, more popular than poetry readings, panels that included Spender and Ransom and Eliot, Allen Tate, Archibald MacLeish, John Holmes, John Ciardi, perhaps Marianne Moore, but very few other women with the exception, now and then, of Louise Bogan or May Sarton. This was still, after all, the age of the New Criticism—all male.

Alfred speaks also of a fairly regular all-male dinner group that met in one of the private dining rooms above the Locke-Ober Café in downtown Boston, including Robert Frost and others. Edwin Muir, the visiting Charles Eliot Norton Lecturer at Harvard in 1955–1956, would have attended, and in a later letter to the notoriously competitive Theodore Roethke, Lowell "[remembers] Edwin Muir arguing with me that there is no rivalry in poetry. Well, there is. No matter what one has done or hasn't done . . . one feels each blow, each turning of the wind, each up and down grading of the critics. . . . There's a strange fact about the poets of roughly our age, and one that doesn't exactly seem to have always been true. It's this, that to write we seem to have to go at it with such single-minded intensity that we are always on the point of drowning."[8] Lord knows this applied to Jarrell, Berryman, Delmore Schwartz, and Theodore Roethke as well as to Lowell himself.

In the fall of 1955 Lowell began teaching at Boston University, and his stature as a Pulitzer Prize winner, a Lowell, excitingly unstable, attracted all sorts of students. One, that first year, was Helen Hennessey (later Vendler), a chemistry student who, shifting to English, sat in on the course but was somewhat bewildered by Lowell at the time, though twenty years later she shrewdly described his teaching: "Those who have heard Lowell's conversation, and know the apparent diffidence and drawl concealing a mind of ferocious force and outrageous irreverence, will know the submerged authority present even in his most offhand remarks, whether they were remarks on life or on art."[9] Yet other pupils, like Anne Sexton and Sylvia Plath, as we have seen, took differing views; and younger women others still, e.g.: "Lowell was a great teacher of literature and an awful workshop teacher."[10] And Lowell was known, despite his powerful attraction for them, not to think highly of women poets, even after teaching and befriending a number of them: "Can I make this generalization? Only four stand with our best men: Emily Dickinson, Marianne Moore, Elizabeth Bishop, and Sylvia Plath."[11] Note the omission of Adrienne Rich and Anne Sexton from this characteristic "grading" of poets in 1971.

During these two settled years in Boston, 1955–1956, the Lowells also struck up a host of new friendships: Stephen and Agatha Fassett, William and Dido Merwin, Peter and Esther Brooks. Esther Brooks was a ballet dancer (I was for an inept while her pupil) and a discerning observer:

> When Cal was well he was enormous fun to be with. His way of looking at things was so completely original that you yourself began to see everything from a different perspective. Hours meant nothing to him when he was interested. Day turned into night and night back into day while he, with his seemingly limitless stamina, worried an idea, rejected it, discovered another, built mental pyramids, tore them down, discoursed on the habits of wolves, the Punic Wars, Dante, Napoleon, Shakespeare, Alexander the Great, politics, his friends, religion, his work, or the great noyade at Nantes. . . .

I think he was probably the most entirely cerebral person I have ever known. His creativity was not diffuse as it so often is with great artists. There were no signs that his talent spilled over into other fields. He didn't sing, didn't play an instrument, didn't draw. He wasn't a linguist. He couldn't dance, nor did he have, in spite of his unusual physical strength, any athletic skill other than a puffy game of tennis. In other words all his genius was concentrated entirely in his mind— a mind so original, so perceptive, so finely wrought, that seemed able to intuit sensory experience without reacting directly to it. He could discourse on music as brilliantly as any trained musician but he could not hear whether a note was higher or lower when played for him on a piano. He had only the meanest, most rudimentary grasp of foreign languages and yet he translated foreign poetry brilliantly. He had an extraordinary sense of metre but no physical sense of rhythm. . . . With Cal it would seem that whatever he encountered he thought about it first, then he turned it into metaphor, and then he reacted with feeling toward that abstraction. In other words the feeling, though no less intense, was once removed from the actual experience.[12]

Lowell's most recent book of poems, *The Mills of the Kavanaughs*, had been published in 1951. However, since about the time of his father's death in 1950, his muse had become inaccessible—"Five messy poems in five years"[13] —and often disabled by violent mental breakdowns, clouds of unknowing that the death of his parents had cast over his psyche. Now, in Boston and in the first summers in Castine, he still could not seem to make poems happen. But, "always a prodigious reader, in these years he began taking in armloads of the western world's best poetry and possessing it by translating it—Juvenal, Racine, Villon,

Baudelaire, Leopardi, Montale."[14] He turned to transla-
tions from languages he thought he knew, like Italian and
French, or from those he knew he did not know: as he said
once, candidly arrogant, "What I did was take other English
translations and translate them into English."[15] Even some
of the few poems he was writing emerged from translations,
e.g., "Sailing Home from Rapallo," the elegy to his mother
which, according to W. S. Merwin, began as a Baudelaire
translation,[16] and "To Speak of Woe That Is in Marriage,"
which Merwin remembers seeing at about this time, began
as a translation from Catullus.

He had also begun writing his autobiography, for which
he requested a contract from Robert Giroux in April 1955.
"It is impossible not to connect his sudden interest in writ-
ing his autobiography with the shock of his mother's death
in Rapallo the previous year," Robert Giroux commented
later on. "I am writing my autobiography literally to 'pass
the time,' " Lowell wrote, in a convalescent mood in 1957.
"I almost doubt if the time would pass at all otherwise.
However, I also hope the result will supply me with swad-
dling clothes, with a sort of immense bandage of grace and
ambergris for my hurt nerves. Therefore, this book will stop
with the summer of 1934. A few months after the end of
this book, I *found* myself."[17] Though this sounds as though
Lowell finished his book, which he never did—it merely
stalled in midstream—its composition had tremendous ef-
fects. "Like Bishop," David Kalstone says, "Lowell in the
1950s was discovering through his work in prose a new way
of writing poetry,"[18] and Elizabeth Hardwick wrote Peter
Taylor about Lowell's prose pieces, "They are reminis-
cences of childhood—that is the closest I can come—and
I think of extraordinary beauty and interest."[19]

The autobiographical passages dealt with the weaknesses
of his father, both as a naval officer, and then, after the
family's taking up residence at 91 Revere Street, and the
father's retirement from the Navy on a trust fund when

Robert was ten, they focussed on his mother's snobbish dominance of the family.

In the twenty-two years Father lived after he resigned from the Navy, he never again deserted Boston and never became Bostonian. He survived to drift from job to job, to be displaced, to be grimly and literally that old cliché, a fish out of water. . . .

In 1924 people still lived in cities. Late that summer, we bought the 91 Revere Street house, looking out on an unbuttoned part of Beacon Hill bounded by the North End slums, though reassuringly only four blocks away from my Grandfather Winslow's brown pillared house at 18 Chestnut Street. . . . A few doors to our south the householders spoke "Beacon Hill British" or the flat *nay nay* of the Boston Brahmin. The parents of the children a few doors north spoke mostly in Italian.

My mother felt a horrified giddiness about the adventure of our address. She once said, "We are barely perched on the outer rim of the hub of decency." We were less than fifty yards from Louisburg Square, the cynosure of old historic Boston's plain-spoken, cold roast elite—the Hub of the Hub of the Universe. Fifty yards! . . .

Boys were a sideline at my Brimmer School. . . . On bright spring days, Mr. Newell, a submerged young man from Boston University, took us on botanical hikes through the Arboretum . . . and one rainy afternoon broke all rules by herding us into the South Boston Aquarium in order to give an unhealthy, eager little lecture on the sewage consumption of the conger eel. . . . Saint Mark's was the boarding school for which I had been enrolled at birth, and was due to enter in 1930. . . . On sunny March and April afternoons . . . our teachers took us for strolls on the polite, landscaped walks of the Public Garden. There I'd loiter by the old iron fence and gape longingly across Charles Street at the historic Boston Common, a now largely wrong-side-of-the-tracks park. On the Common there were mossy bronze reliefs of Union soldiers, and a captured German tank filled with smelly wads of newspapers.[20]

Lowell's literary work went on both in Boston and in Castine, in Boston in a spacious study crammed with books on the top floor of 239 Marlborough Street, and in Castine in the barn at the edge of the harbor, where he could stare out across the weedy flats at low tide or watch the wind whip the whitecaps at the flood. "I'm sitting in a little barn my Cousin Harriet made over and painted (against all town advice) with aluminum paint a sort of pewter color inside. It's right on the bay, which on one side looks like a print of Japan and on the other like a lake in Michigan as the rocky islands with pine trees ease off into birches and meadows."[21] The imagery of water, and of the ocean seen from its western shore, began to heal his imagination, which had from its earliest manifestations been hospitable to deep and shallow salt water, to sailors, whales, marshes, shores, and bays; but first he had to adopt the village of Castine.

Native Philip Booth was a great help here, but importation also took place. As he had done in 1946, with Jean Stafford in Damariscotta Mills, Lowell attempted to recruit to his new colony all those who most interested him in a literary way, and they reciprocated. Philip Booth reported, "People come to talk with Cal, to listen to how his brilliance works. What's remarkable is how steadily, even with visitors, Cal keeps to his writing routine. Almost daily, Cal's day moves from the old isolation of poems to the strong refreshment of people. Breakfast, postoffice, Barn; work and lunch there until it is time for tennis and people again. People come to talk with Cal; they also come to share Elizabeth's own brilliance, to share her table, to be part of her house."[22] The energy of Lowell's literary conversation amazed Booth: "He plays a dinner party at the pitch at which he plays tennis. Given an audience of more than one, Cal turns conversation into his best competitive sport. Cal is immensely knowing in all sorts of worlds beyond Castine: poetry, politics, women—in every possible permutation and combination. He has many appetites but the surest of these is for talk. Cal serves with high wit; his wild intelligence never misses an opportunity to score. The dinner table is, for him, center court at Longwood. As if in total relief from writing, or from shop talk, Cal tries every shot in the book: dropshot, lob, slam."[23]

Despite this somewhat hyperactive social activity, which went on winter and summer, Lowell for two years rather calmly gave himself over to Boston, translation, autobiography, and family, rummaging through the ancestral records of the Winslows and Lowells, the Traills and Spences; and also through the great creations of European poetry. He kept up with two of his most revered mentors, Robert Frost, whom he would see in Cambridge during the winter ("Here one night [Frost] was talking about the suicide of a young friend, and said that sometimes, when he was excited and full of himself, he came back by thinking how little good his health could do those who were close to him"[24]), and William Carlos Williams, with whom he corresponded frequently, and whom he heard read, he says, at Wellesley for the last time in 1957:

I think about three thousand students attended. It couldn't have been more crowded in the wide-galleried hall and I had to sit in the aisle. The poet appeared, one whole side partly paralyzed, his voice just audible, and here and there a word misread. No one stirred. In the silence he read his great poem "Of Asphodel,

That Greeny Flower," a triumph of simple confession
—somehow he delivered to us what was impossible,
something that was both poetry and beyond poetry."[25]

During the autumn of 1956, the second contest between
Eisenhower and Stevenson for the presidency took place,
as did the Suez crisis that toppled Anthony Eden from
power as Britain's prime minister, and the Soviet invasion
of Hungary. At this time Lowell and Merwin used to see a
good deal of one another. Elizabeth Hardwick was preg-
nant, and working on her own writing. On October 23 Low-
ell and Merwin went together to the last Stevenson rally in
Boston and found themselves sinking from real hope to a
real disillusion. Merwin remembers "coming out and say-
ing that he was selling out, he's trimming sail in the wrong
way. He's hedging on the whole nuclear issue, because he
thinks he might lose the election, but he's going to lose
anyway, and he ought to press it harder." The two poets
were talking a lot about translation and poetry: "Cal was
interested in my family poems and wanted me to read them
and would come around to the apartment and ask me,
Would you read that poem over again, could I have cop-
ies?"[26] Lowell was also interested in Merwin's plays and
read them: he was especially interested in his play on Buf-
falo Bill, and in the marine darknesses of *Favor Island*.
Whether Lowell stored away some clues from Merwin's
family poems as he continued to write his own prose mem-
oirs seems quite likely.

On January 4, 1957, Harriet Winslow Lowell was born
in Boston, and an exciting if disruptive phase in the Lowells'
life began. Robert Lowell seems always to have been a
tender and attentive father, even in his distracted phases.
Elizabeth Hardwick was forty. As the spring wore on, the
changes in Lowell's attitude toward his own writing began
to alter in an internal fashion. In March, while on a two-

week reading tour of the West Coast, Lowell, when reading his poems, began to alter them orally, dropping syllables here, rhymes there; he seemed to feel discontent with their crowdedness:

> I had been giving readings on the West Coast, often reading six days a week and sometimes twice on a single day, I was in San Francisco, the era and setting of Allen Ginsberg and all about, very modest poets were waking up prophets. I became sorely aware of how few poems I had written, and that these few had been finished at the latest three or four years earlier. Their style seemed distant, symbol-ridden, and willfully difficult. I began to paraphrase my Latin quotations, and to add extra syllables to a line to make it clearer and more colloquial. I felt my old poems hid what they were really about, and many times offered a stiff, humorless, and even impenetrable surface. I am no convert to the "beats." I know well, too, that the best poems are not necessarily poems that read aloud. Many of the greatest poems can only be read to one's self, for inspiration is no substitute for humor, shock, narrative, and a hypnotic voice, the four musts for oral performance. Still, my own poems seemed like prehistoric monsters dragged down into the bog and death by their ponderous armor. I was reciting what I no longer felt.[27]

> I was still reading my old New Criticism religious, symbolic poems, many published during the war. I found—it's no criticism—that audiences just didn't understand, and I didn't always understand myself while reading. Much good poetry is unsuited to audience performance; mine was incomprehensible.[28] [Having recently listened to an early Lowell recording of "The Quaker Graveyard in Nantucket," I can only agree with his assessment.—P.D.]

During his western journey Lowell came into contact with a number of the Beat poets ("The Beats were a breakthrough. They had little interest, most of them, in experience but had a great interest in stirring utterance. *Howl* doesn't seem to have much to do with the stir of life but it is a stirring sermon"[29]) and their intense admiration for William Carlos Williams, which Lowell had of course long shared. After Lowell wrote Williams about his journey, Williams replied that the "wild-eyed radicals" were not "so wild as they think themselves,"[30] but he read, while travelling, in an early copy of *New Poets of England and America*, "Heart's Needle," by his old Iowa student W. D. Snodgrass, a poem which conveyed with great emotional simplicity but technical dexterity the theme of a poet being separated from his young daughter by divorce—a theme which must, in his separation from little Harriet, have touched Lowell on the quick. In May Williams came to Boston to perform at the Brandeis Arts Festival, and he and his wife stayed with the Lowells on Marlborough Street.[31] And, in late May or early June, Lowell had a long-postponed reunion with Elizabeth Bishop, who after five years in Brazil was making an extended visit to the United States with her beloved companion Lota de Macedo Soares. She visited the Lowells in Boston in June, and Lowell, hearing her read "Sunday, Four A.M." and "The Armadillo," two poems in gently formal verse, at once personal, intimate, and ingratiating, found they had as pronounced an effect on him as "Heart's Needle." He even became slightly amorous, harking back to a frustrated and inappropriate episode in 1948.

He now attempted to get back to writing poems, but found little but discontent in his new efforts: he kept lapsing back into the "inertia of our old rhetoric and habits"[32] and realized that his prose had been far more satisfactory. Ian Hamilton assesses him at this turning point:

He had learned how to give voice to a wide range of what might be called the moderate emotions: affection, regret, nostalgia, embarrassment, and so on. He had become expert at contriving sentences that could be elevated and yet speakable, and had found a literary voice that could encompass something of his social self—that is to say, the teasing, mischievous, gently sardonic side of his own nature. The obvious next step for Lowell was to perceive that some, if not all, of these considerable gains could be carried over into poetry. . . .

And, of course, Lowell's prose "studies" not only suggested a new style; they also offered an almost limitless new subject. . . . In his first three books, autobiography had been oblique, almost clandestine; now he was free to be both distorting and direct. It seems never to have occurred to him that his personal history might not be of considerable public interest.[33]

But, regardless of the inner alterations in his attitude expressed in letters and in conversation with Williams, Bishop, Merwin, and others, the change in his poetry would not come until he had returned to Castine for the summer, which, perhaps the most intense social summer he spent there, included visits from William Alfred ("very brief: I can't stand the country") and Peter and Esther Brooks, and a visit from Elizabeth Bishop and Lota de Macedo Soares, who stayed in a separate house on the shore near Lowell's barn/workplace.

Philip Booth remembers very distinctly Lowell's asking him, in anticipation of Bishop's visit, "where he could get a rowboat with an outboard on it, which he should have known and did know but had forgotten, so that he could take Elizabeth fishing. They did not catch a tremendous fish. They had to be helped to start the engine and they went off across the harbor, and whatever occurred during that fishing trip I have no idea."[34] It seems more happened than met the eye. According to David Kalstone, the day in the boat revived all of Lowell's amorous compulsions, and Elizabeth Bishop, sensing that Lowell was perhaps beginning to develop a manic "high," determined to cut her visit short, though Booth remembers a big dinner party a day or two after the fishing expedition, when he helped Bishop wash dishes while they talked about the younger poets.

A few days later, Bishop and de Macedo Soares returned to New York, leaving on August 8. Lowell presented her with an 1859 edition of her favorite poet, George Herbert, which had belonged to his grandfather, with an inscription including his holograph of Herbert's line "Thy mouth was open, but thou couldst not sing," and accompanied it with a letter of apology as she left: "I see clearly now that for the last few days I have been living in a state of increasing mania—almost off the rails at the end. It almost seems as if I couldn't be with you any length of time without acting with abysmal myopia and lack of consideration. My disease, alas, gives one (during its seizures) a headless heart."[35]

However, only a few days after Bishop's departure, the poetic breakthrough took place: Lowell began writing, a man possessed: between mid-August and the end of October, Hamilton asserts, he had written eleven poems in free verse, having tried some of them in couplets first. Merwin, who was living in a cottage some distance from town, remembers, perhaps incorrectly, that Lowell dashed back to Boston: "I was puzzled when Cal left. Everything was in such flux, his life, when he wrote *Life Studies*, it was that summer in Castine, and he suddenly left, and Elizabeth was up in Castine, and Cal went back to Boston and holed up and heavens knows what he did, but he started work on *Life Studies*, he used to talk about how long it took him to get to the boil."[36] Elizabeth Hardwick remembers no departure from Castine, though she does remember her chagrin when she found that Lowell had started "versing" his prose autobiography, but she recalls this happening after their return to Boston in September.[37]

On September 10 Lowell wrote to Elizabeth Bishop:

I've been furiously writing at poems, and spent whole blue and golden Maine days in my bedroom with a ghastly utility bedside lamp on, my pajamas turning oily with sweat, and I have six poems started. They beat the big drum too much. [This was presumably before Lowell had converted them from couplets to free verse.—P.D.] There's one in a small voice that's fairly charmingly written I hope (called Skunk Hour, not in your style yet indebted a little to your Armadillo). If I can get two short lines and a word, I'll mail it to you. The others, God willing, will come to something in the course of the winter. At least I feel I have armloads of lines and leads.[38]

In his own account of writing "Skunk Hour," which instigated the two great "lunges" that would produce *Life Studies* by the end of 1958, Lowell says that the last part of the poem was written first: "first the last two stanzas, I think, and then the next-to-last two. Anyway, there was a time when I had the last four stanzas much as they now are and nothing before them."[39] If so, here are the first lines of "Skunk Hour" as written:

One dark night,
my Tudor Ford climbed the hill's skull;
I watched for love-cars. Lights turned down,
they lay together, hull to hull,
where the graveyard shelves on the town. . . .
My mind's not right.

A car radio bleats,
"Love, O careless Love. . . ." I hear

my ill-spirit sob in each blood cell,
as if my hand were at its throat. . . .
I myself am hell;
nobody's here—

only skunks, that search
in the moonlight for a bite to eat.
They march on their soles up Main Street:
white stripes, moonstruck eyes' red fire
under the chalk-dry and spar spire
of the Trinitarian Church.

I stand on top
of our back steps and breathe the rich air—
a mother skunk with her column of kittens swills the
    garbage pail.
She jabs her wedge-head in a cup
of sour cream, drops her ostrich tail,
and will not scare.[40]

This would seem to be the August version of the poem; but, although this was clearly a new voice for him, a voice speaking straight from the center, Lowell could not leave it there. Earlier that year, when he had been struggling with his prose, his wife had asked him a question that would echo through his work for the rest of his life, and make a final appearance in the last poem he ever published: "Why not say what really happened?"[41] Now he somewhat regretted the intimacy of the four stanzas he had written, and later explained its development as follows:

I found the bleak personal violence repellent. All was too close, though watching the lovers was not mine, but from an anecdote about Walt Whitman in his old age. I began to feel that real poetry came, not from fierce confessions, but from something almost meaningless but imagined. I was haunted by an image of a blue china doorknob. I never used the doorknob,* or knew what it meant, yet somehow it started the current of images in my opening stanzas. They were written in reverse order, and at last gave my poem an earth to stand on, and space to breathe.[42]

The long drought was over, the block was broken, but Lowell was still in an ascending spiral of excitement. All the while he was writing "Skunk Hour" he was also writing long letters to Bishop recalling their past together, as well as poems to her which he would not publish for some years to come. The letters were full of such manic expressions as "Asking you [to marry me] is *the* might have been for me, the one towering change, the other life that might have been had."[43] Bishop kept her distance from Lowell for the rest of her stay in the United States, except for a short visit to Boston in late September, when she first saw "Skunk Hour," and she left for Brazil on October 18. By late October Lowell had worked his way through the "versing" of a number of the family poems for his book, and he mailed a group of them to Brazil for Elizabeth Bishop to see: "My Last Afternoon with Uncle Devereux Winslow," "Commander Lowell," "Terminal Days at Beverly Farms" (all of which were versified autobiography), "Sailing Home from Rapallo" (the poem on his mother's death), "Memories of West Street and Lepke," "Man and Wife," "To Speak of Woe That Is in Marriage," the Catullan.offshoot of "Man and Wife," and, of course, "Skunk Hour," by now dedicated to Elizabeth Bishop. When she arrived in Brazil she found a parcel containing this first "lunge" of *Life Studies* and responded: "Really superb, Cal . . . A wonderful and impressive drama . . . I am green with envy of your

---

* Kalstone says he got the image from Bishop's poem "Cape Breton." He did not use the image in this poem, but it does turn up in the 1965 version of "Near the Ocean": "Empty, irresolute, ashamed,/when the sacred texts are named,/I lie here on my bed apart,/and when I look into my heart,/I discover none of the great/subjects: death, friendship, love and hate—/only old china doorknobs, sad,/ slight, useless things to calm the mad."—P.D.

kind of assurance. I feel I could write in as much detail about my Uncle Artie, say—but what would be the significance? Nothing at all. . . . The fact that it seems significant, illustrative, American, etc. gives you, I think, the confidence you display about tackling any idea or theme, *seriously*, in both writing and conversation. In some ways you are the luckiest poet I know!"[44]

"Skunk Hour" seems to have had its public premiere under remarkable circumstances: Lowell read it aloud to his friends at a burlesque theatre, as William Alfred recalls: "The Casino, was it? Dick Wilbur and Roethke had told Cal there were two things he couldn't miss, and one was an old baggy-pants comedian at the Casino, and a wonderful dancer, they said, about six foot nine, stark naked, redheaded woman named Tempest Storm . . . and there were wild-eyed sailors, it was still Scollay Square. And there was a break, while they sold the fake watches, and then Cal recited 'Skunk Hour,' in the break."[45] Imagine the reaction of the intermission audience as Lowell's nasal voice recited:

Nautilus Island's hermit
heiress still lives through winter in her Spartan cottage;
her sheep still graze above the sea.
Her son's a bishop. Her farmer
is first selectman in our village;
she's in her dotage. . . .

It was clear that the autumn was giving rise to a tide of disturbance. Another episode illuminating Lowell's mental state this autumn comes from W. S. Merwin:

Cal and I went to Brewster to see Conrad Aiken. I had an incredible car. This is one of the few times in my life that I really felt attraction to cars. When I was in college the '48 Chrysler came out, and one morning down on West Cedar Street below the house there was

a beautiful blue 1948 Chrysler convertible for sale—
for ninety dollars, and I bought it. That was the car
that I had till I left Boston. And Cal kept thinking of
places we could go in my car, because Cal of course
was not allowed to drive. And one place we went very
soon was to go down to see Conrad Aiken. Cal per-
suaded Conrad to read his new most recent poems,
and then he fell asleep while Aiken was reading them.
There were interesting things about Cal that I learned
that day. We had a flat tire on the way home, and Cal
just wandered about as though I were his garage me-
chanic, never offered to help at all. And when we got
back to Boston we'd had a few drinks here and there
and he was feeling pretty manic, and he wanted to go
to go-go bars wherever they were. We didn't go to the
Old Howard, we did go to one bar where there was a
sort of stripper. Cal was so drunk I had to take him
back home. It got back to Cal that I had told somebody,
and he was just furious. As he says in one of his poems,
when he was coming out of it, "I'm nicest when I'm
depressed." There were periods when we seemed to
be very close, but even then I was a little cautious,
suspicious of Cal, and then I reached a point when I
felt very distrustful of Cal and it became very hard to
remain friends. By the time I left Boston I wasn't sure
I really liked him. I wasn't sure that I trusted him. He
was liable to say very very mischievous things, and I
think the destructive side of him was just waiting and
watching for you to give him an opening. I think he
really wanted to be the number one center of attention
and that meant eliminating anyone else. He used to
do something that I was openly annoyed with him
about, all the time, that game about ranking poets,
which one was number one, and so on. There were a
couple of times when I said, "Cal, I just don't want to
hear that garbage anymore."[46]

At the same time, Lowell was sending his first lunge of new poems to other friends—Jarrell, Berryman, William Carlos Williams, Allen Tate—and received nothing but praise from all of them except Tate, who, all too familiar with the phases of Lowell's moon, suggested that the new poems, with the exceptions of "Skunk Hour" and "Inauguration Day: January 1953," were too autobiographical, "definitely *bad.* I do not think you ought to publish them. . . . They have no public or literary interest."[47] Whether it was this blow, from the man who had influenced Lowell's work more than any other, or merely the spiralling ascension of Lowell's "enthusiasm," as he liked to call the manic phase of his bipolar disease, his energies escalated shortly thereafter, and his mania became so intense that it resulted in his hospitalization by the end of the year. The most notorious event was the "nightmarish cocktail party" in early December which William Alfred describes as follows:

an enormous party when he didn't tell Elizabeth but he invited all these people, Katherine Biddle, who lived on the Cape, and Mr. Frost came. Mary Bundy was there, Bill and Dido Merwin. Cal had just randomly picked up the phone and called everybody: Edmund Wilson. And Elizabeth said, "Keep the drinks flowing," so that everyone wouldn't notice. Then I realized that there was something the matter with Cal. Mr. Frost went up into the study, you know it was on the top floor, and tried to engage him in conversation, but then Lowell would come down every once in a while. He tried to calm him down. That's what I mean about Mr. Frost. He was just a very good man. He didn't have to do that. Bill Merwin kept following Cal around and saying, "Tell me, what do you really think of my work?" Cal kept trying not to answer. And then: "I think you're a very very good second-rate poet." And

I said, "Oh, Jesus." And the face fell. But now I know this was a thing he would never say if he wasn't manic. And I got people so drunk that they wouldn't notice, that stately Katherine Biddle fell down the front steps in the street and her hat fell off.[48]

Merwin does not remember the insult, only these events:

Cal came down. He had been upstairs for a long time, and in the meantime Edmund Wilson was in the back room and he fell down and banged his head on the floor. The *Nation* issue about Hiss had just come out, the Fred Cook issue, and he said that nobody ever proved it against Hiss, and that the government's case was completely phony, based on fake evidence, and that Hiss was framed. I had been talking to both Cal and Elizabeth about this. Elizabeth, who was one of the *Partisan Review* people, was very defensive, and it was very important to Elizabeth that Hiss was guilty. And Cal came down, and there was this glass coffee table, and it was loaded with drinks, and everyone was standing around, and Elizabeth and I were talking. You know what a big man he was, Cal threw himself down, sort of pushing people out of the way, threw his legs up onto the coffee table, knocking off about twenty drinks, which got a lot of attention, looked up at the two of us, and said, "Bill thinks Hiss was innocent." And Elizabeth turned on me and said, "How can you say such a thing," and I began arguing with Elizabeth, who had I think by that time had a few drinks, and was very upset and started to cry, and Arthur Schlesinger came over and led her away, giving me a filthy look as though I had started the whole thing. That was Cal's doing the most mischievous thing he could think of. Every time the door opened Elizabeth would look down and groan, because Cal had not warned her about anything.[49]

And all the while Ivor and Dorothea Richards were sitting on a sofa in the middle of the room; she was saying, "What a lovely party. Everybody's having such fun!"[50]

But this was the absurdly comic side of a dangerous state of affairs: Lowell's illness became rapidly worse, and within three or four days he had to be taken to the Boston Psychopathic Hospital; neither his wife—whom he expelled from the house on a cold night—nor his doctors, whom he refused to talk to, could do anything with him. It was a close friend, William Alfred—as in the past it had so often been Peter Taylor or Blair Clark—who persuaded him to go into the hospital:

> He said that he would go into the hospital if he could sit with Harriet for a little while. Her nursery was right up by his study. He was very well behaved. He sat by her, and she was asleep in her crib: she was about a year old. And then the police came up. He started down the stairs and I was right behind him, and Harriet woke up and looked over her crib, and that's when I broke down. It was the only time I ever had a ride in a police van.[51]

> And I remember the look on Cal's face—it was as if the real Cal, the Cal I knew, were looking out at me from within the mania. It was very moving. I'd never seen him crazy. Then when we got to the police station they treated him very roughly—they wouldn't even give him a glass of water. But his school friend arrived then, and he told the cop: "You will give Mr. Lowell a glass of water and you will keep a civil tongue in your head!" It was a bit better after that. Then we took him to the hospital. It was like taking a kid to a boarding school and then having to walk away, having to leave him there. They took his clothes away. When I left, he was standing there in his underclothes.[52]

It was characteristic of Lowell's breakdowns that they began with an infatuation, attached to some "girl in summer," as he would later describe it, and the declaration that he wanted to change his life entirely. This phase had begun with Elizabeth Bishop in August, had accelerated into the profuse productivity of the autumn months, and now, in mid-December, exploded into two successive serious breakdowns. The first, which apparently began at the Boston Psychopathic Hospital, found him falling "in love" with a girl whom in his poems he called "Annie Adden." After a while he was released for a few weeks and put under medication. He took a room near Harvard Square, and, although Elizabeth Hardwick did not deem it safe to let him back in the house, he sometimes pleaded to come home. During the month of January he went back to his teaching and did indeed come home, but by the end of January he was once again manic, and this time he was admitted to McLean Hospital in Belmont and placed in a locked ward. He wrote a letter from McLean, indicative of his state of mind, to Ezra Pound in his own mental hospital in Washington: "Do you think a man who has been off his rocker as often as I have been could run for elective office and win? I have in mind the state senatorship from my district. . . ."[53]

During the month of February at McLean he fell in love again, with a different young woman, twenty and the mother of two children, who was as disturbed as he,[54] and began a poem which was later published as "Waking in the Blue." His wife took refuge for a while in New York, with the faithful Blair Clark, who was able to be of some reassurance to her. Yet the siege went on and on; not until his forty-first birthday, March 1, was he allowed to go home even for a weekend, where he began working on a poem called "Home After Three Months Away," which, after a lingering trace of mania in alluding to himself as Shakespeare's Richard II, includes the touching stanza:

Three months, three months!
Is Richard now himself again?
Dimpled with exaltation,
my daughter holds her levee in the tub.
Our noses rub,
each of us pats a stringy lock of hair—
they tell me nothing's gone.
Though I am forty-one,
not forty now, the time I put away
was child's-play. After thirteen weeks
my child still taps her cheeks
to start me shaving. . . .

And then, at the end of the poem, he describes himself, having descended from the manic royal posture struck at the beginning of the poem to the depressive dreariness that enabled him to write:

I keep no rank nor station.
Cured, I am frizzled, stale and small.[55]

The worst, it seemed, was over. Some of the new poems—"Skunk Hour," "Man and Wife," and "Memories of West Street and Lepke"—had appeared in the winter issue of *Partisan Review*. Lowell by the middle of March had been completely freed from the hospital, had returned home, was teaching again, and had "a desk drawer full of fragmentary poems and autobiography."[56] Elizabeth Hardwick later described him at this stage:

Out of the hospital, he returned to his days, which were regular, getting up early in the morning, going to his room or separate place for work. All day long he lay on the bed, propped up on an elbow. And this was his life, reading, studying and writing. The papers piled up on the floor, the books on the bed, the bottles of milk on the window sill, and the ashtray filled. . . . Cal was not the sort of poet, if there are any, for whom beautiful things come drifting down in a snowfall of gift, the labor was merciless. The discipline, the dedication, the endless adding to his *store*, by reading and studying—all of this had, in my view, much that was heroic about it.[57]

By the time Lowell returned to action, the Merwins had departed for England. By May Lowell was well enough to give a poetry reading at Smith College, where Sylvia Plath and Ted Hughes heard him read for the first time on May 5, where they perhaps heard him read some of the new poems, and where the manuscript of Plath's journal describes the poems she was reading as "tough, knotty, blazing with color and fury, most eminently sayable."[58]

In the summer of 1958 the Lowells returned to Castine, and Lowell dedicated himself to the "second lunge," completing and ordering the book he now was calling *Life Studies*, calling the whole after the section of new poems that would conclude the finished text, but he was also shuttling between Castine and teaching in the summer school at Harvard, so that he could see a new psychotherapist in Boston.[59] I can remember hearing Lowell and William Alfred give a joint reading in Sanders Theater on July 22, during which Lowell read mostly poems by other writers, including Robert Frost's "Home Burial" and W. H. Auden's "The Shield of Achilles," while Alfred read from his play-in-progress, *Hogan's Goat*. But I do not recall Lowell's reading any of the *Life Studies* poems.

By the time Lowell returned to Boston in the fall of 1958, Anne Sexton had entered his writing class at Boston University; he had met Stanley Kunitz and was going over the poems in *Life Studies* with him, and by the end of October he was ready to send off the manuscript of the book to Robert Giroux for publication the following spring. Kunitz recalls that, although he and Lowell worked together on the more recent poems in the book, it was actually the earlier poems, those written in the early 1950s, that claimed most of their attention. "Beyond the Alps" was the poem that stuck in the throat, the poem that would open the new book since it was one of the oldest—and most obscure—in the volume, recalling Lowell's first trip to Rome in the Holy Year 1950: his farewell to the Catholic church. Despite the advice that Kunitz gave him, Lowell published yet another version of this poem in *For the Union Dead* in 1964: it was one of the many examples of his compulsive rewriting, which would attain full strength when he came to the *Notebook* and *History* in the 1960s and 1970s, transforming poem after poem into unrhymed fourteen-liners. As Kunitz said later:

[His poems] always were in such rough and ragged drafts, and sloppy. And actually I don't think he had a natural sense of organization. This is, though, mostly aside from looseness in the development of a poem. I could be of most help to him in cutting out excessive extraneous matter. He loved to dump everything in a poem and then, when you told him it didn't really belong, he would put it in *another* poem. Some of those poems I thought were terrific. Some of them were chatty and rather slight, and I still think that, but certainly they gained strength by being put together and they had a sense of a life being written, exposed; and there was an intimacy of tone that had never been present before in Cal's work, and that, I had always felt, was a limitation, even in the most rhetorically successful of the earlier work. I felt there was very little that seemed to touch a quick human, where you felt that suddenly a soul was being opened. "Beyond the Alps" doesn't belong in the context, it doesn't work. I thought that the new development had a degree of accessibility that his work needed, and that it was in these poems he was reclaiming some of the territory that poetry in the nineteenth century had ceded to the novel.[60]

On November 9 Lowell presided over the reading by W. D. Snodgrass at the Poets' Theatre which has already been described on page 139, and which probably brought more of the Boston poets into one room than any other event of the year. He could not make enough of his view that Snodgrass had hit upon "a new kind of poetry. . . . His experience wouldn't be so interesting and valid if it weren't for the whimsy, the music, the balance, everything revised and placed and pondered. All that gives life to those poems on agonizing subjects comes from the craft."[61]

During the autumn of 1958, while he was still working with Kunitz, Lowell was sending copies of the poems in *Life Studies* to those friends whose opinion he had customarily valued (not, perhaps, Allen Tate this time): Randall Jarrell, William Carlos Williams, and Elizabeth Bishop, who wrote an extensive statement that was used in its entirety as a jacket blurb on the American edition, part of which reads:

> . . . with the autobiographical group called *Life Studies* the tone changes. In these poems, heart-breaking, shocking, grotesque and gentle, the unhesitant attack, the imagery and construction, are as brilliant as ever, but the mood is nostalgic and the meter is refined. A poem like *My Last Afternoon with Uncle Devereux Winslow*, or *Skunk Hour*, can tell us as much about the state of society as a volume of Henry James at his best. Whenever I read a poem by Robert Lowell I have a chilling sensation of here-and-now, of exact contemporaneity. . . . Somehow or other, by fair means or foul, and in the middle of our worst century so far, we have produced a magnificent poet.

No other copy appeared on the jacket of the first printing, only the mandatory cover illustration by Lowell's old friend Frank Parker, showing a lion recumbent at the entrance to a long corridor; and on the back a photograph of Lowell by another old friend, Robert Gardner, showing the poet seated in a white shirt and gazing off left through glasses which reflect the light from a window.

As the book was being printed and advance copies sent out to reviewers in early 1959, Lowell gave himself over to the teaching of his Boston University class, with all its talented students. By February, Plath, Sexton, and Starbuck were all attending with some regularity; and in April *Life Studies* was published by Faber and Faber in England, but without the "autobiographical fragment," "91 Revere Street," which made up the central portion of the book for American readers. The powerfully Bostonian gloss which the poignant prose memoir gave the poems did much to stimulate its American reception: the publishers had not erred in giving Lowell a contract to write his autobiography: it paid them back a hundredfold to have this prose section in the center of *Life Studies*, separating the relatively formal poems of the opening section from the more loosely written intimacies of the latter sections. It indeed attracted to this book readers who had long abandoned poetry for prose.

Perhaps it also accounts for the fact that, at the outset, the British response to the book was tepid; while the American reviews, as we have seen in the Prelude, leaped enthusiastically overboard: "Perhaps alone of living poets," wrote John Thompson in *The Kenyon Review*, "he can bear for us the role of the great poet, the man who on a very large scale sees more, feels more, and speaks more bravely about it than we ourselves can do. He can speak now of the most desperate and sordid personal experience with full dignity. Nothing need be explained, accounted for, or moralized."[62]

Lowell, however, was viewing and hearing all this applause from behind the barred windows of McLean Hospital, from which he did not emerge until late June. After he and Elizabeth Hardwick had given a large party to celebrate his cure, they returned to Castine for the summer, with Lowell commuting weekly to Boston to keep up his psychoanalytical therapy and teach a summer school course. His only poem written during the year 1959 was called "The Drinker":

> The cheese wilts in the rat-trap,
> the milk turns to junket in the cornflakes bowl,
> car keys and razor blades
> shine in an ashtray.
>
> Is he killing time? Out on the street,
> two cops on horseback clop through the April rain
> to check the parking meter violations—
> their oilskins yellow as forsythia.[63]

This year, begun in triumph and surviving collapse, was spent in recuperation, celebration, and calm. Perhaps out of revenge for the consequences of the Lowells' move to Boston in 1955, Elizabeth Hardwick, presumably during the summer, wrote a bracing, stinging excoriation of the city which was published in the December 1959 issue of *Harper's* magazine. It was a delicious attack on the decline of Boston, stemming from her own reading of the classic New England authors, and especially the letters of William James, her selection from which was published in 1960 with an introductory essay entitled "William James: An American Hero." Yet her essay on Boston drew on current experience. "There has never been anything quite like Boston as a creation of the American imagination," she wrote, "or perhaps one should say as a creation of the American scene. Some of the legend was once real, surely."

> The importance of Boston was intellectual and as its
> intellectual donations to the country have diminished,

so it has declined from its lofty symbolic meaning, to become a more lowly image, a sort of farce of conservative exclusiveness and snobbish humor. . . . The "nice little dinner party"—for this the Bostonian would sell his soul. . . . There is a curious flimsiness and indifference in the commercial life of Boston. The restaurants are, charitably, to be called mediocre; the famous seafood is only palatable when raw. . . . For the purest eccentricity there is the "famous" restaurant, Durgin-Park, which is run like a boardinghouse in a mining town.

If there were a Bohemia [George Starbuck, Sylvia Plath, Ted Hughes, L. E. Sissman, W. S. and Dido Merwin, Stephen and Agatha Fassett: no Bohemia?— P.D.], its members *would* live on Beacon Hill, the most beautiful part of Boston and, like the older parts of most cities, fundamentally classless, providing space for the rich in the noble mansions and for the people with little money in the rundown alleys. . . . For the city itself, who will live in it after the present human landmarks are gone? No doubt, some of the young people there at the moment will persevere, and as a reward for their fidelity and endurance will themselves later become monuments. . . . Boston is defective, out-of-date, vain, and lazy, but if you're not in a hurry it has a deep, secret appeal. . . . Quick minds hesitate to embrace a region too deeply compromised. They are on their guard against falling for it, but meanwhile they can enjoy its very defects, its backwardness, its slowness, its position as one of the large, possible cities on the Eastern seacoast, its private, residential charm.[64]

This was indeed a throwing down of the gauntlet, and the article caused a *frisson* of Bostonian outrage when it was published; but it has proved misleading in retrospect. The month after its publication, in January 1960, Robert

Lowell, now fully embraced by Boston as a nationally celebrated figure, was invited to deliver a new poem at the annual Boston Arts Festival, to take place in the Boston Public Garden in June. Throughout that spring, members of his Boston University class were treated to advance glimpses of a poem originally entitled "Colonel Shaw and the Massachusetts 54th," a poem that he labored over, to excellent effect, for six months.

Stephen Sandy, a Harvard graduate student of William Alfred's, had joined the auditors at Lowell's Boston University class:

It was a long trip by subway and trolley; the distance seemed to evaporate the exhausted formalities of Harvard so that the ambience of Lowell's classroom—relaxed intensity—meant a refuge that was faintly exotic and very welcome. Casual reflections on class poems were buttressed by comparisons with earlier poems, obscure or great, recalled by Lowell, smoking cigarettes at all times, gesturing above the poems he addressed. He singled out individual lines to dissect; to excoriate and often then, surprisingly, to praise—almost in the same breath. The tone of those hours was set, dominated by Lowell's soft, tentative voice with its educated Boston vowels skewed by the Southern drawl and punctuated by periods of thoughtful stillness. The only writers whose work I knew were Anne Sexton, a regular, and George Starbuck, a rare visitor because he worked at Houghton Mifflin.

It is midday, bright and warm, early May 1960. Today the class meets in a room facing the Charles; Cal sits in front of the high window, his hulking silhouette a dark outline against blue sky beyond. He has been asked to read a poem at the Boston Arts Festival in June, and though he dislikes commission work and is diffident about what he has done, he has written a poem that he would like to share with us; get our views on. It is about to go into *The Atlantic* and final changes must be made. He passes duplicated copies of a four-page text around the seminar table; for an hour we make a few comments (mostly from Sexton on my left) but largely listen, rapt to hear Cal read and then talk about what he is trying to do in "Col. Shaw and the Massachusetts 54th." Several think the title too topical and specific, going along with Cal's worry as to its "footnoteishness." By fall the poem will be called "For the Union Dead."[65]

The finished poem—preceded by the Latin inscription on the Saint-Gaudens bronze, deliberately altered by Lowell from *Relinquit omnia* to the plural, *Relinquunt omnia*, to include the black soldiers as well as Robert Gould Shaw —was read in June to a huge outdoor crowd, which demanded encores, not five hundred yards from its visible subject, the same statuary little Bobby Lowell had stared at in his childhood. It was first published, in November, in the 103rd anniversary issue of *The Atlantic Monthly*, but by the time it appeared, the Lowells had gone to New York— provisionally but in fact permanently—to return hereafter only as visitors, lecturers, celebrities. They had exchanged their Marlborough Street house for Eric Bentley's New York apartment; the next year they sold their house and took an apartment on West Sixty-seventh Street. When I interviewed Elizabeth Hardwick there recently, she told me that the decision to move from Boston to New York was her husband's, not her own. Boston had lost its Hamlet, its Falstaff, its Tamburlaine. The era had come to an end, but the great poem would always hover around the Shaw memorial near Charles Bulfinch's State House, the permanent poem across the street. Lowell, in baring his personal agony in *Life Studies*, had seemed to embody the city of his past and his ancestry. For decades into the future, readers of

For the Union Dead would discover that he had now summoned Boston's abolitionist past, for the first time, into his poetry. It was not for nothing that he had been born in the neighborhood of the poet who wrote "The Battle Hymn of the Republic." The vexed and intractable paradox of race, in the words of his poem, still "sticks like a fishbone in the city's throat."

During that winter I was invited to the Fassetts' house on Chestnut Street to hear Eric Bentley read aloud the English text of Lowell's latest and most ambitious "imitation," Racine's *Phèdre*. Two dozen friends of the poet sat around the living room in the half-dark, while Bentley rather melodramatically pronounced the lines of Lowell's extreme version of Racine's *tirades*, pausing now and then to revel in their theatrical qualities. It was an affecting performance in absentia: Lowell had left his American birthplace, turned his face eastward to the European culture that had always fascinated him, and dedicated his talents for a while to the theatre. I think he knew his talent—whether in his versions of Hawthorne and Melville, or in his *Oresteia*—would never be at home there. The theatre was no place for a poet who had to think his way into emotion. He reflected upon the subject and said so himself: "Our stage is half fish and half man, half mass culture and half a thing for the intellect. Perhaps it has the best of both worlds, but sometimes one looks on it with a yellow eye and wonders if anyone is really delighted."[66]

Life went on; Lowell in New York in 1961, like Lowell in Boston, fell "in love" again and determined to change his life once more; Elizabeth Hardwick considered returning to Boston, but thought better of it, and a reconciliation eventually took place. The rest of his life followed the bipolar pattern of destructive mania followed by depressive creativity; "I am tired. Everyone's tired of my turmoil."[67] "Pity the monsters!/Pity the monsters!"[68] In 1963 he even began coming back to Harvard to teach once a week, until, in 1970, he left Elizabeth Hardwick and moved to England to embark on a truly new life with Caroline Blackwood, which lasted about six years. Finally he returned in 1976 to share his last months with Elizabeth Hardwick in Castine and with Harvard. There, the last time I saw him, at a dinner party, he pronounced for a while on the two marriages of Thomas Hardy, and compared them to those of Robert Penn Warren. Always literary, always connecting the present to the past, and—as I swear he was in this instance—however inventive, quite wrong.

As Robert Fitzgerald, who succeeded him at Harvard, said of Lowell after his death, "Later he became, in Frost's phrase, 'easy in his harness,' and a splendid and more expansive new period began, I should say at about the time of *For the Union Dead*. At least I remember thinking and writing to him that he had made a breakthrough with that beautifully piercing meditation."[69] But that poem was Lowell's last literary effort to penetrate to the heart of Boston. His elegy to the great monument opposite the State House represents the end of the era that he presided over. After 1960 Robert Lowell's Boston was limited to Harvard, which is another country.

Chronology

Bibliography

Notes

Index

Chronology, 1954–1963

1954

JANUARY 24: L. E. Sissman, living at 35 Anderson Street, takes a job with John P. Dowd, Advertising, Boston.

JANUARY 31: Sylvia Plath returns to Smith College after recovering from suicidal breakdown.

FEBRUARY 14: Robert Lowell, teaching in Cincinnati, hears of Charlotte Lowell's stroke in Rapallo. She dies an hour before Lowell's arrival.

MARCH 21: Robert Lowell: "Mother's death . . . has about doubled my income and given some fifty thousand dollars in cash. . . . Elizabeth and I are separating."

MARCH 24: Robert Frost's eightieth-birthday celebrations.

APRIL 8: Lowell committed to Jewish Hospital in Cincinnati.

MAY: Lowell is moved to Payne Whitney Clinic in New York, starts writing prose sketches for "almost four years."

MAY 7: Fall of Dien Bien Phu in Indo-China.

MAY 17: U.S. Supreme Court hands down decision in *Brown* v. *Board of Education*.

MAY–JUNE: Televised Army-McCarthy hearings.

SUMMER: Sylvia Plath living in Cambridge with Nancy Hunter.

SEPTEMBER: Donald Hall becomes a Junior Fellow at Harvard.

Philip Booth begins to teach at Wellesley College.

W. S. Merwin publishes *The Dancing Bears* and buys a ruined farmhouse in Lacan de Loubressac, in France.

George Starbuck enters graduate study at the University of Chicago.

Richard Wilbur is assistant professor at Harvard.

Sylvia Plath, Smith senior, is studying with Alfred Kazin.

DECEMBER 2: Senator Joseph McCarthy censured by U.S. Senate.

1955

JANUARY 7: Peter Davison meets Sylvia Plath at Smith College.

FEBRUARY 10: Robert Lowell, living with Elizabeth Hardwick in Boston, is "his old self again," and is back to prose pieces.

MARCH 26: Robert Giroux leaves Harcourt, Brace to join Farrar, Straus & Cudahy.

MARCH 28: Adrienne Rich bears her first child, on her father's birthday.

APRIL: Robert Giroux sends Robert Lowell a contract for an autobiography.

SPRING–SUMMER: W. S. Merwin, now married to Dido Milroy, begins refurbishing house in Lacan.

SUMMER: Robert and Elizabeth Lowell spend summer partly in Castine, Maine. They decide to buy a house in Boston at 239 Marlborough Street.

JUNE 27: Peter Davison leaves his job at Harcourt, Brace in New York on his twenty-seventh birthday to take a position in Cambridge as assistant to the director of Harvard University Press.

JULY 23: Peter Davison and Sylvia Plath begin brief romance in Cambridge.

AUGUST 4: Joyce Ladd Sexton born. Anne Sexton soon enters psychiatric treatment with Martha Brunner-Orne to deal with spells of postpartum depression.

AUGUST 23: Sylvia Plath terminates relationship with Peter Davison.

SEPTEMBER: Robert Lowell begins teaching at Boston University. Richard Wilbur begins teaching at Wellesley College.
Sylvia Plath leaves for England.
Edwin Muir arrives to deliver the Charles Eliot Norton Lectures at Harvard.

OCTOBER 31: Richard Wilbur's translation of *The Misanthrope* opens at the Poets' Theatre, to run till November 12, Peter Davison as Alceste.

NOVEMBER 12: Robert Lowell readmitted to the Episcopalian church.

LATE FALL: Lowells move into 239 Marlborough Street, Boston.

DECEMBER 3: *Finnegans Wake*, adapted by Mary Manning Howe, is running at the Poets' Theatre.

DECEMBER 18: Peter Davison and V. R. Lang engage in a tryout play-reading at the Poets' Theatre.

1955 LAMONT POETRY SELECTION: Donald Hall, *Exiles and Marriages* (Viking).

The Diamond Cutters by Adrienne Rich published by Harper & Row.

1956

JANUARY 23: Peter Davison enters psychotherapy, lasting till 1959.

FEBRUARY 25: Sylvia Plath, at Cambridge University, depressed, seeks psychiatric help.

FEBRUARY 26: Sylvia Plath meets Ted Hughes at party.

FEBRUARY 27: Sylvia Plath writes "Pursuit."

MARCH 23: Sylvia Plath spends night with Hughes in London, then leaves for Paris.

APRIL 2: Peter Davison accepts job as editor at Atlantic Monthly Press, Boston, to begin in September.

APRIL 4: Rehearsals begin for *The Compromise* by John Ashbery, played by V. R. Lang, Robert J. Lurtsema, Peter Davison, Frank O'Hara, et al., at the Poets' Theatre.

APRIL 13: Sylvia Plath leaves Rome to rejoin Ted Hughes.

JUNE 16: Sylvia Plath marries Ted Hughes in London.

JULY 19: Death of V. R. Lang in Boston, from Hodgkin's disease.

JULY 19: John Foster Dulles cancels loan to Egypt for Aswan High Dam.

JULY 26: Abdel Nasser seizes Suez Canal.

AUGUST 3: Anne Sexton, patient in Westwood Lodge, becomes patient of Dr. Martin Orne.

AUGUST 27: W. S. Merwin flies from London to Boston to take up Rockefeller Foundation fellowship at Poets' Theatre, promptly settling in at 76 West Cedar Street, Beacon Hill.

SEPTEMBER (DATE UNCERTAIN): W. S. Merwin reads his poems at Wellesley, arranged by Philip Booth; first meets Donald Hall and Adrienne Rich.

SEPTEMBER 4: Peter Davison begins work at the Atlantic Monthly Press.

SEPTEMBER 30: Sylvia Plath writes long letter to Davison regarding Ted Hughes, etc.

OCTOBER: Hungarian uprising.

OCTOBER 3: Peter Davison and W. S. Merwin meet for the first time.

OCTOBER 23: W. S. Merwin and Robert Lowell attend last rally for Adlai Stevenson's presidential campaign.

OCTOBER 29–NOVEMBER 6: Suez Canal crisis, ending in Anglo-French withdrawal and resignation of Anthony Eden.

NOVEMBER 4: Soviet repression of Hungarian uprising.

NOVEMBER 6: Dwight Eisenhower wins second presidential term by a landslide; Adlai Stevenson carries only seven states.

NOVEMBER 8: Anne Sexton's first suicide attempt, the day before her twenty-eighth birthday.

NOVEMBER 17: Opening night in Boston of *Candide*, book by Lillian Hellman, lyrics by Richard Wilbur, music by Leonard Bernstein.

DECEMBER (DATE UNCERTAIN): Anne Sexton tunes in to I. A. Richards' TV broadcast on "the sonnet" and writes her first.

DECEMBER 26: L. E. Sissman, now working at Kenyon & Eckhart advertising, deeply interested in sports cars and rallies.

1956 LAMONT POETRY SELECTION: *Letter from a Distant Land* by Philip Booth (Viking).

1956 YALE YOUNGER POET: John Ashbery, *Some Trees*.

Things of This World by Richard Wilbur published by Harcourt, Brace. Elizabeth Bishop wins Pulitzer Prize for *Poems* (Houghton Mifflin).

1957

Severe economic recession in 1957–1958.

JANUARY: Publication of *New Poets of England and America*, edited by Donald Hall, Louis Simpson, and Robert Pack.

JANUARY: Anne Sexton brings her first poems to her psychiatrist.

JANUARY 4: Birth of Harriet Winslow Lowell.

JANUARY 20: Anne Sexton joins John Holmes' class at Boston Center for Adult Education and meets Maxine Kumin.

FEBRUARY 27: Ted Hughes' *The Hawk in the Rain* wins the first Harper & Row publication contest. Sylvia Plath: "I am so glad Ted is first."

MARCH: Robert Lowell tours West Coast and encounters Beat poets.

MARCH 11: Charles Van Doren gets the "wrong" answer on "The $64,000 Question."

MARCH 18: Randall Jarrell lectures at Brandeis University.

LATE MARCH: George Kirstein writes W. S. Merwin regarding his sea poems in *Green with Beasts* (1956).

APRIL: Fidel Castro visits the United States.

Mary Gray Harvey, Anne Sexton's mother, undergoes radical mastectomy.

APRIL OR MAY: William Carlos Williams reads at "Wellesley," Robert Lowell sitting in the aisle; three thousand present.

MAY: William Carlos and Floss Williams stay with Lowells in Boston.

LATE MAY: Elizabeth Bishop, visiting Lowells in Boston, reads her poem "The Armadillo" to them.

MAY 27: Anne Sexton attempts suicide.

JUNE: Lowells to Castine for the summer.

LATE JUNE: W. S. Merwin embarks with George Kirstein on hurricane-threatened voyage from Mamaroneck, New York, to Tenants Harbor, Maine.

JUNE 29: Aurelia Plath gives open house for Ted Hughes and Sylvia Plath in Wellesley on their arrival in U.S.

JUNE/JULY: Donald Hall leaves Harvard for the University of Michigan; Richard Wilbur leaves Wellesley College for Wesleyan University.

JULY 1: Peter Davison moves to 76 Buckingham Street, Cambridge.

JULY: Richard Wilbur recommends Stanley Kunitz' *Selected Poems* to the Atlantic Monthly Press.

LATE JULY: Merwins living in shack outside Castine; Elizabeth Bishop visits the Lowells there with Lota de Macedo Soares. Peter Davison, reading the manuscript of Stanley Kunitz' *Selected Poems*, writes his own first poem, "The Winner."

AUGUST 9: Elizabeth Bishop cuts short her stay in Castine, owing to Lowell's "mania." He starts feverishly writing poems.

MID-AUGUST–OCTOBER: Lowell "completed eleven poems in verse."

SEPTEMBER: William Alfred and others hear Robert Lowell reciting "Skunk Hour" at the Casino Burlesque.

SEPTEMBER: Maxine Kumin and Anne Sexton begin new term in Holmes' poetry class by exchanging phone numbers and reading poems to each other.

George Starbuck and his family arrive in Boston, take an apartment on Pinckney Street, and Starbuck studies with Archibald MacLeish at Harvard.

W. S. Merwin reads his poems at the DeCordova Museum in Lincoln.

SEPTEMBER 20: U.S. publication of *The Hawk in the Rain* by Ted Hughes, warmly reviewed by Merwin in *The New York Times Book Review* on October 6.

OCTOBER 11: Lowell writes to Jarrell, admiring Philip Larkin and enclosing "Skunk Hour." On October 24 he recommends W. D. Snodgrass' "Heart's Needle" to Jarrell.

OCTOBER 31: L. E. Sissman divorces Barbara Klauer, having moved into new apartment at 58 Anderson Street. Anne Klauer, newly divorced, is living at 63 West Cedar Street, across from W. S. Merwin.

DECEMBER 3: Allen Tate writes Lowell disapproving his new poems.

DECEMBER, DATE UNKNOWN: Nightmarish party at 239 Marlborough Street sprung by Robert Lowell, including Robert Frost, Edmund and Elena Wilson, William and Dido Merwin, Katherine Biddle, William Alfred, Arthur Schlesinger, McGeorge and Mary Bundy, Ivor and Dorothea Richards, et al.

DECEMBER 14: Elizabeth Bishop writes Lowell admiringly from Brazil about the new *Life Studies.*

DECEMBER, DATE UNKNOWN: Lowell's discharge from Boston Psychopathic Hospital.

DECEMBER 20: Centennial banquet for *The Atlantic Monthly,* founded 1857.

1957 LAMONT POETRY SELECTION: Daniel Berrigan, *Time Without Number* (Macmillan).

1957 YALE YOUNGER POET: James Wright, *The Green Wall.*

1958

JANUARY: Philip Booth sits in for John Holmes at the Boston Center for Adult Education.

The Partisan Review publishes Lowell's "Man and Wife," "Memories of West Street and Lepke," and "Skunk Hour."

JANUARY 4: Sylvia Plath has decided "to stop teaching and start writing."

LATE JANUARY: Robert Lowell, having returned to teaching and to Marlborough Street, begins a new outside love affair.

FEBRUARY: Peter Davison's first published poem, "The Winner," appears in *The Atlantic Monthly.*

FEBRUARY 2: Robert Lowell committed to McLean Hospital, begins writing "Waking in the Blue."

MARCH 2: Lowell, hospitalized but granted weekend furloughs, begins writing "Home After Three Months Away" and translating Montale.

MARCH 8: Publication of Archibald MacLeish's play *J.B.*

MARCH 15: Lowell is released from McLean's.
Sexton reads "Heart's Needle," begins correspondence with Snodgrass.

LATE MARCH: W. S. and Dido Merwin leave Boston to return to Europe.
L. E. Sissman and Anne Klauer move to Still River (near Harvard, Massachusetts).

MARCH 30: Peter Davison entertains Sylvia Plath and Ted Hughes.

APRIL: Anne Sexton's first publication, "Eden Revisited." She also brings her second daughter home from her husband's parents' house.
Archibald MacLeish's *J.B.* produced at Yale.

APRIL 11: Ted Hughes reads poems at Harvard; Adrienne Rich and Sylvia Plath meet.

APRIL 18: Ezra Pound released from St. Elizabeth's Hospital, Washington, D.C.

MAY 5: Lowell reads his poetry at Smith, event attended by Sylvia Plath and Ted Hughes.

LATE MAY: Anne Sexton, finishing her term with John Holmes, has written sixty-five poems.

JUNE: Philip Booth begins Guggenheim Fellowship.

JUNE 13: Sylvia Plath records her poems for the Woodberry Poetry Room Collection at Harvard.

JUNE 20: Sylvia Plath battling depression in Northampton, Massachusetts.

JUNE 21: Stanley Kunitz marries Elise Asher.

JUNE 30: Ezra Pound sails for Italy.

JULY–AUGUST: Robert Lowell shuttling between Harvard summer school and Castine. In second "lunge" completes the manuscript of *Life Studies*.

JULY 15–19: United States troops land in Lebanon.

JULY 22: Robert Lowell and William Alfred give joint reading at Sanders Theater, Harvard.

AUGUST: Peter Davison travels to the Caribbean, returning August 18 to find his mother in the hospital with cancer.

MID-AUGUST: Sexton goes to Antioch Writers' Conference to work with Snodgrass.

SEPTEMBER: Stanley Kunitz, visiting at Brandeis part-time for the academic year, takes an apartment in Cambridge, at 1200 Massachusetts Avenue, and soon meets Robert Lowell.

Anne Sexton joins Robert Lowell's Boston University writing class.

Maxine Kumin begins teaching at Tufts.

John Holmes begins private writing group, including Sexton, Kumin, Starbuck.

SEPTEMBER 1: Sylvia Plath and Ted Hughes move to Boston, 9 Willow Street, Beacon Hill.

SEPTEMBER 11: Sylvia Plath reports, "Already I look at job ads."

SEPTEMBER 16: Peter Davison visits Sylvia Plath and Ted Hughes on Willow Street.

SEPTEMBER 28: Ted Hughes reads at Poets' Theatre.

OCTOBER 7: Sylvia Plath starts job at Massachusetts General Hospital.

Peter Davison meets Jane Truslow in New York.

OCTOBER 31: Robert Lowell has sent *Life Studies* to Robert Giroux, at Farrar, Straus & Cudahy.

NOVEMBER: Anne Sexton's father has a stroke. Her mother's breast cancer metastasizes. Sexton herself is hospitalized, while writing "The Double Image."

NOVEMBER 4: John F. Kennedy elected to second senatorial term by a landslide.

NOVEMBER 9: W. D. Snodgrass reads his poems at the Poets' Theatre, introduced by Robert Lowell.

NOVEMBER 16: Robert Frost, Sylvia Plath, Ted Hughes, et al. at Peter Davison's house.

NOVEMBER 27: L. E. Sissman and Anne Klauer are married in New Hampshire.

NOVEMBER 28: John Malcolm Brinnin host to a party where Peter Davison and Jane Truslow meet Philip Booth, Howard Moss, and others.

DECEMBER 4: William Carlos Williams writes Robert Lowell approving *Life Studies*.

DECEMBER 10: Sylvia Plath has entered psychotherapy with Dr. Ruth Beuscher.

DECEMBER 11: *J.B.* by Archibald MacLeish opens at the ANTA Theater in New York.

DECEMBER 17: Sylvia Plath has a "tirade with Ted over Jane Truslow."

DECEMBER 26: Peter Davison and Jane Truslow are engaged.

DECEMBER 30: *The Hudson Review* accepts Anne Sexton's "The Double Image."

1958 LAMONT POETRY SELECTION: Ned O'Gorman, *The Night of the Hammer* (Harcourt).

1958 YALE YOUNGER POET: John Hollander, *A Crackling of Thorns*.

1959

JANUARY 2: Fidel Castro takes control of Havana.

JANUARY 3: Alaska admitted to Union as forty-ninth state.

JANUARY 10: *Yale Review* rejects Sylvia Plath's "Johnny Panic and the Bible of Dreams."

JANUARY 13–15: Anne Sexton hospitalized.

JANUARY 28: The Lowells are entertained at dinner by the Hugheses.

Sylvia Plath reads *The Diamond Cutters*.

FEBRUARY: Sylvia Plath begins attending Lowell's class.

FEBRUARY 8: John Holmes writes Sexton advising her not to publish *To Bedlam and Part Way Back*, and she responds with "For John, Who Begs Me Not to Enquire Further."

FEBRUARY 15: Reading by Richard Wilbur at Harvard. Party afterward at John Holmes' house, including Lowell, Kunitz, Brinnin, Isabella Gardner, Wilbur, Holmes, David Ferry, Philip Booth, Maxine Kumin, Starbuck, Hughes and Plath, Sexton, et al.

FEBRUARY 22: Sylvia Plath records her poems (the second time) for Stephen Fassett.

MARCH 1: Anne Sexton's first public reading at the Poets' Theatre, with Arthur Freeman, Maxine Kumin, George Starbuck, presided over by William Alfred. Repeated following week.

MARCH 6: Peter Davison terminates psychotherapy.

MARCH 7: Peter Davison and Jane Truslow are married in New York, depart for honeymoon in Vermont, returning to Cambridge March 20.

MARCH 8: Sylvia Plath visits her father's grave in Winthrop, writes "Electra on Azalea Path."

MARCH 10: Anne Sexton's mother dies of cancer.

APRIL: Publication of *Life Studies* in England.
Sexton/Starbuck/Plath friendship blossoms in cocktail sessions after Lowell classes, probably on April 1, 7, 14, 21, 28.

APRIL 10: Ted Hughes learns he has won Guggenheim Fellowship. Sylvia Plath and Ted Hughes receive notice of admission to Yaddo for autumn visit.

APRIL 28: Probable date of Lowell's breakdown in class at Boston University.

MAY 1: Lowell back in McLean's.

MAY 3: Plath reports, "Felt our triple-martini afternoons at the Ritz breaking up."

MAY 11: Official publication date of *Life Studies*. Also the date of announcement of Pulitzer Prize in poetry for 1958 to Stanley Kunitz.

MAY 12: Stanley Kunitz reads at Tufts University.

MAY 19: Anne Sexton's *To Bedlam and Part Way Back* accepted for publication by Houghton Mifflin.

MAY 24: Death of John Foster Dulles.

MAY 31: Plath and Hughes dine at house of Peter and Jane Davison.

JUNE: Lowell released from McLean.
Kunitz departs Cambridge for Cape Cod and New York.

JUNE 3: Anne Sexton's father dies of a stroke.

MID-JUNE: Lowells give a big party, where Anne Sexton and Adrienne Rich meet for the only time.

LATE JUNE: Hugheses leave for transcontinental auto trip.

JUNE 25: Davison's *Atlantic Monthly* review of *Life Studies*: "The reader remains more fascinated by Lowell's life than by his poems."

JULY 17: Sexton begins writing "All My Pretty Ones."

AUGUST: Sexton and Starbuck are at Bread Loaf Writers' Conference together. Lowell writes blurb for *Bedlam*.

AUGUST 7: *Macbeth* performed at Opera House by Bristol Old Vic. Davison and Lowell attend, discuss play at intermission.

AUGUST 21: Hawaii admitted to Union as fiftieth state.

SEPTEMBER: Davison writing poems in premonitory shadow of his mother's death.

SEPTEMBER 10: Sylvia Plath and Ted Hughes arrive at Yaddo.

SEPTEMBER 24: Natalie Davison dies of cancer.

OCTOBER: Anne Sexton undergoes surgery, writes "Dancing the Jig," and "The Operation."

OCTOBER 19: Plath writes "The Manor Garden" and "The Colossus" at Yaddo.

NOVEMBER 11: Davison finishes "Not Forgotten."

NOVEMBER 19: Sexton finishes "All My Pretty Ones."

LATE NOVEMBER: Plath and Hughes leave Yaddo before Thanksgiving.

NOVEMBER 25: Elizabeth Hardwick's "Boston: A Lost Ideal" appears in *Harper's*, and, later, in *Encounter*.

DECEMBER 10: Anne Sexton gives Morris Gray Poetry Reading at Harvard.

DECEMBER 25: Doris Holmes presents her husband "A Christmas Garland for John Holmes," celebratory verses written by most New England poets.

1959 LAMONT POETRY SELECTION: Donald Justice, *The Summer Anniversaries* (Wesleyan).

1959 YALE YOUNGER POET: William Dickey, *Of the Festivity.*

1960

JANUARY 3: Robert Lowell working on a poem commissioned by the Boston Arts Festival, while his wife edits and introduces *The Selected Letters of William James.*

JANUARY 25: Davison's "To a Mad Friend" appears in the February *Harper's*.

FEBRUARY: Anne Sexton begins correspondence with James Wright. James Michie of William Heinemann Ltd. accepts Sylvia Plath's *The Colossus and Other Poems* for U.K. publication.

SPRING: Sit-ins for civil rights begin in the South, spread rapidly.

MARCH (DATE UNCERTAIN): Anne Sexton's husband's father killed in an auto accident.

MARCH 18: Ted Hughes' *Lupercal* published in London.

MARCH 23: Robert Lowell receives National Book Award for *Life Studies*, delivers remarks on "cooked" and "raw" poetry.

APRIL: Theodore Roethke reads at Harvard, Brandeis, Wellesley.

APRIL 1: Frieda Hughes born in London.

APRIL 22: Sexton's *To Bedlam and Part Way Back* is published.

MAY: Anne Sexton has an abortion.

MAY 2: Ted Hughes and Sylvia Plath dine with Peter and Jane Davison in London.

JUNE 4: Robert Lowell reads "For the Union Dead" at the Boston

Arts Festival in the Boston Public Garden, then repairs to Castine.

JULY 12: John F. Kennedy nominated for presidency at Democratic party convention in Los Angeles.

LATE JULY: Anne Sexton and James Wright go to Long Island for a poetry festival.

AUGUST 9: James Michie submits *The Colossus* to Atlantic Monthly Press for U.S. publication.

SEPTEMBER: The Lowells (his decision) move to New York, exchanging their Boston house for Eric Bentley's apartment at 194 Riverside Drive.

SEPTEMBER 18: Peter Davison declines *The Colossus*.

FALL 1960: W. S. Merwin returns to New York, living on the Lower East Side.

OCTOBER 25: "For the Union Dead" appears in *The Atlantic Monthly*'s November issue.

(DATE UNCERTAIN): Merwin's *The Drunk in the Furnace* is published by Macmillan.

DECEMBER: Lowell resigns from Boston University. Hardwick finds them a New York apartment on West Sixty-seventh Street before the turn of the year.

1960 YALE YOUNGER POET: George Starbuck, *Bone Thoughts*.

1960 LAMONT POETRY SELECTION: Robert Mezey, *The Lovemaker* (Hillside Press, Mt. Vernon, Iowa).

1961

FEBRUARY: Robert Lowell falls in love again, resulting in his hospitalization on March 3 at New York Presbyterian Hospital for six weeks. His *Imitations* is published by Farrar, Straus.

APRIL 19: Anne Sexton, Peter Davison, and George Starbuck give poetry readings at the Cornell University Arts Festival, concurrently with the Bay of Pigs disaster.

JUNE 30: The Lowells retreat to Castine; the Marlborough Street house is sold.

SEPTEMBER: Peter Davison reviews Hughes' *Lupercal* and Merwin's *The Drunk in the Furnace* in *The Atlantic Monthly*. Stanley Kunitz reviews *Lupercal* in *Harper's*.

Philip Booth leaves Wellesley to take up a professorship at Syracuse University. His book *The Islanders* published by Viking.

1961 LAMONT POETRY SELECTION: X. J. Kennedy, *Nude Descending a Staircase* (Doubleday).
1961 YALE YOUNGER POET: Alan Dugan, *Poems*.

1962

JANUARY 22: Robinson Jeffers dies.
JUNE 22: John Holmes dies.
New Poets of England and America: Second Selection is published, including Booth, Merwin, Plath, Rich, Sexton, Starbuck.
NOVEMBER 16: Sylvia Plath sends thirteen poems to Peter Davison at *The Atlantic Monthly*, six of which were published in *Ariel* (1966), four in *Winter Trees* (1972), and three of which were not published until *The Collected Poems* (1981). (*The Atlantic Monthly* accepted "The Arrival of the Bee Box" and "Wintering" on December 4. These were the last poems accepted by any magazine during Sylvia Plath's lifetime. They appeared in the April 1963 *Atlantic Monthly* after Sylvia Plath's death.)

1963

JANUARY 14: *The Bell Jar*, by "Victoria Lucas," published in London by William Heinemann Ltd.
JANUARY 29: Robert Frost dies.
FEBRUARY 11: Sylvia Plath dies.
MARCH 4: William Carlos Williams dies.
JUNE: L. E. Sissman starts publishing his accumulated poems and writing new ones at a rapidly accelerating rate.
AUGUST 4: Theodore Roethke dies.

Bibliography

I. Books

Alexander, Paul. *Rough Magic: A Biography of Sylvia Plath.* New York: Viking Penguin, 1991.

———, ed. *Ariel Ascending: Writings about Sylvia Plath.* New York: Harper & Row, 1985.

Birkerts, Sven. *The Electric Life: Essays on Modern Poetry.* New York: William Morrow, 1989.

Bishop, Elizabeth. *The Complete Poems 1927–1979.* New York: Farrar, Straus, Giroux, 1983.

———. *One Art: Elizabeth Bishop Letters.* Selected and edited by Robert Giroux. New York: Farrar, Straus, Giroux, 1994.

Booth, Philip. *Relations: Selected Poems, 1950–1985.* New York: Viking Press, 1986.

Brinnin, John Malcolm. *Dylan Thomas in America: An Intimate Journal.* Boston: Atlantic-Little, Brown, 1955.

———, and Bill Reid, eds. *The Modern Poets: An American-British Anthology.* Photographs by Rollie McKenna. 2nd ed. New York: McGraw-Hill, 1970.

Brunner, Edward J. *Poetry as Labor and Privilege: The Writings of W. S. Merwin.* Urbana and Chicago: University of Illinois Press, 1991.

Butscher, Edward. *Sylvia Plath: Method and Madness.* New York: Seabury Press, 1976.

———, ed. *Sylvia Plath: The Woman and the Work.* New York: Dodd Mead, 1977.

Colburn, Steven E., ed. *Anne Sexton: Telling the Tale.* Ann Arbor: University of Michigan Press, 1988.

Coles, Robert. *The Call of Stories: Teaching and the Moral Imagination.* Boston: Houghton Mifflin Company, A Peter Davison Book, 1989.

Cooper, Jane Roberta, ed. *Reading Adrienne Rich: Reviews and Re-Visions, 1951–1981.* Ann Arbor: University of Michigan Press, 1984.

Davison, Peter. *The Breaking of the Day and Other Poems*. Preface by Dudley Fitts. New Haven: Yale University Press, 1964.

—. *The City and the Island*. New York: Atheneum Publishers, 1966.

—. *The Great Ledge*. New York: Alfred A. Knopf, 1989.

—. *Half Remembered: A Personal History*. Revised edition. Brownsville, Oregon: Story Line Press, 1991.

—. *One of the Dangerous Trades: Essays on the Work and Workings of Poetry*. Ann Arbor: University of Michigan Press, 1991.

—. *Praying Wrong: New and Selected Poems, 1957–1984*. New York: Atheneum Publishers, 1984.

Donaldson, Scott. *Archibald MacLeish: An American Life*. Boston: Houghton Mifflin Company, A Peter Davison Book, 1992.

Frost, Robert. *Complete Poems of Robert Frost*. New York: Henry Holt & Company, 1949.

—. *In the Clearing*. New York: Holt, Rinehart & Winston, 1962.

Gooch, Brad. *City Poet: The Life and Times of Frank O'Hara*. New York: Alfred A. Knopf, 1993.

Hall, Donald. *Old and New Poems*. New York: Ticknor & Fields, 1990.

—, *Their Ancient Glittering Eyes: Remembering Poets and More Poets*. New York: Ticknor & Fields, 1992.

Hall, Donald, and Robert Pack, eds. *New Poets of England and America: Second Selection*. New York: Meridian Books, 1962.

—, Robert Pack, and Louis Simpson, eds. *New Poets of England and America*. Introduction by Robert Frost. New York: Meridian Books, 1957.

Hecht, Anthony. *Obbligati: Essays in Criticism*. New York: Atheneum Publishers, 1986.

Heilbrun, Carolyn G. *Writing a Woman's Life*. New York: W. W. Norton, 1988.

Hillier, Brett C. *Elizabeth Bishop: Life and the Memory of It*. Berkeley: University of California Press, 1993.

Howard, Richard. *Alone With America: Essays on the Art of Poetry in the United States Since 1950*. New York: Atheneum Publishers, 1969.

Hulbert, Ann. *The Interior Castle: The Art and Life of Jean Stafford*. New York: Alfred A. Knopf, 1992.

Kalstone, David. *Becoming a Poet: Elizabeth Bishop with Mar-*

ianne Moore and Robert Lowell. New York: Farrar, Straus & Giroux, Noonday Press, 1991.

Kroll, Judith. *Chapters in a Mythology: The Poetry of Sylvia Plath.* New York: Harper/Colophon, 1976.

Kumin, Maxine. *Halfway.* New York: Holt, Rinehart & Winston, 1961.

———. *Our Ground Time Here Will Be Brief.* New York: Viking, 1982.

———. *The Privilege.* New York: Harper & Row, 1965.

———. *To Make a Prairie: Essays on Poets, Poetry, and Country Living.* Ann Arbor: University of Michigan Press, 1979.

Kunitz, Stanley. *Interviews and Encounters with Stanley Kunitz.* Edited by Stanley Moss. New York: Sheep Meadow Press, 1993.

———. *A Kind of Order, a Kind of Folly: Essays and Conversations.* Boston: Atlantic-Little, Brown, 1975.

———. *Next-to-Last Things: New Poems and Essays.* Boston/New York: Atlantic Monthly Press, 1985.

———. *The Poems of Stanley Kunitz, 1928–1978.* Boston: Atlantic-Little, Brown, 1979.

———. *Selected Poems, 1928–1958.* Boston: Atlantic-Little, Brown, 1958.

Lang, V. R. *Poems & Plays.* Preface by Alison Lurie. New York: Random House, 1975.

Langer, Elinor. *Josephine Herbst: The Story She Could Never Tell.* Boston: Atlantic-Little, Brown, 1984.

Lowell, Robert. *Collected Prose.* Edited and introduced by Robert Giroux. New York: Farrar, Straus & Giroux, 1987.

———. *For the Union Dead.* New York: Farrar, Straus & Giroux, 1964.

———. *Imitations.* 2nd ed. New York: Farrar, Straus & Giroux, Noonday Press, 1963.

———. *Life Studies.* New York, Farrar, Straus & Cudahy, 1959.

———. *Lord Weary's Castle.* New York: Harcourt, Brace, 1946.

———. *The Mills of the Kavanaughs.* New York: Harcourt, Brace, 1951.

———. *Selected Poems.* New York: Farrar, Straus & Giroux, 1976.

MacLeish, Archibald. *J.B.: A Play in Verse.* Boston: Houghton Mifflin Company, 1958.

———. *Letters of Archibald MacLeish, 1907–1981.* Edited by R. H. Winnick. Boston: Houghton Mifflin Company, 1982.

————. *New and Collected Poems, 1917–1976*. Boston: Houghton Mifflin Company, 1976.

Malcolm, Janet. *The Silent Woman: Sylvia Plath & Ted Hughes*. New York: Alfred A. Knopf, 1994.

Mariani, Paul. *William Carlos Williams: A New World Naked*. New York: McGraw-Hill, 1981.

Merwin, W. S. *The Drunk in the Furnace*. New York: Macmillan, 1960.

————. *The First Four Books of Poems*. New York: Atheneum Publishers, 1975.

————. *Houses and Travellers: Prose*. New York: Atheneum Publishers, 1977.

————. *The Lost Upland*. New York: Alfred A. Knopf, 1992.

————. *The Moving Target*. New York: Atheneum Publishers, 1963.

————. *The Rain in the Trees*. New York: Alfred A. Knopf, 1990.

————. *Regions of Memory: Uncollected Prose, 1949–82*. Edited and with an introduction by Ed Folsom and Cary Nelson. Urbana and Chicago: University of Illinois Press, 1987.

————. *Selected Poems*. New York: Atheneum Publishers, 1988.

————. *Travels: Poems*. New York: Alfred A. Knopf, 1993.

————. *Unframed Originals: Recollections*. New York: Atheneum Publishers, 1982.

Meyers, Jeffrey. *Manic Power: Robert Lowell and His Circle*. New York: Arbor House, 1987.

————, ed. *Robert Lowell: Interviews and Memoirs*. Ann Arbor: University of Michigan Press, 1988.

Michelson, Bruce. *Wilbur's Poetry: Music in a Scattering Time*. Amherst: University of Massachusetts Press, 1991.

Middlebrook, Diane Wood. *Anne Sexton: A Biography*. Boston: Houghton Mifflin Company, A Peter Davison Book, 1991.

————, and Marilyn Yalom, eds. *Coming to Light: American Women Poets in the Twentieth Century*. Ann Arbor: University of Michigan Press, 1985.

Molière [Jean Baptiste Poquelin]. *The Misanthrope*. Translated by Richard Wilbur. New York: Harcourt, Brace, 1955.

O'Connell, Shaun. *Imagining Boston: A Literary Landscape*. Boston: Beacon Press, 1990.

Ostriker, Alicia. *Stealing the Language: The Emergence of Women's Poetry in America*. Boston: Beacon Press, 1986.

———. *Writing Like a Woman*. Ann Arbor: University of Michigan Press, 1983.

Plath, Sylvia. *Ariel*. New York: Harper & Row, 1966.

——— [Victoria Lucas, pseudonym]. *The Bell Jar*, London: Heinemann, 1963.

———. *The Collected Poems*. Edited by Ted Hughes. New York: Harper & Row, 1981.

———. *The Colossus and Other Poems*. New York: Alfred A. Knopf, 1962.

———. *Crossing the Water*. London: Faber & Faber, 1971.

———. *Johnny Panic and the Bible of Dreams: Short Stories, Prose, and Diary Extracts*. New York: Harper & Row, 1979.

———. *The Journals of Sylvia Plath*. Foreword by Ted Hughes; Ted Hughes, consulting editor, and Frances McCullough, editor. New York: Dial Press, 1982.

———. *Letters Home: Correspondence 1950–1963*. Selected and edited with commentary by Aurelia Schober Plath. New York: Harper & Row, 1975.

———. *Winter Trees*. New York: Harper & Row, 1972.

Prunty, Wyatt. *"Fallen from the Symboled World": Precedents for the New Formalism*. New York and Oxford: Oxford University Press, 1990.

Rector, Liam, ed. *The Day I Was Older: On the Poetry of Donald Hall*. Santa Cruz, California: Story Line Press, 1989.

Rich, Adrienne. *An Atlas of the Difficult World: Poems 1988–1991*. New York: W. W. Norton, 1991.

———. *Blood, Bread, and Poetry: Selected Prose, 1979–1985*. New York: W. W. Norton, 1986.

———. *The Fact of a Doorframe: Poems, Selected and New, 1950–1984*. New York: W. W. Norton, 1984.

———. *Of Woman Born: Motherhood as Experience and Institution*. 10th anniversary edition. New York: W. W. Norton, 1986.

———. *On Lies, Secrets, and Silence: Selected Prose 1966–1978*, New York: W. W. Norton, 1979.

———. *Your Native Land, Your Life: Poems*. New York: W. W. Norton, 1986.

———. *Time's Power: Poems 1985–1988*. New York: W. W. Norton, 1989.

———. *What Is Found There: Notebooks on Poetry and Politics*. New York: W. W. Norton, 1993.

Rose, Jacqueline. *The Haunting of Sylvia Plath.* London: Virago Press, 1991.

Rotella, Guy. *Three Contemporary Poets of New England: William Meredith, Philip Booth, and Peter Davison.* Boston: Twayne/ G. K. Hall, 1983.

Ruddick, Sara, and Pamela Daniels, eds. *Working It Out: 23 Women Writers, Artists, Scientists, and Scholars Talk About Their Lives and Work.* Foreword by Adrienne Rich. New York: Pantheon Books, 1977.

Rudman, Mark. *Robert Lowell: An Introduction to the Poetry.* New York: Columbia University Press, 1983.

Salinger, Wendy, ed. *Richard Wilbur's Creation.* Ann Arbor: University of Michigan Press, 1983.

Sexton, Anne. *The Complete Poems of Anne Sexton.* Foreword by Maxine Kumin. Boston: Houghton Mifflin Company, 1981.

———. *No Evil Star: Selected Essays, Interviews, and Prose.* Edited by Steven E. Colburn. Ann Arbor: University of Michigan Press, 1985.

———. *Selected Poems of Anne Sexton.* Edited with an introduction by Diane Wood Middlebrook and Diana Hume George. Boston: Houghton Mifflin Company, 1988.

———. *A Self-Portrait in Letters.* Edited by Linda Sexton and Lois Ames. Boston: Houghton Mifflin Company, 1977.

———. *To Bedlam and Part Way Back.* Boston: Houghton Mifflin Company, 1960.

Simpson, Eileen. *Poets in Their Youth: A Memoir.* New York: Farrar, Straus & Giroux, Noonday Press, 1990.

Sissman, L. E. *Dying: An Introduction.* Boston: Atlantic-Little, Brown, 1967.

———. *Hello, Darkness: The Collected Poems of L. E. Sissman.* Edited and with a preface by Peter Davison. Boston: Atlantic-Little, Brown, 1978.

———. *Innocent Bystander: The Scene from the 70's* (essays). Foreword by John Updike. New York: Vanguard Press, 1975.

Slobodkin, Salem. *Meditations on a Great Man Gone and Other Poems.* Preface by Richard Eberhart. Freeport, Maine: Bond Wheelwright Company, 1965.

Starbuck, George. *The Argot Merchant Disaster: Poems New and Selected.* Boston: Atlantic-Little, Brown, 1982.

———. *Bone Thoughts.* Introduction by Dudley Fitts. New Haven: Yale University Press, 1960.

———. *White Paper: Poems.* Boston: Atlantic-Little, Brown, 1966.

Steiner, Nancy Hunter. *A Closer Look at Ariel: A Memory of Sylvia Plath*. Introduction by George Stade. New York: Harper's Magazine Press, 1973.

Stevenson, Anne. *Bitter Fame: A Life of Sylvia Plath*. Boston: Houghton Mifflin Company, A Peter Davison Book, 1989. (I have used the 1990 Houghton Mifflin paperback edition, which contains some useful corrections.)

Updike, John. *Collected Poems*. New York: Alfred A. Knopf, 1993.

————. *Self-Consciousness: Memoirs*. New York: Alfred A. Knopf, 1989.

Van Dyne, Susan R. *Women's Voices in American Poetry: "the beauty of inflections/or the beauty of innuendoes."* Northampton, Massachusetts: Friends of the Smith College Library, 1981.

Wagner-Martin, Linda. *Sylvia Plath: A Biography*. New York: Simon & Schuster, 1987.

Warren, Robert Penn. Introduction to *Fifty Years of American Poetry*. Anniversary volume for the Academy of American Poets. Wood Engravings by Barry Moser. New York: Harry N. Abrams, 1984.

————. *Poetry and Democracy*. Cambridge: Harvard University Press, 1975.

Wilbur, Richard. *Advice to a Prophet and Other Poems*. New York: Harcourt, Brace, 1961.

————. *New and Collected Poems*. New York: Harcourt Brace Jovanovich, 1988.

————. *Things of This World*. New York: Harcourt, Brace, 1956.

II. Articles

Acocella, Joan. "Perfectly Frank, Brad Gooch's 'City Poet.' " *The New Yorker*, July 19, 1993.

Kumin, Maxine. "A Poet in Secret: Writing Poems in the Interstices of Life." In *The Writer on Her Work*, vol. 2, edited and with an introduction by Janet Sternberg. New York: W. W. Norton, 1991.

Malcolm, Janet. "The Silent Woman." *The New Yorker*, August 23 and 30, 1993.

Merwin, W. S. "In the Wake of the Blackfish: A Memoir of George Kirstein." *The Paris Review*, vol. 32, no. 115 (Summer 1990).

Stitt, Peter (interviewer). "Donald Hall: The Art of Poetry XLIII." *The Paris Review* 120 (Fall 1991).

Thompson, Catherine. " 'Dawn Poems in Blood': Sylvia Plath and PMS." *Triquarterly* 80 (Winter 1990–91).

III. Archives

Robert Lowell Archives, Houghton Library, Harvard University.
Sylvia Plath Archives, Rare Book Room, Neilson Library, Smith College.
Poets' Theatre Archives, Theatre Collection, Pusey Library. Harvard University.
L. E. Sissman Archives, Houghton Library, Harvard University.

IV. Recordings

Philip Booth. Vol. 15 of *The Spoken Arts Treasury of 100 Modern American Poets* [hereafter *Spoken Arts*].
Peter Davison. Vol. 17 of *Spoken Arts*.
———. "Paradise as a Garden." Watershed Tape C-168.
Robert Frost. Vol. 1 of *Spoken Arts*.
———. *The Poet's Voice*. Harvard University Press, 1978 [hereafter *Poet's Voice*]. Recorded December 7, 1960.
———. *Robert Frost Reads from His Own Words*. Yale Series of Recorded Poets [hereafter *Yale Series*] DL 9127.
Donald Hall. Vol. 17 of *Spoken Arts*.
———. "Names of Horses." Watershed Tape C-189.
Stanley Kunitz. Vol. 9 of *Spoken Arts*.
———. *Yale Series*, YP 302.
———. "The Only Dance." Watershed Tape C-153.
Robert Lowell. Vol. 13 of *Spoken Arts*.
———. *Poet's Voice*.
———. *Robert Lowell Reading His Own Poems*. Library of Congress, PL 32–33.
Sylvia Plath. Vol. 18 of *Spoken Arts*.
———. *Plath Reads Plath*. Credo 3, Cambridge, 1975.
Adrienne Rich. Vol. 17 of *Spoken Arts*.
Anne Sexton. Vol. 17 of *Spoken Arts*.
———. *Poet's Voice*. Caedmon Records.
George Starbuck. *George Starbuck Reads from His Own Poems*. Yale Series, DL 9137.
Richard Wilbur. Vol. 14 of *Spoken Arts*.

Notes

Prelude

1. Peter Davison, "To a Mad Friend," in *The Breaking of the Day* (New Haven and London: Yale University Press, 1964), p. 37.

2. Allen Tate, letter to Robert Lowell, December 3, 1957, quoted in Ian Hamilton, *Robert Lowell: A Biography* (New York: Random House, 1982), p. 237.

3. Edmund Wilson, jacket blurb for *For the Union Dead*, by Robert Lowell (New York: Farrar, Straus & Giroux, 1964).

4. John Thompson, "Two Poets," *The Kenyon Review* 21 (Summer 1959): p. 492ff.

5. Mark Rudman, *Robert Lowell: An Introduction to the Poetry* (New York: Columbia University Press, 1983), pp. 53–94.

6. Robert Lowell, quoted in Stanley Kunitz, "Poet: 'A Slightly Laughable and Glamorous Word': A Conversation with Robert Lowell," in *A Kind of Order, A Kind of Folly: Essays and Conversations* (Boston: Atlantic-Little, Brown, 1975), p. 154.

7. Anne Sexton, "Classroom at Boston University," *Harvard Advocate* 145 (November 1961): pp. 13–14.

8. Robert Lowell, "Sylvia Plath's *Ariel*," in *Collected Prose* (New York: Farrar, Straus & Giroux, 1987), p. 124.

9. Kathleen Spivack, "Poets and Friends," in *Anne Sexton: Telling the Tale*, edited by Steven E. Colburn (Ann Arbor: University of Michigan Press, 1988), p. 28.

10. "Elegy in the Classroom," in *The Complete Poems of Anne Sexton* (Boston: Houghton Mifflin Company, 1981), p. 32.

11. This was Sexton's view of the matter, but both Plath and Starbuck played down the frequency and the intensity of the drinking bouts. Starbuck, in an interview with Diane Middlebrook, suggests there were no more than three or four "meetings."

12. *The Journals of Sylvia Plath*, May 3, 1959 (New York: Dial Press, 1982), p. 302.

13. Anthony Hecht, "Robert Lowell," in *Obbligati: Essays in Criticism* (New York: Atheneum Publishers, 1986), p. 269.
14. Stanley Kunitz, interview with author, March 28, 1991.

Chapter 1

1. "Design," in *Complete Poems of Robert Frost* (New York: Henry Holt & Company, 1949), p. 396.
2. Randall Jarrell, quoted in Lowell, "Randall Jarrell," in *Collected Prose*, p. 93.
3. Ibid.
4. Lowell, "Stanley Kunitz," in *Collected Prose*, p. 85.
5. Elizabeth Hardwick, "Boston," in *A View of My Own: Essays on Literature and Society* (New York: Farrar, Straus & Cudahy, 1962), p. 145.
6. David Kalstone, *Becoming a Poet: Elizabeth Bishop with Marianne Moore and Robert Lowell*, edited, with a preface, by Robert Hemenway, afterword by James Merrill (New York: Farrar, Straus & Giroux, Noonday Press, 1989), p. 157.
7. First published in *A Remembrance Collection of New Poems* (New York, 1959), with the dedicatory lines: "This to the memory of my great friend/Ahmed Bokhari who had me down/from Vermont to view his lump of/purest iron ore at the United Nations/in the room for meditation on/Tools and Weapons"; see *The Poetry of Robert Frost*, edited by Edward Connery Lathem (New York: Holt, Rinehart & Winston, 1969), pp. 468, 580.
8. Robert Frost, "The Objection to Being Stepped On," in *In the Clearing* (New York: Holt, Rinehart & Winston, 1962), p. 70.
9. First published in *In the Clearing* (1962); written in 1957 according to Lathem, ed., *The Poetry of Robert Frost* (1969).
10. Lowell, "Robert Frost," in *Collected Prose*, p. 207.
11. Robert Frost, unpublished manuscript letter to Edward Davison, in the Dartmouth College Library, sent from "South Shaftsbury, Vermont, October 20, 1927." Quoted by permission of the Estate of Robert Frost.
12. Diane Wood Middlebrook, *Anne Sexton: A Biography* (Boston: Houghton Mifflin, A Peter Davison Book, 1991), pp. 100, 415.
13. Philip Booth, interview with author, May 29, 1992.
14. Doris Holmes Eyges, interview with author, June 22, 1992.

15. Philip Booth, interview with author, May 29, 1992.

16. Doris Holmes Eyges, interview with author, June 22, 1992.

17. Ibid.

18. Maxine Kumin, quoted in Middlebrook, *Anne Sexton: A Biography*, p. 100.

19. Lowell, "Poets and the Theater," in *Collected Prose*, pp. 176–78.

20. Donald Hall, interview with author, September 30, 1992.

21. Alison Lurie, in Introduction to *Poems & Plays*, by V. R. Lang (New York: Random House, 1975), p. 17. This is the finest and most irreverent portrait of the theatre as well as of Violet.

22. John Malcolm Brinnin, *Dylan Thomas in America* (Boston: Atlantic-Little, Brown, 1955), p. 201.

23. William Alfred, interview with author, June 5, 1991.

24. James Schuyler, quoted in Brad Gooch, *City Poet: The Life and Times of Frank O'Hara* (New York: Alfred A. Knopf, 1993), p. 200.

25. Frank O'Hara, letter to Grace Hartigan, February 11, 1956, quoted in Gooch, *City Poet*, p. 281.

Chapter 2

1. I. A. Richards, letter to the author, March 14, 1970. (The spelling and punctuation are characteristic.)

2. I have written about this inner struggle at length in *Half Remembered: A Personal History* (New York: Harper & Row, 1973; revised and expanded paperback edition, Brownsville, Oregon: Story Line Press, 1991) and in *One of the Dangerous Trades: Essays on the Work and Workings of Poetry* (Ann Arbor: University of Michigan Press, 1991).

3. It resembled in tone Plath's letter to "E." of December 28, 1953, published in *Letters Home: Correspondence 1950–1963* (New York: Harper & Row, 1975), p. 129.

4. *The Journals of Sylvia Plath*, February 25, 1956, pp. 106–7.

5. Molière, *The Misanthrope*, translated by Richard Wilbur (New York: Harcourt, Brace, 1955), pp. 6–7.

6. Richard Wilbur, "Advice to a Prophet," in *New and Collected Poems* (New York: Harcourt Brace Jovanovich, 1988), p. 182.

7. Edwin Muir, "The Combat," in *Collected Poems* (New York: Oxford University Press, 1965), pp. 179–80.

8. T. S. Eliot, Preface to *Collected Poems*, by Edwin Muir, p. 6.

9. Stanley Kunitz, "Open the Gates," in *Selected Poems, 1928–1958* (Boston: Atlantic-Little, Brown, 1958), p. 41.

10. Kunitz, "Father and Son," in *Selected Poems*, p. 46.

11. Davison, "The Winner," *The Atlantic Monthly*, February 1958; and in *The Breaking of the Day*, p. 46.

12. Robert Penn Warren, *Democracy and Poetry* (Cambridge, Massachusetts, and London, England: Harvard University Press, 1975), p. 68.

13. Ibid., p. 69.

14. Dudley Fitts, Introduction to *The Breaking of the Day*, by Peter Davison.

15. Davison, "Artemis," in *The Breaking of the Day*, p. 48.

16. See note 2.

17. *The Journals of Sylvia Plath*, September 14, 15, and 18, 1958, pp. 259–61.

18. Jane Davison, *The Fall of a Doll's House: Three Generations of American Women and the Houses They Lived In* (New York: Holt, Rinehart & Winston, 1980), expanded and edited by our daughter, Lesley Davison, and published (1994) by Random House under the title *To Make a House a Home: Four Generations . . .*

19. See Anne Stevenson, *Bitter Fame* (Boston: Houghton Mifflin, A Peter Davison Book, 1989), pp. 224, 235, 247.

20. See epigraph to the Prelude.

21. Robert Lowell, undated and unpublished postcard to Peter Davison, 1965.

22. Maxine Kumin, interview with author, June 3, 1991.

23. Kalstone, *Becoming a Poet*, p. 185.

24. "Dialogue over a Ouija Board": see notes to *The Collected Poems of Sylvia Plath*, p. 276ff; also *The Journals of Sylvia Plath*, pp. 170–73.

Chapter 3

1. Richard Wilbur, "Love Calls Us to the Things of This World," in *Things of This World* (New York: Harcourt, Brace, 1956); p. 233 of *New and Collected Poems* (New York: Harcourt, Brace, 1988).

2. Donald Hall, *Goatfoot Milktongue Twinbird* (Ann Arbor: University of Michigan Press, 1978), p. 155.

3. Wilbur, "My Father Paints the Summer," in *New and Collected Poems*, p. 363.

4. Richard Wilbur, interview with author, July 1, 1991.

5. Bruce Michelson, *Wilbur's Poetry: Music in a Scattering Time* (Amherst: University of Massachusetts Press, 1991), p. 156.

6. Ibid., p. 41.

7. Richard Wilbur, interview with author, July 1, 1991.

8. Ibid.

9. Ibid.

10. Ibid.

11. Ibid.

12. Ibid.

13. Ibid.

14. Ibid.

15. Ibid.

16. Donald Hall, quoted in *Richard Wilbur's Creation*, edited and with an introduction by Wendy Salinger (Ann Arbor: University of Michigan Press, 1983; originally published in 1956).

17. Hyam Plutzik, "Recent Poetry," in Salinger, ed., *Richard Wilbur's Creation*, pp. 66–68.

18. Randall Jarrell, *Poetry and the Age* (New York: Vintage Books, 1959), p. 230; "Fifty Years of American Poetry" (1962), in *The Third Book of Criticism* (New York: Farrar, Straus & Giroux, 1969), pp. 331–32.

19. Richard Wilbur, interview with author, July 1, 1991.

20. Ibid.

21. Wilbur, "Ballade for the Duke of Orléans," in *New and Collected Poems*, p. 211.

22. Wilbur, "A Fire-Truck," in *New and Collected Poems*, p. 207.

23. Wilbur, "Advice to a Prophet," from *Advice to a Prophet*, in *New and Collected Poems*, p. 183.

24. Hecht, *Obbligati*, p. 130.

25. Richard Wilbur, interview with author, July 1, 1991.

26. *The Journals of Sylvia Plath*, February 19, 1959, p. 296.

27. Ibid., January 27, 1959, p. 293.

28. Lowell, "The Drinker," in *For the Union Dead*, p. 36.

29. Wilbur, "Leaving," in *New and Collected Poems*, p. 15.

30. Richard Wilbur, interview with author, July 1, 1991.

31. Wilbur, "The Death of a Toad," from *Ceremony*, in *New and Collected Poems*, p. 320.

32. Wilbur, "The Eye," in *New and Collected Poems*, p. 57.

Chapter 4

1. W. S. Merwin, "The Native," in *The Drunk in the Furnace* (New York: Macmillan, 1960), p. 45.

2. W. S. Merwin, "Flight Home," in *Regions of Memory: Uncollected Prose, 1949–82* (Urbana and Chicago: University of Illinois Press, 1984), edited and with an introduction by Ed Folsom and Cary Nelson, p. 179; first published in *Paris Review*, 1958.

3. W. S. Merwin, "In the Wake of the Blackfish: A Memoir of George Kirstein," *Paris Review*, vol. 32, no. 115 (Summer 1990): p. 279.

4. Poets' Theatre Archives, Pusey Library, Harvard University.

5. W. S. Merwin, interview with author, November 13, 1991.

6. Ibid.

7. William Alfred, interview with author, June 8, 1991.

8. W. S. Merwin, interview with author, November 13, 1991.

9. W. S. Merwin, "Variation on a Line by Emerson," in *The First Four Books of Poems* (New York: Atheneum Publishers, 1975), p. 31.

10. Merwin, "Song," in *The First Four Books of Poems*, p. 60.

11. Merwin, "East of the Sun and West of the Moon," in *The First Four Books of Poems*, p. 89.

12. W. S. Merwin, *Unframed Originals: Recollections* (New York: Atheneum Publishers, 1988), p. 12.

13. Ibid., pp. 111–12.

14. W. S. Merwin, "Another Place," in *Travels: Poems* (New York: Alfred A. Knopf, 1993), p. 116.

15. Merwin, *Unframed Originals*, p. 109.

16. W. S. Merwin, quoted from *Contemporary Authors*, vols. 13–16, in *Regions of Memory*, p. 301.

17. Merwin, "Learning a Dead Language," in *The First Four Books of Poetry*, p. 176.

18. Merwin, *Unframed Originals*, pp. 173–76.

19. W. S. Merwin, interview with author, November 13, 1991.

20. Stevenson, *Bitter Fame*, p. 193; W. S. Merwin, interview with author, November 13, 1991.

21. Merwin, *Unframed Originals*, p. 154ff.

22. E.g., Merwin, *Unframed Originals*, pp. 155–70; and *The Lost Upland* (New York: Alfred A. Knopf, 1992), *passim*.

23. Merwin, "In Stony Country," from *The Drunk in the Furnace*, in *The First Four Books of Poems*, p. 226.

24. W. S. Merwin, interview with author, November 13, 1991.

25. Ibid.

26. According to Donald Hall, in author's interview September 30, 1992.

27. Robert Frost, "Maturity No Object," Introduction to *New Poets of England and America*, edited by Donald Hall, Robert Pack, and Louis Simpson (New York: Meridian Books, 1957).

28. Donald Hall, interview with author, September 30, 1992.

29. Edward J. Brunner, *Poetry as Labor and Privilege: The Writings of W. S. Merwin* (Urbana and Chicago, University of Illinois Press, 1991), p. 68ff.

30. W. S. Merwin, interview with author, November 13, 1991.

31. Ibid.

32. Merwin, "In the Wake of the Blackfish," p. 283.

33. W. S. Merwin, interview with author, November 13, 1991.

34. Ibid.

35. Merwin, "Pool Room in the Lions' Club," in *The First Four Books of Poems*, p. 244.

36. Merwin, review of *The Hawk in the Rain*, by Ted Hughes, *The New York Times Book Review*, October 6, 1957.

37. Stevenson, *Bitter Fame*, p. 117.

38. Ibid.

39. Dido Merwin, "Vessel of Wrath: A Memoir of Sylvia Plath," Appendix 2 to *Bitter Fame*, by Anne Stevenson, p. 322.

40. Merwin, "Bell Buoy," in *The First Four Books of Poems*, p. 214.

41. W. S. Merwin, interview with author, November 13, 1991.

42. Merwin, "The Drunk in the Furnace," in *The First Four Books of Poems*, p. 261.

43. W. S. Merwin, interviewed by Ed Folsom and Cary Nelson, in *American Poetry Observed: Poets on Their Work*, edited by Joe David Bellamy (Urbana and Chicago: University of Illinois Press, 1984), pp. 179–80.

44. W. S. Merwin, "Lemuel's Blessing," in *The Moving Target* (New York: Atheneum, 1963), p. 8.

45. Merwin, "For Now," in *The Moving Target*, p. 93.

46. See Dido Merwin, Appendix 2 to *Bitter Fame*, by Anne Stevenson, for a full account; also Janet Malcolm, *The Silent Woman: Sylvia Plath & Ted Hughes* (New York: Alfred A. Knopf, 1994), pp. 18–19, 75, *passim*.

Chapter 5

1. Anne Sexton, *No Evil Star: Selected Essays, Interviews, and Prose*, edited by Steven E. Colburn (Ann Arbor: University of Michigan Press, 1985), p. 174.

2. Maxine Kumin, "Halfway," in *Halfway* (New York: Holt, Rinehart & Winston, 1961), p. 16.

3. *The Modern Poets: An American-British Anthology*, edited by John Malcolm Brinnin and Bill Read, both of Boston University, and with photographs by Rollie McKenna. The second edition (1970) contained work by every poet discussed at length in this book—except for Maxine Kumin and Adrienne Rich.

4. Maxine Kumin, "A Poet in Secret: Writing Poems in the Interstices of Life," *Boston Review*, April 1991.

5. Ibid.

6. Maxine Kumin, "An Interview with Joan Norris," in *To Make a Prairie: Essays on Poets, Poetry, and Country Living* (Ann Arbor: University of Michigan Press, 1979), pp. 12–13.

7. Louis Simpson, *A Revolution in Taste* (New York: Macmillan, 1978), p. xvi.

8. Adrienne Rich, *What Is Found There: Notebooks on Poetry and Politics* (New York: W. W. Norton, 1993), p. 191.

9. Maxine Kumin, interview with author, June 3, 1991.

10. Middlebrook, *Anne Sexton: A Biography*, p. 123.

11. Donald Hall, "Digging," in *Old and New Poems* (New York: Ticknor & Fields, 1990), p. 76.

12. Donald Hall, "Education of the Poet," a lecture delivered October 1, 1991, as part of an annual series sponsored by the Academy of American Poets, *Poetry Pilot*, July–August 1992.

13. Donald Hall, interview with author, September 30, 1992.

14. Donald Hall, *Their Ancient Glittering Eyes: Remembering Poets and More Poets* (New York: Ticknor & Fields, 1992), p. 146.

15. Donald Hall, quoted in Scott Donaldson, *Archibald MacLeish: An American Life* (Boston: Houghton Mifflin, A Peter Davison Book, 1992), p. 406.

16. Hall, *Their Ancient Glittering Eyes*, p. 118.

17. Ibid., p. 117.

18. William Arrowsmith, review of *Exiles and Marriages*, by Donald Hall, *The Hudson Review*, vol. 9, no. 2 (Summer 1956); and in *The Day I Was Older: On the Poetry of Donald Hall*, edited by Liam Rector (Santa Cruz, California: Story Line Press, 1989), p. 206.

19. Donald Hall, interview with author, September 30, 1992.

20. Philip Booth, interview with author, May 29, 1992.

21. Donald Hall, interview with author, September 30, 1992.

22. Ibid.

23. Donald Hall, "Sestina," in *The Dark Houses* (New York, Viking Press, 1958), p. 47.

24. Donald Hall, interview with author, September 30, 1992.

25. W. D. Snodgrass, "The Immutability of the Quick-Change Artist: Donald Hall," in Rector, ed., *The Day I Was Older*, p. 51.

26. Robert McDowell, untitled commentary, in *Contemporary Poets*, fifth edition, edited by Tracy Chevalier (Chicago and London: St. James Press, fifth edition, 1991), p. 373–74.

27. William Matthews, "Some Notes on the Alligator Bride," in *The Day I Was Older*, p. 224.

28. Philip Booth, interview with author, May 29, 1992.

29. Ibid.

30. Philip Booth, "Summers in Castine/Contact Prints: 1955–1965," *Salmagundi* 37 (Spring 1977), p. 41.

31. Ibid., p. 40.

32. Philip Booth, quoted in Guy Rotella, *Three Contemporary Poets of New England: Meredith, Booth, and Davison* (Boston: Twayne/G. K. Hall, 1983), p. 65; also Philip Booth, interview with author, May 29, 1992.

33. Philip Booth, *The Islanders* (New York: The Viking Press, 1961), p. 54.

Chapter 6

1. "For John, Who Begs Me Not to Enquire Further," in *To Bedlam and Part Way Back* (Boston: Houghton Mifflin Company, 1960), and in *The Complete Poems of Anne Sexton*, pp. 34–35.

2. Arthur Freeman, quoted in Diane Wood Middlebrook, *Anne Sexton: A Biography* (Boston: Houghton Mifflin Company, A Peter Davison Book, 1991), p. 118.

3. Middlebrook, *Anne Sexton: A Biography*.

4. Diane Wood Middlebrook, "Becoming Anne Sexton," in Colburn, ed., *Anne Sexton: Telling the Tale*, p. 9.

5. Martin T. Orne, Foreword to *Anne Sexton: A Biography*, by Diane Wood Middlebrook, p. xiii.

6. Middlebrook, "Becoming Anne Sexton," in Colburn, ed., *Anne Sexton: Telling the Tale*, p. 9.

7. "You, Doctor Martin," in *The Complete Poems of Anne Sexton*, p. 3.

8. Maxine Kumin, interview with author, June 3, 1991.

9. "Music Swims Back to Me," in *The Complete Poems of Anne Sexton*, p. 6.

10. Maxine Kumin, "How It Was: Maxine Kumin on Anne Sexton," Foreword to *The Complete Poems of Anne Sexton*, p. xxiii. In the foreword Kumin puts this episode in January 1957 but Diane Middlebrook has dated the first draft of "Music Swims Back to Me" on September 27, 1957, at the opening of the second year of the Holmes workshop.

11. Sexton, *No Evil Star*, ed. Colburn, p. 165.

12. Middlebrook, *Anne Sexton: A Biography*, p. 75.

13. Ibid., p. 61.

14. W. D. Snodgrass, quoted in Middlebrook, *Anne Sexton: A Biography*, p. 81.

15. Anne Sexton, letter to W. D. Snodgrass, March 11, 1959, quoted in Middlebrook, *Anne Sexton: A Biography*, p. 78.

16. Middlebrook, *Anne Sexton: A Biography*, p. 89.

17. "The Double Image," in *The Complete Poems of Anne Sexton*, p. 41.

18. Robert Lowell, letter to Anne Sexton, September 11, 1958, quoted in Middlebrook, *Anne Sexton: A Biography*, p. 91.

19. Anne Sexton, letter to Robert Lowell, September 15, 1958, *A Self-Portrait in Letters* (Boston: Houghton Mifflin Company, 1977), p. 38.

20. Anne Sexton, letter to W. D. Snodgrass, October 6, 1958, *A Self-Portrait in Letters*, p. 39.

21. Elizabeth Hardwick, interview with author, March 22, 1992.

22. Maxine Kumin, interview with author, June 3, 1991.

23. As recounted to author by Stephen Sandy, who frequently saw Starbuck there.

24. George Starbuck, "A Tapestry for Bayeux," published in *The Saturday Review* by John Ciardi, and in *Bone Thoughts* (1960) by Yale University Press.

25. George Starbuck, "War Story," in *Bone Thoughts* (New Haven: Yale University Press, 1960), p. 56.

26. Sexton, *No Evil Star*, ed. Colburn, pp. 164–65.

27. Middlebrook, *Anne Sexton: A Biography*, p. 127.

28. For additional verification: Middlebrook, *Anne Sexton: A Biography*, p. 107ff.; *The Journals of Sylvia Plath*, p. 302ff.; Kathleen Spivack, "Poets and Friends," *Boston Globe Magazine*, August 9, 1981, p. 11.

29. Maxine Kumin, interview with author, June 3, 1991.

30. Sexton, "Classroom at Boston University," in *No Evil Star*, p. 3.

31. John Holmes, letter to Anne Sexton, February 8, 1959, quoted in Middlebrook, *Anne Sexton: A Biography*, p. 98.

32. Sexton, letter to Nolan Miller, February 15, 1959, in *A Self-Portrait in Letters*, p. 61.

33. Harry Ford, personal information supplied to the author, 1993.

34. Anne Sexton, letter to W. D. Snodgrass, March 11, 1959, in *A Self-Portrait in Letters*, p. 67.

35. Anne Sexton, letter to W. D. Snodgrass, February 24, 1959, in *A Self-Portrait in Letters*, p. 64.

36. Anne Sexton, letter to W. D. Snodgrass, April 1959, in *A Self-Portrait in Letters*, pp. 71–74.

37. "Young Girl" (in part), from "Doors, Doors, Doors," in *The Complete Poems of Anne Sexton*, p. 80.

38. Anne Sexton, letter to Carolyn Kizer, "April Fool," 1959, in *A Self-Portrait in Letters*, pp. 68–71.

39. *The Journals of Sylvia Plath*, May 3, 1959, p. 302.

40. Starbuck, *Bone Thoughts*, dedication page.

41. Anne Sexton to Martin Orne, therapy tape, April 25, 1961, quoted in Middlebrook, *Anne Sexton: A Biography*, p. 140.
42. It is also the epigraph to *To Bedlam and Part Way Back.*
43. Peter Davison, "One of the Muses," in *The City and the Island* (New York: Atheneum Publishers, 1966), p. 50.

Chapter 7

1. "The Colossus," in *The Collected Poems of Sylvia Plath*, no. 117, p. 129; written at Yaddo October 19, 1959.
2. "The Manor Garden," in *The Collected Poems of Sylvia Plath*, no. 113, p. 125; written at Yaddo, October 19, 1959.
3. Alfred Kazin, *New York Jew* (New York: Alfred A. Knopf, 1978), pp. 226–28.
4. Sylvia Plath, letter to Lynne Lawner, June 8, 1955, *Antaeus* 28 (Winter 1978), p. 32.
5. Malcolm, *The Silent Woman: Sylvia Plath & Ted Hughes* (New York: Alfred A. Knopf, 1994), p. 192.
6. See Stevenson, *Bitter Fame*, pp. 59–72.
7. First published in *The Atlantic Monthly*, January 1957; omitted from *The Colossus*, and not published in book form till 1981: *The Collected Poems of Sylvia Plath*, no. 3, p. 22.
8. *The Journals of Sylvia Plath*, pp. 108–44; see also a more orderly, and less bowdlerized, description of the events of these weeks in Stevenson, *Bitter Fame*, chapters 4 and 5, and especially Janet Malcolm's rereading of these journals in *The Silent Woman*, pp. 35–42, *et passim.*
9. Sylvia Plath, letter to her mother, April 19, 1956, in *Letters Home*, p. 234.
10. Sylvia Plath, letter to her brother, April 23, 1956, in *Letters Home*, p. 240.
11. Stevenson, *Bitter Fame*, p. 90.
12. "Ode for Ted," in *The Collected Poems of Sylvia Plath*, no. 10, p. 29.
13. Sylvia Plath, unpublished letter to Peter Davison, September 30, 1956. Reprinted by permission of Ted Hughes.
14. Sylvia Plath, unpublished, undated Christmas card to Peter Davison. Reprinted by permission of Ted Hughes.
15. Sylvia Plath, letter to her mother, March 12, 1957, in *Letters Home*, p. 300.

16. Sylvia Plath, letter to her mother, February 15, 1955, in *Letters Home*, p. 163.

17. *The Journals of Sylvia Plath*, January 10, 1959, p. 290.

18. Ibid., July 17, 1957, p. 165.

19. Maureen Howard, conversation in person with author, 1980.

20. Daniel Aaron, interview with author, July 22, 1992.

21. Edwin Muir, review of *The Hawk in the Rain*, by Ted Hughes, in *The New Statesman*, September 28, 1957.

22. Stevenson, *Bitter Fame*, p. 117.

23. *The Journals of Sylvia Plath*, January 4, 1958, p. 182.

24. Ibid., January 20, 1958, pp. 185–86. She had a point. In addition to Swenson and Rich, the other American women poets were Catherine Davis, Elizabeth B. Harrod, Ellen de Young Kay, and Vassar Miller, only the last of whom would be remembered today. Donald Hall and Robert Pack would remedy the quality, though not the proportion, of women poets in their second, 1962, edition, which included only Jane Cooper, Carolyn Kizer, Denise Levertov, Vassar Miller, Sylvia Plath, Adrienne Rich, and Anne Sexton, out of thirty-five Americans born after 1922. Footnote: Ted Hughes was also included only in the second volume. Elizabeth Jennings was the only English woman poet in either volume.

25. Ibid., March 20, 1958, pp. 211–12.

26. Ted Hughes, unpublished letter to Peter Davison, April 27, 1958.

27. *The Journals of Sylvia Plath*, p. 217.

28. Ibid., May 5, 1958, p. 222.

29. Ibid., May 11, 1958, "Mother's Day," p. 223.

30. This reading is noted in my diary, and in the Poets' Theatre executive committee minutes. I cannot recall being present. I was probably in New York, visiting my mother in the hospital, where she had recently been operated on for cancer of the kidney.

31. Sylvia Plath, *Johnny Panic and the Bible of Dreams: Short Stories, Prose, and Diary Extracts* (New York: Harper & Row, 1979), p. 152ff.

32. Ibid., p. 157.

33. Ibid., p. 166.

34. *The Journals of Sylvia Plath*, editorial note, p. 266.

35. "Point Shirley," in *The Collected Poems of Sylvia Plath*, no. 94, p. 110.

36. *The Journals of Sylvia Plath*, January 20, 1959, pp. 292–93.

37. Stanley Kunitz, interview with author, March 28, 1991.

38. *The Journals of Sylvia Plath*, February 25, 1959, p. 298.

39. Ibid., January 28, 1959, pp. 294–95.

40. Ibid., February 19, 1959, p. 296.

41. Ibid., p. 297.

42. Ibid., March 20, 1959, pp. 299–301.

43. "Electra on Azalea Path," in *The Collected Poems of Sylvia Plath*, no. 193, p. 117. This poem seems not to have been published in book form until 1981.

44. Sylvia Plath, letter to Lynne Lawner, March 11, 1959, in *Antaeus* 28 (Winter 1978), p. 45.

45. Robert Lowell, Foreword to the American edition of *Ariel*, by Sylvia Plath (New York, Harper & Row, 1966), p. xi. Further on, Lowell quotes, as having been shown to his class in the spring, a line that was not written until October 19 at Yaddo: "The pears fatten like little buddhas."

46. George Starbuck, quoted in Middlebrook, *Anne Sexton: A Biography*, p. 107.

47. Middlebrook, *Anne Sexton: A Biography*, pp. 107–108.

48. *The Journals of Sylvia Plath*, May 20, 1959, p. 306.

49. Sexton, "Classroom at Boston University," in *No Evil Star*, ed. Colburn, p. 7.

50. Philip Booth, interview with author, May 29, 1992.

51. *The Journals of Sylvia Plath*, June 20, 1959, pp. 311–12.

52. Catherine Thompson, " 'Dawn Poems in Blood': Sylvia Plath and PMS," *Triquarterly* 80 (1990–91): p. 221ff.

53. *The Journals of Sylvia Plath*, September 29, 1959, p. 317.

54. Ibid., October 6, 1959, p. 320.

55. Ibid., September 29, 1959, p. 317.

56. Ibid., October 22, 1959, p. 325.

57. "The Manor Garden," in *The Collected Poems of Sylvia Plath*, no. 113, p. 125.

58. "The Colossus," in *The Collected Poems of Sylvia Plath*, no. 117, pp. 129–30.

59. "The Stones," from "Poem for a Birthday," in *The Collected Poems of Sylvia Plath*, no. 119, pp. 136–37.

60. See my *One of the Dangerous Trades: Essays on the Work and Working of Poetry* (Ann Arbor: University of Michigan Press, 1991), "Sylvia Plath 2: *Crossing the Water*" (1972), in which I dilate on the "desert of death" in these poems of the middle period.

61. "Berck-Plage," in *The Collected Poems of Sylvia Plath*, no. 167, p. 196.

62. "The Applicant," in *The Collected Poems of Sylvia Plath*, no. 182, p. 221.

63. "Thalidomide," in *The Collected Poems of Sylvia Plath*, no. 203, p. 252.

64. "Mystic," in *The Collected Poems of Sylvia Plath*, February 1, 1963, no. 219, p. 268.

65. "Kindness," in *The Collected Poems of Sylvia Plath*, February 1, 1963, no. 220, p. 270.

66. "Edge," in *The Collected Poems of Sylvia Plath*, February 5, 1963, no. 224, p. 273.

67. May Swenson, undated and unpublished diary notes, reprinted by permission of the Estate of May Swenson, Rozeanne Knudson, Executor.

68. *The Journals of Sylvia Plath*, November 7, 1959, p. 328.

69. Ibid., November 12, 1959, p. 331.

70. Sylvia Plath, letter to her mother, February 11, 1960, in *Letters Home*, p. 366.

71. A. Alvarez, "Sylvia Plath, A Memoir," in *Ariel Ascending: Writings about Sylvia Plath*, edited by Paul Alexander (New York: Harper & Row, 1985), p. 190.

72. Stanley Kunitz, interview with author, March 28, 1991. Before *The Colossus* was published in the U.S.A. in 1962, eight other poems were dropped from the English version, and one poem, "Frog Autumn," was inserted into the American version that had not appeared in the English. Of all Plath's poetry books published in both countries, only *Collected Poems* contained the same poems on both sides of the ocean. Her *oeuvre* is a bibliographer's nightmare.

73. Ted Hughes, Foreword to *The Journals of Sylvia Plath*, p. xii.

Chapter 8

1. Adrienne Rich: "Snapshots of a Daughter-in-Law," in *The Fact of a Doorframe: Poems Selected and New, 1950–1984* (New York: W. W. Norton, 1984), pp. 35–39.

2. W. H. Auden, Foreword to *A Change of World*, by Adrienne Rich (New Haven: Yale University Press, 1951), reprinted in Jane Roberta Cooper, *Reading Adrienne Rich*, p. 211.

3. Randall Jarrell, review of *The Diamond Cutters*, by Adrienne Rich, *Yale Review*, Autumn 1956.

4. Richard Wilbur, interview with author, July 1, 1991.

5. Adrienne Rich, interviewed by Elly Bulkin, in Bellamy, ed., *American Poetry Observed*, p. 191.

6. Adrienne Rich, "Blood, Bread, and Poetry: The Location of the Poet," in *Blood, Bread, and Poetry: Selected Prose 1979–1985* (New York: W. W. Norton, 1986), p. 181.

7. Rich, *What Is Found There*, p. 23.

8. Ibid., p. 184.

9. Rich, "Split at the Root," in *Blood, Bread, and Poetry*, pp. 101–14, *passim*.

10. Rich, "Blood, Bread, and Poetry," in *Blood, Bread, and Poetry*, p. 168.

11. Adrienne Rich, "Taking Women Students Seriously," in *On Lies, Secrets, and Silence: Selected Prose 1966–1978* (New York: W. W. Norton, 1979), p. 238.

12. Rich, "Blood, Bread, and Poetry," in *Blood, Bread, and Poetry*, p. 175.

13. Adrienne Rich, letter to the author, June 1, 1993.

14. Rich, *Blood, Bread, and Poetry*, op. cit., p. 176.

15. Rich: "An Unsaid Word," in *The Fact of a Doorframe*, p. 5.

16. Rich, *What Is Found There*, p. 229.

17. Rich, "A Walk by the Charles," in *The Fact of a Doorframe*, p. 19.

18. Adrienne Rich, *Of Woman Born: Motherhood as Experience and Institution*, 10th anniversary edition (New York and London: W. W. Norton, 1986), p. 15.

19. Adrienne Rich, letter to the author, June 1, 1993.

20. Ibid.

21. Rich, "Split at the Root," in *Blood, Bread, and Poetry*, p. 114.

22. Donald Hall, interview with author, September 15, 1992.

23. Philip Booth, interview with author, May 29, 1992.

24. William Alfred, interview with author, June 8, 1991.

25. W. S. Merwin, interview with author, November 22, 1991.

26. Rich, *Of Woman Born*, p. 40.

27. Ibid., pp. 26–29, *passim*.

28. Kathleen Spivack, "Robert Lowell: A Memoir," in *Robert Lowell: Interviews and Memoirs*, edited by Jeffrey Meyers (Ann Arbor: University of Michigan Press, 1988), p. 355.

29. Elizabeth Hardwick, interview with author, March 22, 1992.

30. Adrienne Rich, quoted in Middlebrook, *Anne Sexton: A Biography*, pp. 110–11.

31. Ibid., p. 111.

32. Adrienne Rich's account of this event was vividly conveyed at a Cambridge poetry reading in 1992 at which I was present.

33. Rich, "When We Dead Awaken: Writing as Re-Vision," in *On Lies, Secrets, and Silences*, p. 42.

34. Adrienne Rich, letter to the author, June 1, 1993.

35. Rich, Foreword to *The Fact of a Doorframe*, p. xv.

36. Adrienne Rich, interview with Diane Middlebrook, May 19, 1983; with thanks to both participants.

37. Rich, "When We Dead Awaken: Writing as Re-Vision" (1971), in *On Lies, Secrets, and Silence*, p. 44.

38. Rich, op. cit., p. 40.

39. Alicia Ostriker, *Stealing the Language: The Emergence of Women's Poetry in America* (Boston: Beacon Press, 1986), p. 68.

40. Rich, "Twenty-One Love Poems," no. 8, in *The Fact of a Doorframe*, p. 240.

Chapter 9

1. *Hello, Darkness: The Collected Poems of L. E. Sissman* (Boston: Atlantic-Little, Brown, 1978), pp. 20–21.

2. L. E. Sissman, "Adoptive Son," *Innocent Bystander: The Scene from the 70's*, with a foreword by John Updike (New York: Vanguard Books, 1975), p. 41.

3. Anne Sissman, interview with author, June 12, 1992; and Barbara Klauer Sissman Boger, interview with author, June 2, 1993.

4. Sissman, "Confessions of an Ex-Quiz Kid: A Vote for Children's Lib," in *Innocent Bystander*, pp. 3–6, *passim*.

5. Albert C. Cook, interview with author, September 3, 1993.

6. Barbara Klauer Sissman Boger, interview with author, June 2, 1993.

7. According to Sissman's college friend Albert Cook, whose wife was also a stack clerk at the library at the time.

8. Sissman, "Quare Fellows," in *Innocent Bystander*, p. 12.

9. Ibid., p. 13.

10. Ibid., pp. 13–14.

11. Barbara Klauer Sissman Boger, interview with author, June 2, 1993.

12. Ibid.

13. Sissman, "East Cambridge, 1949," from "A War Requiem," in *Hello, Darkness*, p. 134.

14. These, as well as Theodore Morrison's comments, can be seen pencilled on the manuscripts in the Sissman Archives at Harvard's Houghton Library.

15. Donald Hall, interview with author, September 30, 1992.

16. Sissman, "Just a Whack at Empson," in *Hello, Darkness*, p. 51.

17. Sissman, "Canzone: Aubade," in *Hello, Darkness*, p. 88. ·

18. Sissman, "The Village: The Seasons," in *Hello, Darkness*, p. 121.

19. Barbara Klauer Sissman Boger, interview with author, June 2, 1993.

20. L. E. Sissman, letter to Edward and Marie Sissman, December 26, 1956.

21. Saul Touster, personal information supplied to the author, August 3, 1993.

22. Sissman, "A Marriage, 1958," from "A War Requiem," in *Hello, Darkness*, p. 139.

23. Robert Coles, *The Call of Stories: Teaching and the Moral Imagination* (Boston: Houghton Mifflin Company, A Peter Davison Book, 1989), p. 94.

24. Sissman, "Writing, 1963," in *Hello, Darkness*, p. 140.

25. Elizabeth Hardwick, interview with author, March 22, 1992.

Chapter 10

1. "Robin Redbreast," from *The Testing-Tree* (1971), in *The Poems of Stanley Kunitz, 1928–1978* (Boston: Atlantic-Little, Brown, 1979), p. 56; written in 1959 according to Kunitz in an interview with me, March 1991.

2. "The Portrait," from *The Testing-Tree* (1971), in *The Poems of Stanley Kunitz*, p. 86.

3. *Interviews and Encounters with Stanley Kunitz* (New York: Sheep Meadow Press), p. 178.

4. Ibid., p. 186.

5. "The Portrait," in *The Poems of Stanley Kunitz*, p. 86.

6. Stanley Kunitz, *Next-to-Last Things* (Boston/New York: Atlantic Monthly Press, 1985), p. 74.

7. *Interviews and Encounters with Stanley Kunitz*, p. 182.

8. Ibid., p. 61.

9. Ibid., p. 174.

10. Stanley Kunitz, personal information supplied to the author, 1993.

11. *Interviews and Encounters with Stanley Kunitz*, p. 168.

12. Louise Glück, "The Difficult Journey," *Antaeus* 37 (Spring 1980): p. 106.

13. "Poem," in *The Poems of Stanley Kunitz*, p. 198.

14. *Interviews and Encounters with Stanley Kunitz*, p. 125.

15. Ibid., p. 166.

16. Stanley Kunitz, interview with Christopher Busa, *Provincetown Arts* 8 (1992): p. 10.

17. *Interviews and Encounters with Stanley Kunitz*, p. 22.

18. Kunitz, "Remembering Roethke," *A Kind of Order, A Kind of Folly*, pp. 78–79.

19. *Interviews and Encounters with Stanley Kunitz*, pp. 49–50.

20. Kunitz, *Next-to-Last Things*, p. 92.

21. Stanley Kunitz, interview with Christopher Busa, loc. cit., p. 11.

22. Ibid., p. 93.

23. Robert Hass, *Twentieth Century Pleasures: Prose on Poetry* (New York: The Ecco Press, 1984), p. 98.

24. "Father and Son," in *The Poems of Stanley Kunitz*, pp. 157–58.

25. *Interviews and Encounters with Stanley Kunitz*, p. 184.

26. Gregory Orr, *Stanley Kunitz: An Introduction to the Poetry* (New York: Columbia University Press, 1985), p. 123.

27. Kunitz, "News of the Riot," in *A Kind of Order, A Kind of Folly*, p. 82; originally published in *Poetry*.

28. For an eloquent version of the agonized complexities of this affair, see Elinor Langer, *Josephine Herbst: The Story She Could Never Tell* (Boston: Atlantic-Little, Brown, 1984), pp. 290–96; and many of the poems in "This Garland, Danger," the section of new poems published in Kunitz' *Selected Poems, 1928–1958*.

29. Gregory Orr, *Stanley Kunitz*, p. 134.

30. "The Approach to Thebes," in *The Poems of Stanley Kunitz*, p. 112.

31. *Interviews and Encounters with Stanley Kunitz*, p. 169.

32. "End of Summer," in *The Poems of Stanley Kunitz*, p. 119.

33. Stanley Kunitz, "The Poet on His Work: Awake after Midnight," *Christian Science Monitor*, April 26, 1966.

34. Stanley Kunitz, interview with author, March 28, 1991.

35. Ibid.

36. Ibid.

37. Kunitz, "A Conversation with Robert Lowell" (1964), in *A Kind of Order, A Kind of Folly*, p. 155.

38. Kunitz, "Poet of Terribilità," *A Kind of Order, A Kind of Folly*, p. 249.

39. Kunitz, *Next-to-Last Things*, pp. 41–46.

40. Stanley Kunitz, interview with author, March 28, 1991.

41. Stanley Kunitz, letter to the author, March 10, 1991.

42. "The Testing-Tree," in *The Poems of Stanley Kunitz*, p. 92.

43. Stanley Kunitz, "Proteus," *The New Yorker*, July 26, 1993.

Chapter 11

1. Lowell, "For the Union Dead," in *For the Union Dead*, p. 70. There are minute differences between the book version and *The Atlantic Monthly*'s version.

2. Lowell, "A Conversation with Ian Hamilton," in *Collected Prose*, pp. 276–77.

3. Kunitz, *Next-to-Last Things*, p. 46.

4. Robert Lowell, undated and uncancelled postcard to the author, from Castine, Maine, probably summer 1965. My contribution included "Not Forgotten," the elegy to my mother quoted as epigraph to chapter 2.

5. William Alfred, interview with author, June 8, 1991.

6. Hamilton, *Robert Lowell: A Biography*, p. 206.

7. Elizabeth Hardwick, letter to Harriet Winslow, April 22, 1955, quoted in Hamilton, *Robert Lowell: A Biography*, p. 222.

8. Robert Lowell, letter to Theodore Roethke, July 10, 1963, quoted in Hamilton, *Robert Lowell: A Biography*, pp. 336–37.

9. Helen Vendler, "Lowell in the Classroom," in Meyers, ed., *Robert Lowell: Interviews and Memoirs*, pp. 294–95.

10. Judith Baumel, "Robert Lowell: The Teacher," in Meyers, ed., *Robert Lowell: Interviews and Memoirs*, p. 277.

11. Lowell, "A Conversation with Ian Hamilton," in *Collected Prose*, p. 287.

12. Esther Brooks, from *Robert Lowell: A Tribute*, edited by Rolando Anzilotto (Pisa: Nistri-Lischi) as excerpted in Meyers, ed., *Robert Lowell: Interviews and Memoirs*, pp. 281–83.

13. Lowell, "A Conversation with Ian Hamilton," in *Collected Prose*, p. 269.

14. Robert Fitzgerald, "The Things of the Eye," in Meyers, ed., *Robert Lowell: Interviews and Memoirs*, p. 227.

15. In his spoken commentary during a reading at the Library of Congress, May 5, 1969, Library of Congress Recording PL32-33.

16. W. S. Merwin, interview with author, November 13, 1991.

17. Lowell, "Near the Unbalanced Aquarium," in *Collected Prose*, p. 362.

18. Kalstone, *Becoming a Poet*, p. 171.

19. Elizabeth Hardwick, letter to Peter Taylor, February 10, 1955, quoted in Hamilton, *Robert Lowell: A Biography*, p. 220.

20. Lowell, "91 Revere Street," in *Collected Prose*, pp. 313, 316, 323, 324, 326, 329.

21. Robert Lowell, letter to William Carlos Williams, June 24, 1957, quoted in Hamilton, *Robert Lowell: A Biography*, p. 223. Anyone who has seen this barn and its surround would support Merwin's claim that Lowell had no powers of observation.

22. Philip Booth, "Summers in Castine: Contact Prints, 1955–1965," *Salmagundi* 37 (Spring 1977), p. 49.

23. Booth, "Summers in Castine," p. 43.

24. Lowell, "Robert Frost," in *Collected Prose*, p. 11.

25. Lowell, "William Carlos Williams," in *Collected Prose*, p. 44; see also Paul Mariani, *William Carlos Williams: A New World Naked* (New York: McGraw-Hill, 1981), p. 678.

26. W. S. Merwin, interview with author, November 13, 1991.

27. Lowell, "On 'Skunk Hour'" (1964), in *Collected Prose*, p. 227.

28. Lowell, "A Conversation with Ian Hamilton" (1971), in *Collected Prose*, p. 284.

29. Ibid., p. 286.

30. William Carlos Williams, letter to Robert Lowell, April 20, 1957, quoted in Mariani, *William Carlos Williams*, p. 731.

31. Mariani, *William Carlos Williams*, p. 732.

32. Robert Lowell, letter to Randall Jarrell, October 24, 1957, quoted in Hamilton, *Robert Lowell: A Biography*, p. 232.

33. Hamilton, *Robert Lowell: A Biography* pp. 232–33.

34. Philip Booth, interview with author, May 29, 1992.

35. Robert Lowell, letter to Elizabeth Bishop, August 8/9, 1957, quoted in Kalstone, *Becoming a Poet*, p. 176.

36. W. S. Merwin, interview with author, November 13, 1991.

37. Elizabeth Hardwick, interview with author, March 27, 1992.

38. Robert Lowell, letter to Elizabeth Bishop, September 10, 1957, quoted in Kalstone, *Becoming a Poet*, p. 185.

39. Lowell, "On 'Skunk Hour,' " in *Collected Prose*, p. 228.

40. The last four stanzas of "Skunk Hour," *Life Studies*, first printing (New York: Farrar, Straus & Cudahy, 1959), p. 90.

41. Robert Lowell, interview with A. Alvarez, "Robert Lowell in Conversation," in Meyers, ed., *Robert Lowell: Interviews and Memoirs*, p. 75; Lowell, "Epilogue," in *Day by Day* (New York: Farrar, Straus & Giroux, 1977), p. 127.

42. Lowell, "On 'Skunk Hour,' " in *Collected Prose*, p. 228.

43. Robert Lowell, letter to Elizabeth Bishop, August 15, 1957, quoted in Brett C. Millier, *Elizabeth Bishop: Life and the Memory of It* (Berkeley: University of California Press, 1993), p. 294.

44. Elizabeth Bishop, letter to Robert Lowell, December 14, 1957, in *One Art: Elizabeth Bishop Letters*. Selected and edited by Robert Giroux. (New York: Farrar, Straus, Giroux, 1994), pp. 351–52.

45. William Alfred, interview with author, June 5, 1991.

46. W. S. Merwin, interview with author, November 13, 1991.

47. Allen Tate, letter to Robert Lowell, December 3, 1957, quoted at length in Hamilton, *Robert Lowell: A Biography*, p. 237.

48. William Alfred, interview with author, June 5, 1991.

49. W. S. Merwin, interview with author, November 13, 1991.

50. Dido Merwin, quoted in Hamilton, *Robert Lowell: A Biography*, p. 239.

51. William Alfred, interview with author, June 5, 1991.

52. William Alfred, quoted in Hamilton, *Robert Lowell: A Biography*, p. 240.

53. Robert Lowell, letter to Ezra Pound, January 29, 1958, quoted in Hamilton, *Robert Lowell: A Biography*, p. 252.

54. Personal information.

55. Lowell, *Life Studies*, p. 83.

56. Robert Lowell, letter to Peter Taylor, March 15, 1958, quoted in Hamilton, *Robert Lowell: A Biography*, p. 253.

57. Elizabeth Hardwick, quoted in Hamilton, *Robert Lowell: A Biography*, p. 258.

58. *The Journals of Sylvia Plath*, May 5, 1958, p. 222.

59. Hamilton, *Robert Lowell: A Biography*, p. 258.

60. Stanley Kunitz, interview with author, March 28, 1991.

61. Robert Lowell, interview with Fred Seidel in Boston, probably (judging from internal evidence) in early 1960, but published in *The Paris Review*, Winter–Spring 1961; reprinted in Meyers, ed., *Robert Lowell: Interviews and Memoirs*, p. 56.

62. Thompson, "Two Poets," quoted in Hamilton, *Robert Lowell: A Biography*, p. 272.

63. Robert Lowell, "The Drinker," in *Selected Poems* (New York: Farrar, Straus & Giroux, 1976), pp. 116–17.

64. Elizabeth Hardwick, "Boston: A Lost Ideal," *Harper's*, December 1959, *passim*.

65. Stephen Sandy, unpublished manuscript, quoted by permission.

66. Lowell, "Poets and the Theater," in *Collected Prose*, p. 176.

67. Lowell, "Eye and Tooth," in *For the Union Dead*, p. 19.

68. Lowell, "Florence," in *For the Union Dead*, p. 14.

69. Robert Fitzgerald, "Robert Lowell, 1917–1977," in *The Harvard Advocate Commemorative to Robert Lowell*, November 1979; reprinted from *The New Republic*.

Index

Permissions Acknowledgments

Grateful acknowledgment is made to the following for permission to reprint previously published and unpublished material:

Georges Borchardt, Inc.: Excerpts from *The First Four Books of Poems* by W. S. Merwin (Atheneum Publishers), copyright © 1952, 1954, 1955, 1956, 1957, 1958, 1959, 1960, 1975 by W. S. Merwin; excerpts from *The Moving Target* (Atheneum Publishers), copyright © 1963 by W. S. Merwin; excerpts from *Unframed Originals: Recollections* by W. S. Merwin (Atheneum Publishers), copyright © 1980, 1981, 1982 by W. S. Merwin. Reprinted by permission of Georges Borchardt, Inc.

Darhansoff & Verrill Literary Agency: Excerpts from *The Poems of Stanley Kunitz, 1928–1978* (Atlantic-Little, Brown), copyright © 1930, 1944, 1958, 1971, 1973, 1974, 1976, 1978, 1979 by Stanley Kunitz; excerpts from *A Kind of Order, A Kind of Folly: Essays and Conversations* by Stanley Kunitz (Atlantic-Little, Brown), copyright © 1935, 1937, 1938, 1941, 1942, 1947, 1949, 1957, 1963, 1964, 1965, 1966, 1967, 1970, 1971, 1972, 1973, 1975 by Stanley Kunitz; excerpts from *Next-to-Last Things: New Poems and Essays* (Atlantic Monthly Press), copyright © 1985 by Stanley Kunitz. Reprinted by permission of Darhansoff & Verrill Literary Agency on behalf of Stanley Kunitz.

Peter Davison: Excerpts from *The Breaking of the Day and Other Poems* by Peter Davison (Yale University Press, 1964), excerpts from *The City and the Island* by Peter Davison (Atheneum Publishers, 1966), and excerpts from *Praying Wrong: New and Selected Poems, 1957–1984* by Peter Davison (Atheneum Publishers, 1984), copyright © 1958, 1959, 1960, 1961, 1963, 1964, 1965, 1966, 1984 by Peter Davison. Reprinted by permission of the author.

Doubleday and *Faber and Faber Limited*: Excerpts from *The Journals of Sylvia Plath*, edited by Ted Hughes and Frances McCullough, copyright © 1982 by Ted Hughes as Executor of the Estate of Sylvia Plath. Rights in the United Kingdom administered by Faber and Faber Limited, London. Reprinted by permission of Doubleday, a division of Bantam Doubleday Dell Publishing Group, Inc., and Faber and Faber Limited on behalf of Frieda Hughes and Nicholas Hughes.

Faber and Faber Limited: Excerpts from letter of September 30, 1956, from Sylvia Plath to Peter Davison; excerpt from Christmas card, 1956, from Sylvia Plath to Peter Davison; excerpts from letter from Sylvia Plath to Lynne Lawner (*Antaeus* 28, Winter 1978); excerpts from letter of March 11, 1959, from Sylvia Plath to Lynne Lawner (*Antaeus* 28, Winter 1978). Reprinted by permission of Faber and Faber Limited.

Farrar, Straus & Giroux, Inc. and *Faber and Faber Limited*: Excerpts from *Life Studies* by Robert Lowell (Farrar, Straus & Cudahy, 1959), copyright © 1956, 1959 by Robert Lowell; "For the Union Dead" from *For the Union Dead* by Robert Lowell, copyright © 1956, 1960, 1961, 1963, 1964 by Robert Lowell; excerpts from *Collected Prose* by Robert Lowell, edited and introduced by Robert Giroux, copyright © 1987 by Caroline Lowell, Harriet Lowell, and Sheridan

Lowell, Introduction copyright © 1987 by Robert Giroux. Rights in the United Kingdom administered by Faber and Faber Limited, London. Reprinted by permission of Farrar, Straus & Giroux, Inc., and Faber and Faber Limited.

The Estate of Robert Lee Frost: Excerpt from an October 20, 1927, letter from Robert Frost to Edward Davison. Reprinted by permission of Peter A. Gilbert, Executor and Trustee, on behalf of The Estate of Robert Lee Frost.

Harcourt Brace & Company: "Ballade for the Duke of Orléans" from *Advice to a Prophet and Other Poems* by Richard Wilbur, copyright © 1961, copyright renewed 1989 by Richard Wilbur; "The Death of a Toad" from *Ceremony and Other Poems* by Richard Wilbur, copyright © 1950, copyright renewed 1978 by Richard Wilbur; excerpt from *The Misanthrope* by Molière, translated by Richard Wilbur, copyright © 1955, copyright renewed 1983 by Richard Wilbur. Reprinted by permission of Harcourt Brace & Company.

Harcourt Brace & Company and *Faber and Faber Limited*: Excerpt from "My Father Paints the Summer" from *The Beautiful Changes and Other Poems* by Richard Wilbur, copyright © 1947, copyright renewed 1975 by Richard Wilbur; "Love Calls Us to the Things of This World" from *Things of This World* by Richard Wilbur, copyright © 1956, copyright renewed 1984 by Richard Wilbur; excerpt from "The Eye" from *The Mind-Reader* by Richard Wilbur, copyright © 1975 by Richard Wilbur. Rights in the United Kingdom from *New and Collected Poems* by Richard Wilbur administered by Faber and Faber Limited, London. Reprinted by permission of Harcourt Brace & Company and Faber and Faber Limited.

HarperCollins Publishers, Inc.: Excerpt from "Ode for Ted" from *Letters Home by Sylvia Plath: Correspondence 1950–1963* by Aurelia Schober Plath, copyright © 1975 by Aurelia Schober Plath. Reprinted by permission of HarperCollins Publishers, Inc.

HarperCollins Publishers, Inc., and *Faber and Faber Limited*: Excerpts from "The Applicant," "Berck-Plage," "Edge," and "Kindness" from *Ariel* by Sylvia Plath, copyright © 1963 by Ted Hughes, copyright renewed; excerpts from "Electra on Azalea Path" and from "Pursuit" from *The Collected Poems of Sylvia Plath*, edited by Ted Hughes, copyright © 1960, 1965, 1971, 1981 by the Estate of Sylvia Plath, editorial material copyright © 1981 by Ted Hughes; excerpts from "Mystic" and from "Thalidomide" from *Winter Trees* by Sylvia Plath, copyright © 1963 by Ted Hughes, copyright renewed. Rights outside the United States from *The Collected Poems of Sylvia Plath*, edited by Ted Hughes, administered by Faber and Faber Limited, London. Reprinted by permission of HarperCollins Publishers, Inc., and Faber and Faber Limited on behalf of Frieda Hughes and Nicholas Hughes.

Henry Holt and Company, Inc., and *Jonathan Cape Limited*: "The Draft Horse," "From Iron," excerpt from "Design," and excerpt from "The Objection to Being Stepped On" from *The Poetry of Robert Frost*, edited by Edward Connery Lathem, copyright © 1936, 1962 by Robert Frost, copyright © 1964 by Lesley Frost Ballantine, copyright © 1969 by Henry Holt and Company, Inc. Rights in the United Kingdom administered by Jonathan Cape Limited, London, on behalf of the Estate of Robert Frost. Reprinted by permission of Henry Holt and Company, Inc., and Jonathan Cape Limited.

Houghton Mifflin Company: Excerpt from *Anne Sexton: A Biography* by Diane Wood Middlebrook, copyright © 1991 by Diane Wood Middlebrook; "Digging"

Permissions Acknowledgments

from *Old and New Poems* by Donald Hall, copyright © 1990 by Donald Hall. Reprinted by permission of Houghton Mifflin Company. All rights reserved.

Houghton Mifflin Company and *Sterling Lord Literistic*: Excerpt from "Young Girl" from *All My Pretty Ones* by Anne Sexton, copyright © 1962 by Anne Sexton, copyright renewed 1990 by Linda G. Sexton; "Elegy in the Classroom," "For John, Who Begs Me Not to Inquire Further," excerpt from "The Double Image," part 7, and excerpt from "Music Swims Back to Me" from *To Bedlam and Part Way Back* by Anne Sexton, copyright © 1960 by Anne Sexton, copyright renewed 1988 by Linda G. Sexton. Rights in the United Kingdom administered by Sterling Lord Literistic, Inc. Reprinted by permission of Houghton Mifflin Company. All rights reserved.

Alfred A. Knopf, Inc., and *Faber and Faber Limited*: "The Colossus" and "The Manor Garden" from *The Colossus and Other Poems* by Sylvia Plath, copyright © 1962 by Sylvia Plath. Rights outside the United States from *The Collected Poems of Sylvia Plath*, edited by Ted Hughes, administered by Faber and Faber Limited, London. Reprinted by permission of Alfred A. Knopf, Inc., and Faber and Faber Limited on behalf of Frieda Hughes and Nicholas Hughes.

Little, Brown and Company and *Martin Secker and Warburg Limited*: Excerpt from "War Story" from *The Argot Merchant Disaster: Poems, New and Selected* by George Starbuck, copyright © 1960 by George Starbuck. Rights in the United Kingdom administered by Martin Secker and Warburg Limited, London. Reprinted by permission of Little, Brown and Company and Martin Secker and Warburg Limited.

The Estate of Robert Lowell: Postcard from Robert Lowell to Peter Davison. Reprinted by permission of Robert Giroux on behalf of The Estate of Robert Lowell.

Richard Luckett: Excerpt from letter of March 14, 1970, from I.A.R. to Peter Davison. Reprinted by permission of Richard Luckett, Literary Executor, on behalf of The Estate of I. A. Richards.

W. W. Norton & Company, Inc., and *Adrienne Rich*: "An Unsaid Word," excerpt from "Snapshots of a Daughter-in-Law," excerpt from "A Walk by the Charles," excerpt from Part VIII of "Twenty-One Love Poems," and an excerpt from the "Foreword" from *The Fact of a Doorframe, Poems Selected and New, 1950–1984* by Adrienne Rich, copyright © 1984 by Adrienne Rich, copyright © 1975, 1978 by W. W. Norton & Company, Inc., copyright © 1981 by Adrienne Rich; excerpts from *On Lies, Secrets, and Silence, Selected Prose 1966–1978* by Adrienne Rich, copyright © 1979 by W. W. Norton & Company, Inc. Reprinted by permission of the author and W. W. Norton & Company, Inc.

W. W. Norton & Company, Inc., Adrienne Rich, and *Virago Press Limited*: Excerpts from *Of Woman Born: Motherhood as Experience and Institution* by Adrienne Rich, copyright © 1976, 1986 by W. W. Norton & Company, Inc. Rights in the United Kingdom administered by Virago Press Limited, London. Reprinted by permission of the author, W. W. Norton & Company, Inc., and Virago Press Limited.

Penguin USA: "Builder" from *The Islanders* by Philip Booth, copyright © 1952, 1956, 1957, 1958, 1959, 1960, 1961 by Philip Booth; "Night Notes on an Old Dream" from *Relations: New and Selected Poems* by Philip Booth, copyright ©

345

1986 by Philip Booth; "Halfway" from *Our Ground Time Here Will be Brief* by Maxine Kumin, copyright © 1957–1965, 1970–1982 by Maxine Kumin. Reprinted by permission of Viking Penguin, a division of Penguin Books USA Inc.

Random House, Inc., and *Aitken, Stone & Wylie Limited*: Excerpts from *Robert Lowell: A Biography* by Ian Hamilton, copyright © 1982 by Ian Hamilton. Rights in the United Kingdom administered by Aitken, Stone & Wylie Limited, London. Reprinted by permission of Random House, Inc., and Aitken, Stone & Wylie Limited.

The Sheep Meadow Press: Excerpts from *Interviews and Encounters with Stanley Kunitz*, edited by Stanley Moss, copyright © 1993 by Stanley Kunitz. Reprinted by permission of The Sheep Meadow Press.

Anne B. Sissman: Excerpts from *Hello, Darkness: The Collected Poems of L. E. Sissman* (Atlantic-Little, Brown, 1979), copyright © 1963, 1964, 1965, 1966, 1967, 1968, 1969, 1970, 1971 by L. E. Sissman, copyright © 1971, 1972, 1973, 1974, 1976, 1977, 1978 by Anne B. Sissman; excerpts from *Innocent Bystander* by L. E. Sissman, copyright © 1975 by L. E. Sissman. Reprinted by permission of Anne B. Sissman.

The University of Michigan Press: Excerpts from *Robert Lowell: Interviews and Memoirs*, edited by Jeffrey Meyers, copyright © 1988 by the University of Michigan Press. Reprinted by permission of the University of Michigan Press.

A Note About the Author

Peter Davison was born in New York City in 1928, son of the English poet Edward Davison, who had emigrated to the United States a few years earlier, and who had a long career as a teacher, initially at the University of Colorado at Boulder, where Peter Davison was raised. He served at sixteen as a page in the U.S. Senate, and subsequently attended Harvard University and Cambridge in England. He became an editor at Harcourt, Brace at the age of twenty-two, moving to Boston in 1955 to work at Harvard University Press and then at Atlantic Monthly Press, where he remained for the next twenty-nine years, latterly as its editor-in-chief and director. His career as a poet began in 1963 when his first book, *The Breaking of the Day*, was chosen as the Yale Series of Younger Poets volume for that year. Since then he has published eight other books of poems. He is also the author of an autobiographical volume, *Half Remembered: A Personal History*, and a book of essays, *One of the Dangerous Trades: Essays on the Work and Workings of Poetry*. In 1985 he severed connections with Atlantic Monthly Press (although he remains poetry editor of the magazine) and joined Houghton Mifflin with his own imprint.